JOURNAL FOR THE STUDY OF THE OLD TESTAMENT
SUPPLEMENT SERIES

51

Editors
David J A Clines
Philip R Davies

JSOT Press
Sheffield

Divine Initiative and Human Response in Ezekiel

Paul Joyce

Journal for the Study of the Old Testament
Supplement Series 51

For Ali

Copyright © 1989 Sheffield Academic Press

Published by JSOT Press
JSOT Press is an imprint of
Sheffield Academic Press Ltd
The University of Sheffield
343 Fulwood Road
Sheffield S10 3BP
England

Printed in Great Britain
by Billing & Sons Ltd
Worcester

British Library Cataloguing in Publication Data

Joyce, P.M.
    Divine initiative and human response.
    1. Bible. O.T. Ezekiel
    I. Title II. Series
    224'20.4

ISSN 0309-0787
ISBN 1-85075-041-6

CONTENTS

PREFACE

This book represents a development of work for which the degree of D.Phil. in the University of Oxford was awarded in 1983. It is a pleasure to record my gratitude to John Barton, who first aroused my interest in the Old Testament and who subsequently supervised my work with great wisdom and patience. I am grateful also to Ripon College, Cuddesdon, for making possible two terms of sabbatical leave, to the British Trust for the Ecumenical Institute, Tantur, whose generosity enabled me to spend a period in Jerusalem, and to Donn Morgan and the Church Divinity School of the Pacific, Berkeley. Finally, special thanks are due to a number of people whose support has been more important than they know: to my mother and father, to David and Pam Wilcox and to John and Pauline Garton.

PAUL JOYCE
Ripon College, Cuddesdon, Oxford
April 1988

ABBREVIATIONS

The following list does not include:

(i) standard abbreviations such as 'cf.' and 'e.g.'
(ii) standard abbreviations for the books of the Bible.
(iii) abbreviated titles occasionally used in the notes where a book has already been cited; these are self-explanatory.

ASTI	*Annual of the Swedish Theological Institute*
ATANT	Abhandlungen zur Theologie des Alten und Neuen Testaments
ATD	Das Alte Testament Deutsch
BDB	*A Hebrew and English Lexicon of the Old Testament*, ed. F. Brown, S.R. Driver, and C.A. Briggs (Oxford, 1907)
BhEvTh	Beihefte zur evangelischen Theologie
BH3	*Biblia Hebraica*, ed. R. Kittel (3rd edn; Stuttgart, 1937) (Ezekiel text prepared by J.A. Bewer)
BHS	*Biblia Hebraica Stuttgartensia*, ed. K. Elliger and W. Rudolph (Stuttgart, 1977) (Ezekiel text prepared by K. Elliger)
BJRL	*The Bulletin of the John Rylands Library*
BK	Biblischer Kommentar Altes Testament, ed. M. Noth, H.W. Wolff and S. Herrmann
BWANT	Beiträge zur Wissenschaft vom Alten und Neuen Testament
BZ	*Biblische Zeitschrift*
BZAW	Beihefte zur Zeitschrift für die alttestamentliche Wissenschaft
CBQ	*Catholic Biblical Quarterly*
EHPhR	Études d'Histoire et de Philosophie Religieuse
Eng.	English
ET	English Translation (when not italicised)
ET	*Expository Times* (when italicised)
FRLANT	Forschungen zur Religion und Literatur des Alten und Neuen Testaments
G-K	*Gesenius' Hebrew Grammar*, edited and enlarged by E. Kautzsch, translated by A.E. Cowley (2nd edn, Oxford 1910)

HAT	Handbuch zum Alten Testament, ed. O. Eissfeldt
Heb.	Hebrew
HKAT	Handkommentar zum Alten Testament, ed. W. Nowack
HUCA	*Hebrew Union College Annual*
IB	Interpreter's Bible
ICC	The International Critical Commentary
JBL	*Journal of Biblical Literature*
JSOT	*Journal for the Study of the Old Testament*
JSS	*Journal of Semitic Studies*
JTS	*Journal of Theological Studies*
KAT	Kommentar zum Alten Testament, ed. E. Sellin
KeH	Kurzgefasstes exegetisches Handbuch zum Alten Testament
KHC	Kurzer Hand-Commentar zum Alten Testament, ed. K. Marti
LXX	Septuagint
MT	Massoretic Text
NF	Neue Folge (New Series)
RB	*Revue Biblique*
RHPhR	*Revue d'Histoire et de Philosophie Religieuses*
RSV	Revised Standard Version
SBTh	Studies in Biblical Theology
ThB	Theologische Bücherei
ThLZ	*Theologische Literaturzeitung*
ThR	*Theologische Rundschau*
ThZ	*Theologische Zeitschrift*
VT	*Vetus Testamentum*
WMANT	Wissenschaftliche Monographien zum Alten und Neuen Testament
ZAW	*Zeitschrift für die alttestamentliche Wissenschaft*
ZThK	*Zeitschrift für Theologie und Kirche*

INTRODUCTION

'Get yourselves a new heart and a new spirit! Why will you die, O
house of Israel?' (Ezek. 18.31)

'A new heart I will give you, and a new spirit I will put within you;
and I will take out of your flesh the heart of stone and give you a
heart of flesh' (Ezek. 36.26)

What is the connexion between these two declarations? The first,
'Get yourselves a new heart and a new spirit!', marks the culmination
of a chapter devoted to demonstrating the absolute responsibility of
the house of Israel for the disaster of exile. The second, 'A new heart
I will give you, and a new spirit I will put within you', promises as a
gift the very thing that Israel had always been unable to muster for
herself, namely obedient response to the will of Yahweh. How do the
two statements relate to one another?

This is a book about the theology of the Ezekiel tradition. The
purpose of our inquiry is to investigate the twin poles represented by
the two quotations cited above; on the one hand, a strong insistence
upon Israel's responsibility before her God and, on the other, a
remarkable assurance that Yahweh will enable his recalcitrant people
to obey him. A clear understanding of each of these is a prerequisite
for any exploration of the relationship between divine initiative and
human response as presented in Ezekiel.

We set the scene with a consideration of the theological crisis of
exile as the context of the prophet's activity, followed by a discussion
of the unity and authorship of the book of Ezekiel, currently the
subject of lively debate.

The first major section of the book explores in detail the way in
which the responsibility of Israel is expressed in Ezekiel. A close
exegesis of selected key passages (primarily chs. 18, 9 and 14)

demonstrates the complexity of questions relating to the theme. In the course of the inquiry, we reassess the widely held view that the Ezekiel tradition is marked by a strong emphasis on the responsibility of the individual. The discussion is then set in the broader context of the theme of responsibility in the Old Testament as a whole.

The second major section is devoted to an investigation of the activity of Yahweh as portrayed in the book of Ezekiel. This begins with a detailed study of particular formulae: 'You shall know that I am Yahweh', 'In the sight of the nations', 'For the sake of my name' and 'I will vindicate my holiness'. Attention is then focussed upon the point at which the notion of divine activity intersects with that of human moral response: the remarkable motif of Yahweh's gift of a 'new heart' and a 'new spirit' to Israel. The language used here is examined in detail and is considered in relation to similar material in Old Testament literature from broadly the same period (notably the books of Jeremiah and Deuteronomy). In the light of this comparison, we attempt to isolate and identify the distinctive contribution of Ezekiel himself.

Having explored in turn the responsibility of Israel and the activity of Yahweh, we conclude with an assessment of the relationship between divine initiative and human response in the book of Ezekiel.

Note: Quotations from the Bible in English are taken from the Revised Standard Version (RSV). The use of 'the LORD' and 'the Lord GOD' for the divine name in this version is retained in quotations, but in all other cases 'Yahweh' is used as the name of Israel's God.

Chapter 1

THE CONTEXT OF EZEKIEL'S MINISTRY

The Theological Crisis of Exile

The first two decades of the sixth century BCE brought upon Judah a catastrophe of unprecedented scale. In 597 and again in 587 she suffered crushing defeats at the hands of the Babylonians, and a significant proportion of her population was transported a thousand miles to Mesopotamia.[1] Ezekiel was among those deported; these events provide the key to his prophetic message and to the book which bears his name.

It might seem at first sight that conditions for the exiles were not as bad as might have been feared. These Judaean exiles were not scattered, as had been the inhabitants of the northern Kingdom of Israel, deported by the Assyrians in the eighth century. Rather, they were placed in ghetto-like settlements in Babylonia, such as Tel Abib (Ezek. 3.15). They seem to have enjoyed some freedom of association, for the elders are depicted gathering at the house of Ezekiel (8.1; 14.1; 20.1). The letter to the exiles in Jeremiah 29, whether or not it is actually from Jeremiah himself,[2] certainly assumes that the exiled community will enjoy the liberty to 'build houses and live in them; plant gardens and eat their produce; take wives and have sons and daughters' (Jer. 29.5-6).

And yet, even if conditions seem to have been tolerable, in certain respects at least, we must take with full seriousness the anguish reflected in Psalm 137: 'By the waters of Babylon, there we sat down and wept, when we remembered Zion' (Ps. 137.1). The bitterness against Babylon evidenced in v. 9 cannot be ignored: 'Happy shall he be who takes your little ones and dashes them against the rock!' Though the physical events of destruction and exile were certainly devastating, the real key to the disaster lies in its psychological and emotional impact. For within the space of just a few years Judah was robbed of all the major elements in her theological system. In order to appreciate the magnitude of the catastrophe, it is essential to take account of each of these.

'The land' had played a vital part in the identity of the people of Yahweh from the time of the Settlement (c. 1200);[3] indeed, the Patriarchal traditions envisage an association with Canaan long before the Exodus, this land being a central feature of the divine promises to Abraham (Gen. 12.1-3; 17.8). The stories of wanderings in the wilderness are oriented to Canaan as their goal, that land 'flowing with milk and honey' (e.g. Num. 13.27). The link between the worship of Yahweh and this particular territory was a uniquely intimate one. The fugitive David complains, 'They have driven me out this day that I should have no share in the heritage of the LORD, saying, "Go, serve other gods"' (1 Sam. 26.19). Again, Naaman, about to return to his native Syria, pleads with Elisha, 'Let there be given to your servant two mules' burden of earth; for henceforth your servant will not offer burnt offering or sacrifice to any god but the LORD' (2 Kgs 5.17). The annexation of the northern territories by Assyria in c. 721 was indeed a mighty blow, but now to have lost Judah too was a crushing trauma. The land itself lay under Babylonian control, whilst many of its inhabitants had been torn away to live in remote exile. The Psalmist laments, 'How shall we sing the LORD's song in a foreign land?' (Ps. 137.4).

Closely related to possession of the land was the notion that Israel was a special people, chosen by Yahweh. This theme runs through the traditions both of the Patriarchs (Gen. 12.2; 17.7-8) and of the Exodus (Exod. 10.3). Joshua is portrayed as calling the people to reaffirm this identity (Josh. 24), and the military conquests of David are seen as confirmation that Israel was favoured (2 Sam. 5.10, 12). The Deuteronomists gave particular weight to this concept, giving prominence to the Hebrew verb בחר, 'to choose', (e.g. Deut. 7.6-7). It is an irony that it may well have been during the seventh century that increased emphasis was placed upon this theme, so soon before the 'chosen' nation of Yahweh suffered its greatest defeat and humiliation.

The city of Jerusalem was a more recent acquisition than the land, but by 587 it had been in Israelite hands for some 400 years. David had captured the city from the Jebusites (2 Sam. 5.7) and had made it the central capital city of his empire; it may be, though, that even before this Jerusalem had a reputation as a holy city, as the tradition of the pre-Israelite priest-king Melchizedek may attest (Gen. 14.18-20; cf. Ps. 110.4). The Psalter is a treasury of the devotion and grandiose imagery which Jerusalem inspired:

> Great is the LORD and greatly to be praised in the city of our God! His holy mountain, beautiful in elevation, is the joy of all the earth, Mount Zion, in the far north, the city of the great King. Within her citadels God has shown himself a sure defence (Ps. 48.1-3).

By some remarkable if obscure turn of events in about 700, the city was spared from falling to the Assyrians, and this seems to have encouraged the notion that it was in fact impregnable (2 Kgs 19.35-37; cf. Isa. 29.5-8). Yet now Jerusalem lay in ruins; 'How lonely sits the city that was full of people! How like a widow she has become, she that was great among the nations!' (Lam. 1.1).

The pride of Jerusalem was the Temple, built by Solomon in the mid-tenth century. Here was housed the ark of the covenant, which was said to contain the two tables of stone placed there by Moses (cf. 1 Kgs 8.9) and which was thought of as the throne of Yahweh (cf. 1 Kgs 8.13, 'I have built thee an exalted house, a place for thee to dwell in forever'). Again, the Psalter is a rich quarry of elevated language about the Temple: 'A day in thy courts is better than a thousand elsewhere. I would rather be a doorkeeper in the house of my God than dwell in the tents of wickedness' (Ps. 84.10). The importance of the Temple as the focus of the worshipping life of Israel was heightened by the Deuteronomists, whose influence seems to have played a part in the reforms of Josiah, late in the seventh century (cf. 2 Kgs 22-23).[4] The Jerusalem Temple is clearly 'the place which the LORD your God will choose out of all your tribes to put his name and to make his habitation there', referred to in Deuteronomy (e.g. Deut. 12.5). It is indeed a paradox that so soon before the collapse of Jerusalem and its Temple these reforms made this the only legitimate place of sacrifice, for as its significance was enhanced in this way so its vulnerability to historical catastrophe was simultaneously increased. In 587 the Temple was razed to the ground and its treasures ransacked. 'The enemy has stretched out his hands over her precious things; yea, she has seen the nations invade her sanctuary, those whom thou didst forbid to enter thy congregation' (Lam. 1.10).

Monarchy came relatively late to Israel. It was not until some two centuries after the Settlement—perhaps as a means of resisting the threat of the Philistines—that Israel embraced this 'alien' form of government (cf. 1 Sam. 8.19-20). Nathan is presented as enunciating divine promises of permanent blessing upon the royal house (2 Sam. 7). The institution was always to have its critics (cf. Hos. 8.4; Deut. 17.14ff.), but once established it took firm root and, in Judah at least, became the focus of a powerful ideology, to which the so-called 'Royal Psalms' bear eloquent witness. The Davidic King was spoken of as the 'son' of God (Ps. 2.7), sitting at God's 'right hand' (Ps. 110.1); it may be that he is actually addressed as 'God' in Ps. 45.6.[5] Strong language indeed; and yet in 597 the young King Jehoiachin was exiled, and ten years later his successor, King Zedekiah, met the same fate.

Judah had lost her land and with it, it seemed, her status as the chosen people of Yahweh. She had been stripped of her city, her temple, and of not one but two kings. Robbed of all these elements of her identity, it is hardly surprising that profound theological questions were raised in her. For, as Baker puts it, 'the fate of the community formed a central and indispensable part of their faith in God'.[6] Had Yahweh himself been defeated by the Babylonian gods? It does seem that some interpreted imperial conquest as the vanquishing of local gods by foreign gods (cf. 2 Kgs 19.11-13), and there is evidence to suggest that a number of Judaeans in the early sixth century in fact embraced the worship of gods other than Yahweh (Ezek. 8; cf. Jer. 44.18). Some managed to hold on to the belief that Yahweh was powerful and indeed was responsible for what was happening to them; and yet, for many of these, profound questions were raised about the justice of a god who could permit such things (cf. Ezek. 18.29, 'The house of Israel says, "The way of the Lord is not just"'). To quote Baker again, 'Some drew the straightforward conclusion that their god was less powerful than the foreign gods; others decided that he was unjust. In both cases the result was that the nerve of their religion was cut, and that they lapsed into either paganism or despair'.[7]

Too many discussions of the events of these years rush on to speak of the lessons which Israel learned and to show how growth came out of suffering; in so doing they fail to take the depth of the disaster with due seriousness.[8] This catastrophe might well have proved to be the end of Israel as a religious community; that it did not is a very remarkable fact, for which the prophet Ezekiel was in no small part responsible.

Ezekiel, together with Jeremiah, articulated the theological meaning of the national crisis, much as Isaiah of Jerusalem and his prophetic contemporaries had done in response to the Assyrian conquests more than a century earlier. The explanation they gave was that the Babylonian onslaught was Yahweh's powerful and just act, punishing his own people for their sins. This may not seem a very edifying or even a theologically acceptable message to many modern readers, but it offered at least a glimmer of theological light to a people who had lost all, and made possible an initial assimilation of the traumatic disaster which could be the basis of subsequent more positive lessons. Indeed, in due course, it enabled Ezekiel and Jeremiah—and others too—to begin to express hope for the future.

The events of defeat and exile at the hands of the Babylonians and the theological questions which they posed are the essential key to understanding Ezekiel and his tradition; we shall find confirmation of this at numerous points in our study. Nevertheless, it must be acknowledged in passing that, in spite of the wealth of evidence pointing in this direction, not all scholars have regarded the events of the early sixth century as determinative for the book.

In 1930, C.C. Torrey denied the existence of an historical Ezekiel altogether; he argued that the book is a third-century redaction of a pseudepigraphical work purporting to have been written in the reign of the seventh-century king Manasseh.[9] In 1931, J. Smith advanced a theory which was in certain respects similar, but claiming that Ezekiel was an historical character who exercised a prophetic ministry during Manasseh's reign.[10] The work of these scholars illustrates the dangers of over-imaginative theorizing which goes well beyond what is demanded by the evidence of the biblical text. Even so, a comparable hypothesis has been put forward more recently by J. Becker, who considers the book to be a pseudepigraph composed in the fifth century.[11]

It is important to distinguish these extreme views from those of scholars who acknowledge the existence of a sixth-century prophet called Ezekiel (to whom at least some of the words in the book may be attributed), but who regard certain strata as dating from later periods. These will be considered when we turn in our next chapter to discuss questions of unity and authorship.[12]

The Location of Ezekiel's Ministry

We have indicated that the early sixth century provides the temporal context for Ezekiel's activity; but what of geography? Where did he exercise his ministry?

The book of Ezekiel presents his work as taking place in Babylonia from the year 593 onwards (Ezek. 1.2-3).[13] In 33.21 we read, 'In the twelfth year of our exile . . . a man who had escaped from Jerusalem came to me and said, "The city has fallen"'. The biblical text clearly portrays Ezekiel as one of the deportees of 597 who was in Babylonia when Jerusalem fell in 587. There is no reference to his preaching anywhere other than in Babylonia. Accordingly, the majority of commentators believe that Ezekiel's ministry took place entirely in Babylonia;[14] he is the great prophet to the exiles, as Jeremiah is the great prophet to the community in Judah.

However, certain features of the book have led some scholars, notably V. Herntrich,[15] to question this and to suggest that Ezekiel's ministry may have been conducted not in Babylonia but in Jerusalem. The detailed description of the abominations in the Jerusalem Temple in Ezekiel 8 was one such feature stressed by Herntrich. Another was the presence of passages which might be thought to make more sense if spoken in Jerusalem, notably the oracle in Ezekiel 12 concerning 'the prince in Jerusalem and all the house of Israel who are in it' (12.10). This speaks of Ezekiel performing a sign (digging his way out through a wall carrying an exile's baggage), which is said to symbolize the coming exile of the prince and those in Jerusalem. Herntrich claimed that this would be a far more effective sign if performed in the sight of those it concerned in Judah rather than before those already in Babylonia. On the basis of this and similar evidence, he argued that Ezekiel exercised the whole of his ministry in Jerusalem. Herntrich followed certain other scholars, such as Torrey[16] and Smith,[17] in suggesting that at some point redactors had carried out a systematic revision of the book of Ezekiel, giving it a fictional Babylonian setting; such a view has found a measure of support even recently from Garscha.[18] Perhaps more influential than the position of Herntrich, however, has been that particularly associated with Bertholet.[19] This represents a compromise between the traditional view, that Ezekiel's ministry took place entirely in Babylonia, and the view of Herntrich, that the prophet remained in Jerusalem throughout. Bertholet suggested that

Ezekiel had in fact two ministries, one beginning in 593 not in Babylonia but in Jerusalem, and a second conducted in Babylonia after the fall of Jerusalem in 587; in this way Bertholet hoped to do justice to the evidence for both locations. Many scholars have adopted a similar compromise.[20] In passing, we may mention that there have also been more complex theories, such as that of Pfeiffer, who envisaged the prophet moving back and forth a number of times between the two locations.[21]

It is by no means clear, however, that the problems raised by the traditional view are sufficiently serious to justify the alternative theories of Herntrich, Bertholet and those who have followed them. We shall comment briefly on the two passages most commonly cited as presenting difficulties.

The detailed description of the abominations in the Jerusalem Temple found in Ezekiel 8 could certainly have been produced in Babylonia by a man who had been a priest in Jerusalem before his deportation (cf. Ezek. 1.3). The book states clearly that it was 'in visions of God' that Ezekiel was taken to Jerusalem (8.3; cf. 40.2). There is no need to interpret these references as evidence of actual journeys to Jerusalem from Babylonia or, indirectly, as evidence of a ministry in Jerusalem.

As for Ezekiel 12, Zimmerli argued persuasively that even this chapter does not demand a Jerusalem setting: 'Ezekiel speaks in exile about the fate of those who remain in Jerusalem, who are threatened by the divine judgement which the exiles, whose hope depends on the continued existence of Jerusalem, refuse to see'.[22] Thus Zimmerli regarded the chapter as primarily directed to the exiles, even though it speaks of the fate of the community in Judah. It may be appropriate here to draw a comparison with the oracles against foreign nations which are a feature of the book of Ezekiel as of many other prophetic books. As Taylor points out, 'No one has yet insisted that Ezekiel's oracles to the foreign nations should have been delivered on Ammonite territory or in Tyre or Egypt'.[23]

It may be admitted that, taken independently, the material in Ezekiel 8 and 12 might reasonably be read as indicating a Jerusalem setting for at least part of Ezekiel's work. However, the book places the whole of the prophet's ministry in Babylonia and, as we have suggested, the difficulties which are raised by this are not sufficient to demand that it be explained as a fiction. Given the absence of positive indications that redactors have carried out a wholesale fabrication of an exilic setting, it seems probable that Ezekiel's ministry was indeed conducted entirely in Babylonia.[24]

We have argued that the context of the ministry of Ezekiel is the early sixth century and that his message is shaped by the need to respond to the theological questions raised by the Babylonian crisis. We have suggested, moreover, that he made his response from within the community of Judaean exiles in Babylonia. But how much of the book of Ezekiel in fact represents the words of the prophet himself? And what is the relationship of the remaining material to Ezekiel? It is to these keenly debated questions that we must turn in our next chapter.

Chapter 2

QUESTIONS OF UNITY AND AUTHORSHIP

There is considerable debate among scholars as to how much of the book of Ezekiel is actually from the prophet himself and concerning the provenance and date of any secondary material. Ackroyd writes that 'The complexity of the literary and other problems attaching to the book of Ezekiel is such that any discussion ought ideally to be prefaced by a full-scale consideration of the view that is adopted'.[1] The present chapter does not claim to meet that ideal, but represents at least an acknowledgment of the importance of these questions.

Recognition of the Problem

A distinctive feature of the book of Ezekiel is the extent to which it is arranged in a systematic and thematic way: chs. 1–24 are concerned with Yahweh's judgment upon Judah; chs. 25–32 contain oracles against the nations; chs. 33–39 focus upon hopes for the restoration of Judah; chs. 40–48 contain a detailed vision of the restored Temple and its setting. It was largely this orderly format which led most scholars, even up to the early twentieth century, to feel that this book was, for the most part, free of the problems which had already been recognized in the other major prophetic books. R. Smend wrote, 'The whole book is . . . the logical development of a series of ideas in accordance with a well thought-out, and in part quite schematic, plan. We cannot remove any part without disturbing the whole structure'.[2] In the case of Isaiah and Jeremiah, scholars acknowledged at a relatively early date that certain parts of the books might well be from hands other than those of the prophets after whom they were named.[3] However, matters seemed rather different with regard to the book of Ezekiel. Gunkel felt able to describe Ezekiel as 'the first prophet who wrote a book'[4] and G.B. Gray could write 'No other book of the Old Testament is distinguished by such decisive marks of unity of authorship and integrity as this'.[5] 'No critical question arises in connection with the authorship of the book', claimed S.R. Driver, 'It bears unmistakably the stamp of a single mind'.[6]

However, this scholarly consensus was not to remain unchallenged. There had already been hints of an alternative approach in the works of R. Kraetzschmar[7] and J. Herrmann,[8] but it was G. Hölscher who in 1924 first articulated a more critical view of the unity of the book of Ezekiel.[9] He proposed that only one seventh of the book actually came from the prophet; the bulk he attributed to a Zadokite redactor in Jerusalem in the early fifth century. Hölscher's work marked an important turning-point in the history of Ezekiel scholarship. The unity and integrity of the book could never again be taken for granted. A decade or so after Hölscher's crucial contribution, G.A. Cooke wrote that 'In recent years the study of Ezekiel has undergone something like a revolution'. Cooke himself took a relatively conservative position, but he had to admit that 'It is no longer possible to treat the Book as the product of a single mind and a single age'.[10] Hölscher opened the way for others to embark on the difficult task of attempting to distinguish between those parts of the book which may with some certainty be traced back to the prophet himself and those which may be regarded as secondary additions.

An exhaustive chronicle of the ensuing debate is available elsewhere and need not be rehearsed here.[11] More central to our purpose is a review of the major criteria upon which theories about the unity and authorship of the book of Ezekiel have generally been based.

Criteria of Authorship

1. The first criterion to be considered is the distinction between poetry and prose. Hölscher's approach was based primarily upon the theory that poetry or verse was more likely to go back to the prophet himself, prose material being the work of later hands. He sought to rescue Ezekiel the Poet from the book which bore his name.[12] Thus, for example, the whole of chs. 6 and 7 were rejected as secondary prose. Hölscher was here influenced by the work of B. Duhm, who had argued that poetry was the natural mode of expression in the ecstatic state in which the prophets proclaimed their messages.[13]

Rigorously applying this theory to the book of Ezekiel, Hölscher reduced the number of verses attributed to the prophet from the 1273 of the traditional view (i.e. the whole book) to a mere 170.

How helpful is the distinction between poetry and prose as a criterion in determining which parts of a book are primary? Poetic form may indeed in certain cases be an indication of earlier date; for example, many believe that in the book of Jeremiah the poetic oracles are more likely to go back to the prophet himself than is the prose material.[14] However, Jeremiah also illustrates that this criterion can never be applied in a mechanical way, for it seems likely that many of the secondary prose passages have some basis in words of Jeremiah himself, albeit adapted to somewhat different situations.[15]

In the case of Ezekiel the application of this criterion is arguably even more problematic. There are indeed some cases where prose material is probably correctly identified as secondary; for example, 27.12-25, which may have been adapted from a trade document.[16] In general, though, we do not find in the prose material of the book a particularly distinctive style or theology which may easily be contrasted with that of the poetic passages. G.A. Cooke believed that the points of contact between the poetry and the prose were sufficient to 'suggest a common source'.[17] Although he was inclined to underestimate the difficulties involved in the question of unity, these words are an important corrective to Hölscher's excessively rigorous application of his criterion. Chapters 17 and 19 of Ezekiel afford a good example of the continuities between the poetry and the prose of the book. Both contain allegorical treatments of the historical and political background to the prophet's ministry and yet the literary form is rather different in each case, ch. 17 being essentially in prose, ch. 19 in poetry. These two chapters contain, broadly speaking, the same kind of material; the particular content of ch. 19 has led to the adoption of the קינה ('lament') metre, but this poetic format does not in itself give ch. 19 a stronger claim than ch. 17 to be regarded as primary material. Hölscher's analysis failed to do justice to such real continuities between poetry and prose and attempted to provide too simplistic an answer to the question of authorship.

2. A second criterion often employed by scholars relates to the repetition which is a feature of much of the book. For example, in Ezek. 36.1-15, the introductory formula 'Thus says the Lord GOD' occurs no less than seven times (vv. 2, 3, 4, 5, 6, 7, 13), and very

similar concluding formulae occur twice (vv. 14, 15). The most common formula of all in the book, occurring over seventy times in its various forms, is the phrase 'that you may know that I am the LORD' (e.g. Ezek. 35.4, 9, 12, 15). It is often suggested that such repetition is the result of secondary additions and glosses. This view has been taken by Pfeiffer, Bertholet, May and, in an especially extreme form, by Vogt.[18] Some have stressed the importance of the Greek Septuagint (LXX) of the book of Ezekiel, claiming that it reflects a more faithful and less encumbered text than the longer and more repetitive Hebrew Massoretic Text (MT). This was argued in the nineteenth century by Hitzig and Cornill, at the turn of the century by Jahn and, more recently, by Wevers.[19] For example, when considering Ezek. 20.43, Wevers regards the words אשר עשיתם ('that you have committed') as a late addition to the MT unattested by the LXX.[20]

A number of the repetitions in Ezekiel may indeed be the result of scribal errors or deliberate glosses. For example, the repetition in Ezek. 16.6 of the words ואמר לך בדמיך חיי ('I said to you in your blood, "Live"') is widely regarded as a case of accidental dittography.[21] A judicious consideration of such possibilities is to be found in the work of Fohrer,[22] and Zimmerli's commentary exemplifies a careful weighing of the evidence of the LXX in these cases.[23] We should resist, however, the over-confident reconstruction of a concise and unrepetitive 'original' text which Wevers offers, based as it is on the presupposition that 'The true oracle in its original form was concise, even bordering on the cryptic'.[24] Whilst there is probably some truth in this description, it cannot be made to support a dogmatic rule. Recently, a number of scholars have seriously criticized the validity of repetition as a criterion of authorship. Carley and Boadt[25] have argued that repetition and redundancy might well characterize the prophet's own style and cannot of themselves be taken as indicators of a later hand. This problem of discerning whether a particular feature is a characteristic of Ezekiel himself or of some subsequent stage in the tradition is one which occurs with many of the criteria applied to the book; it is a difficulty to which we shall return.

3. A third criterion relates to the occurrence of language which seems to have affinities to that of priestly case law; for example, the use of the phrase צדיק הוא ('He is righteous') in Ezek. 18.9 and the phrase מות יומת ('He shall surely die') in Ezek. 18.13. The major

passages in question are Ezek. 3.17-21; 14.1-20; 18.1-20; 22.1-16 and
33.1-20, all of them passages of particular relevance to the present
study. This material, in whole or in part, is regarded as secondary by
Hölscher, May, Schulz and Garscha.[26] These scholars all regard the
occurrence in Ezekiel of language which seems to be related to
priestly case law as a distinctive mark of the activity of redactors.

It is clear that much material which has strong affinities with
priestly language and vocabulary is to be found in Ezekiel.[27]
However, it is also evident that Ezekiel himself was a priest (Ezek.
1.3), and it seems reasonable to regard at least some of the priestly
features of the book as related to this fact. This is not to say that all
priestly language must derive from the prophet; such features are
certainly found in sections which seem, on other grounds, to be in
part secondary (e.g. chs. 40–48).[28] In fact priestly language characterizes
the book as a whole. It seems to be typical of the form of expression
of the prophet himself, as Reventlow stresses,[29] yet it seems to be
characteristic also of secondary strata. Priestly language is one of
many features shared by Ezekiel and the tradition he shaped; in
short, it is of no independent significance as a criterion of authorship.

4. There is a certain amount of material in Ezekiel which seems to
exhibit similarities to the deuteronomistic literature.[30] For example,
Ezek. 6.13 features subject matter and vocabulary typical of that
tradition: '. . . when their slain lie among their idols, round about
their altars, upon every high hill, on all the mountain tops, under
every green tree and under every leafy oak. . . ' Some scholars have
argued that such material is not to be attributed to the prophet
himself: S. Herrmann has noted the deuteronomistic colouring of
Ezekiel 34–37 in particular. He points, for example, to the recurrent
formula, 'You shall be my people, and I will be your God' (Ezek.
36.28; 37.27; cf. 34.30-31) and also to the use of the word לב ('heart')
in 36.26. Herrmann attributes this material to a deuteronomistic
school active in Palestine during the later part of the exilic period.[31]
This approach has been pursued in further detail by R. Liwak, who
claims to discern in Ezekiel a range of deuteronomistic insertions of
varying length.[32]

The identification of what are probably deuteronomistic elements
in Jeremiah has played an important part in the attempt to trace the
development of that book. It seems, for example, that the prose
sermons are to be attributed, for the most part, to deuteronomistic

hands.[33] However, this is not usually taken to preclude a possible basis for that material in the preaching of the prophet himself.[34] Thus even in Jeremiah no absolute distinction can be made between primary and secondary material on this criterion.

In the case of Ezekiel matters are arguably even less clear-cut. That there are at least some deuteronomistic elements in the book seems undeniable. Even Zimmerli, who tended to minimize these, had to recognize such affinities in Ezek. 6.13.[35] And yet it is very difficult to tell in what way these are related to the words of Ezekiel, since they are often closely juxtaposed to features which are more obviously characteristic of the prophet himself, as we shall attempt to demonstrate later when discussing the promise of a 'new heart' and a 'new spirit' in Ezek. 36.26-27.[36] There is no reason to believe that Ezekiel himself would have been immune to the influence of deuteronomistic theology and style either in his native Jerusalem or in Babylonian exile. Redactors may well be responsible for a proportion of the deuteronomistic features in the book, but it cannot be demonstrated that all must be explained in this way. We must conclude then that deuteronomistic language is, like priestly language, of no independent significance as a criterion of authorship.

5. Another criterion which has been employed in the debate is that of consistency of grammar and motif.[37] For example, Wevers argues that since the judgment oracle in Ezek. 6.3-7 begins 'Behold, I, even I, will . . . ', it should be in the first person throughout and that words which do not conform to this expectation must be accretions to the original text.[38] Here, Wevers bases his argument on consistency of grammar; elsewhere, he focusses on consistency of motif. In ch. 17, Nebuchadrezzar is portrayed as a great eagle in v. 3 and as an east wind in v. 10; Wevers concludes that the latter must be an accretion.[39]

How legitimate are such arguments? First, it is of course reasonable to expect of an author a certain degree of consistency; what appear to be outright contradictions within biblical material, such as in Genesis 37, are rightly regarded as at least raising the question of multiple authorship.[40] However, in Ezekiel it is very difficult to employ the criterion of consistency with any confidence. There are some cases where it may be of help; for example, it is likely that Ezek. 16.44ff. is a secondary addition, since the literary image of the foundling Israel becomes complicated and confused from that point in the chapter.[41] However, apparent inconsistency need not necessarily indicate secondary elaboration. In 34.15, Yahweh himself is spoken of as shepherd of the sheep, whereas it is his servant David who appears as shepherd in v. 23. This shift could be taken as evidence of redaction, but it could equally be read as the use of a characteristic motif by a single author.

Wevers' argument from consistency has much in common with his attempt to trim our text of Ezekiel to a concise 'original' by excising repetitions.[42] On the whole, we should resist the tendency to impose excessively stringent demands of consistency upon texts which are often metaphorical or poetic in nature.[43]

6. Argument from consistency can take another form, namely that based on theological content. A number of the chapters in Ezekiel which are predominantly concerned with judgment conclude on an optimistic note (11.14-21; 16.59-63; 17.22-24; 20.40-44). These passages are often regarded as secondary additions, largely because they disrupt the consistency of theological outlook of the chapters in which they occur.[44] It is of course reasonable to expect some degree of theological consistency. However, it should not be assumed that themes of judgment and promise could not be juxtaposed in the earliest stratum—we shall later advance a case for the early dating of 11.14-21.[45]

The view which a scholar holds concerning questions of unity and authorship in the book of Ezekiel and his understanding of the theology of the prophet are usually closely related; indeed circularity of argument is an ever-present danger. We may contrast the positions of two particular scholars here: S. Herrmann believes that none of the material in the present book of Ezekiel which speaks of the deliverance of Israel derives from the prophet himself; Ezekiel is exclusively a prophet of judgment.[46] T.M. Raitt, on the other hand, regards much of the hopeful material in the book as primary and interprets the shift from judgment to deliverance as a characteristic feature of the theology of Ezekiel himself.[47]

Arguments which are primarily or solely theological can easily become subjective. An important safeguard against this is to draw upon a broad range of evidence, employing various different criteria side by side. Thus we have seen that there may be literary as well as theological arguments for regarding the latter part of ch. 16 as secondary.[48]

The Homogeneity of the Ezekiel Tradition

In addition to illustrating the caution which is always demanded by such discussions, our survey has in fact highlighted a distinctive feature of the book of Ezekiel: the nature of the book is such that it is particularly resistant to any straightforward division between primary and secondary material. This is surely not because the whole book is from the prophet Ezekiel—there are, as we have seen, indications to the contrary—but rather because of the marked homogeneity of the Ezekiel tradition, in which secondary material bears an unusually close 'family resemblance' to primary.

In this respect Ezekiel differs significantly from the other two major prophetic books. In Isaiah, for example, chs. 24–27 and 40–55 stand apart in a distinctive way, both stylistically and theologically.[49] In Jeremiah, as we have noted, the prose sermons have a characteristic style and theology which seems to distinguish them from the primary material in the book.[50] In Ezekiel, however, even the section within which scholars have most commonly discerned secondary material, namely chs. 40–48, exhibits throughout numerous elements of continuity with what are likely to be primary strata of the book.[51] Chapters 1–39 are yet more problematic, being marked by a degree of homogeneity which makes the separation of primary and secondary material unusually difficult.[52]

Reference has been made to the problem of discerning whether a certain distinctive feature is a characteristic of the prophet Ezekiel himself or of some subsequent stage of the tradition. For example, are repetitions the result of accretions or do they represent an important feature of Ezekiel's own style? Such questions do not permit of a straightforward answer. Thus it may be that in the case of, for example, priestly and deuteronomistic affinities we are dealing with features of the words of the prophet which have been heightened in the course of redaction and have become more characteristic of the finished book than of the primary material.

The Polarization of Recent Scholarship

The critical study of Ezekiel has tended to develop in two rather divergent directions in recent years, each, as we shall see, reflecting in a different way the distinctively homogeneous nature of the Ezekiel tradition.[53]

One trend is represented by the attempt to establish a refined stratification of the book, reconstructing its redactional history in minute detail. The work of J. Garscha affords a good example of this approach; he attributes only about 30 verses of the entire book to Ezekiel himself (17.2-10; 23.2-25).[54] He believes that the basic structure of the book and its uniformity of style are the result of the work of a redactor active either in about 485 or in about 460.[55] Garscha goes on to discern a further layer, for which he uses the term 'Deutero-Ezekiel'. This he dates between 400 and 350; it is marked by a sharp polemic against the non-exiles and by the use of the formula 'You shall know that I am Yahweh' and its variants.[56] Next, he isolates a 'Sacral law stratum', from around 300, and to this he ascribes the priestly language of the book.[57] Even later than this stage, a range of further elements were added, the book being completed by about 200.[58]

The grounds for Garscha's stratification must, however, be questioned. It is the alleged lack of stylistic and structural uniformity in the book which leads him to doubt its unity in the first place. He then concedes that some uniformity is nevertheless to be recognized, and this he ascribes primarily to the work of the redactor whom he dates to the first half of the fifth century. And yet Garscha does not demonstrate that these elements of uniformity must be traced to a secondary stratum. Clearly, any such hypothesis should be resisted until it can be shown that stylistic and structural uniformity cannot be from the primary level. Here we do well to follow the example of methodological caution set by Zimmerli: he envisaged a complex elaboration of the tradition by a 'School' of Ezekiel, but was at pains to stress that when a particular distinctive feature is discerned there is to be recognized at least a *prima facie* case for regarding it as a mark of the prophet himself, in the absence of clear evidence to the contrary.[59]

Garscha is by no means the only scholar to discern many layers within the text. Comparable theses are advanced by H. Schulz, H. Simian, F.L. Hossfeld and G. Bettenzoli.[60] The degree of complexity varies, but their analyses, like that of Garscha, would seem to multiply hypotheses unnecessarily and to assert more than our evidence can possibly sustain. Those who adopt this approach are inclined to be over-confident about assigning material to periods of which we know relatively little (such as the fifth century)[61] and all too cavalier about dismissing dates which appear in the text.[62] Moreover, these stratifications tend to become somewhat subjective: Garscha attributes the priestly language of the book to a stratum different from that which he regards as responsible for the character- istic style of the Ezekiel tradition, in spite of the fact that there are good grounds for regarding priestly language as an integral feature of that style. Schulz, like Garscha, speaks of a 'Deutero-Ezekiel', and yet each assigns different materials to the redactor upon whom he bestows the name.[63] As Muilenburg pointed out some years ago, the variety of the conclusions arrived at by the more radical scholars of Ezekiel is itself sufficient to counsel greater caution with regard to such attempts at stratification.[64]

A very different approach is to be found in the work of those scholars who prefer to analyse the text in its present form rather than posit a hypothetical history of its formation. This position is by no means necessarily a flight to naïve conservatism; its proponents are generally skilled in the use of historical-critical methods but believe them no longer adequate to the task, and instead resort to other critical methods, such as structural analysis and rhetorical criticism.

We may take M. Greenberg's 'Holistic Interpretation' as a good example of this trend.[65] He writes, 'There is only one way that gives any hope of eliciting the innate conventions and literary formations of a piece of ancient literature, and that is by listening to it patiently and humbly. The critic must curb all temptations to impose his antecedent judgments on the text'.[66] Greenberg deduces that the book is 'the product of art and intelligent design... A consistent trend of thought expressed in a distinctive style has emerged, giving the impression of an individual mind of powerful and passionate proclivities'.[67] This leads him consistently towards the belief that the 'individual mind' in question is that of Ezekiel: 'The persuasion grows on one as piece after piece falls into the established patterns... that a coherent world of vision is emerging, contemporary with the sixth-century prophet and decisively shaped by him, if not the very words of the prophet Ezekiel himself'.[68] L. Boadt and M. Nobile adopt approaches which are in certain respects similar.[69]

Greenberg's scepticism concerning alleged secondary elaboration provides a very valuable corrective to speculations like those of Garscha. However, such a position all too easily slides from a healthy agnosticism about editorial layers into an implicit assumption of authorship by the prophet himself; this is equally unjustified and fails to take seriously the evidence of redactional activity which is to be discerned.

Neither an elaborate stratification nor a 'Holistic Interpretation' fully recognizes the particular complexity and difficulty of the questions of unity and authorship in the book of Ezekiel. The former goes too far, offering detailed answers where none is legitimately to be sought; the latter does not go far enough and fails to address important questions concerning the historical development or 'depth dimension' of the text. And yet both approaches reflect the distinctive homogeneity which we have seen to characterize the Ezekiel tradition: Garscha's stratifications have to be so minutely detailed (if they are to have any plausibility at all) precisely because there is no clear-cut distinction between the style and theology of Ezekiel and of those who followed him; but it is this same 'family resemblance' between primary and secondary material which allows Greenberg to believe (in effect) that it all comes from the prophet himself.

How then are we to proceed? We must acknowledge that the text has indeed at points been elaborated and modified and that questions are to be asked about its development, but we must conduct our inquiry not in the speculative style of Garscha and those who would offer refined stratifications, but rather in the more careful manner to which Clements has recently recalled us.[70] Our review of criteria illustrated the difficulty of such an enterprise; we saw that all must be used with great caution. We noted that some of these criteria are of no value used in isolation and that, wherever feasible, they should be used together, as part of a cumulative case. We saw this to be of particular importance where theological judgments are involved and, moreover, noted the danger of circular argument which can attend attempts to judge questions of unity and authorship in the light of theological presuppositions about Ezekiel. We must endeavour where possible, then, to discriminate between primary material and secondary elaboration, but we must undertake this task in the realization that assured results will be rare.

With these considerations in mind, we turn now to explore the themes of divine initiative and human response as they appear in the words of Ezekiel and the tradition which he shaped.

Chapter 3

THE RESPONSIBILITY OF ISRAEL: I

We saw in Chapter 1 that the context of the ministry of Ezekiel is the early sixth century, an age beset with profound theological questions posed by the Babylonian crisis. We noted that the catastrophe was so devastating in its theological implications that it might well have meant the end of the people of Israel as a community of faith. That it did not owed everything to a small group of theologians who boldly attempted to account for the disaster within the framework of faith in Yahweh. In Judah, the prophet Jeremiah and also, it seems, the authors of the Deuteronomistic History[1] struggled to give a faithful account of events. Among the exiled community, this task apparently fell to just one person, namely Ezekiel, deported as a priest in 597 and called to prophesy in Babylonia in about 593.

A radical question mark had been put against both the power and the justice of Yahweh; any adequate Yahwist response would have to vindicate both. This was, of course, not the first time that such a task had been faced by the prophets of Israel. A century and a half before, the Assyrian empire had posed a dire threat to the Hebrew kingdoms; indeed, the northern kingdom of Israel fell in about 721 and Judah very nearly suffered the same fate around 700. During that period, four great prophetic figures attempted to give a theological explanation for this historical disaster. Amos and Hosea working in the north and Isaiah and Micah in the south advanced the view that, far from representing the routing of Yahweh by Assyrian gods (cf. 2 Kgs 19.10-13), these events were the powerful and just act of Yahweh who was angry with the sins of his people. Isaiah indeed spoke of Assyria as a 'rod' raised up by Yahweh to beat his recalcitrant people (Isa. 10.5). It is difficult to overstate the importance of this episode in 'sharpening the tools' for the prophetic response to the Babylonian crisis at the start of the sixth century.

Ezekiel and his Yahwistic contemporaries were confronted by a scenario remarkably similar to that which had faced the eighth-century prophets—only this time Jerusalem was not spared. Whereas in the Assyrian crisis the adequacy of the prophetic response was not tested to breaking point, since Judah survived intact (albeit under the shadow of imperial domination), the Babylonian crisis appeared to falsify all the promises of old. The eighth-century prophets had provided invaluable tools, but could the same theological rationale for historical disaster bear all the weight which was now to be placed upon it?

The first twenty-four chapters of the book of Ezekiel contain one of the most sustained and vehement declarations of judgment to be found anywhere in the prophetic literature of the Old Testament. These chapters assert in an unqualified way the responsibility of Israel for the fate which has befallen her. In so doing they offer a rationale for exile which is also a theodicy: Yahweh is indeed still both powerful and just and he is punishing his own people for their outrageous sins. Just as he had raised up Assyria in the eighth century, so now Babylon is the agent of his righteous judgment. Given that everything which constituted the identity of Israel had been lost this time, it is hardly surprising that the theological explanation for this is given in the most thoroughgoing of terms. These chapters speak of 'disaster after disaster' (Ezek. 7.5), in language which is often violent and at times even crude: 'Thus shall my anger spend itself, and I will vent my fury upon them and satisfy myself; and they shall know that I, the LORD, have spoken in my jealousy, when I spend my fury upon them' (5.13). Yahweh's wrath expresses itself in judgment by fire, sword, wind, famine, wild beasts and pestilence (5.2, 16-17). So violent is the language used that the reader might be forgiven for feeling that this section of the book contains a cruel and vindictive message, calling down upon the people the most dreadful calamities imaginable. However, it must be read in the perspective of the catastrophic events which had already come upon Israel, events which demanded theological interpretation. Ezekiel offers a key to understanding the disaster which had engulfed the nation: this is not, he asserts, meaningless chaos; it is the just punishment of a sinful people by their powerful God. 'Because the land is full of bloody crimes and the city is full of violence, I will bring the worst of the nations to take possession of their houses'

(Ezek. 7.23-24)—this was indeed a hard message, but it at least offered theological meaning to a generation which was experiencing the loss of all that defined its identity.

Ezekiel 18

Perhaps the most explicit statement of the responsibility of Israel is that which appears in Ezekiel 18; the theme is here articulated in a more coherent and systematic fashion than in many of the more rhetorical passages of the book. For this reason, the present chapter is devoted to a detailed discussion of Ezekiel 18.[2] We begin by offering a brief sketch of its contents: The prophet addresses an audience who are blaming the sins of previous generations for the disaster of exile; they say, 'The fathers have eaten sour grapes and the children's teeth are set on edge'. He rejects this saying and with it his audience's denial of responsibility for their fate (vv. 1-4). To illustrate his case, he draws an analogy with three generations within a family, showing that each generation is judged independently. In this way Ezekiel emphasizes the responsibility of the present generation of Israel for what is happening to them (vv. 5-20). The final section of the chapter explores the theme of repentance; again by analogy to particular cases, the prophet argues that God always wants his people to repent. 'Get yourselves a new heart and a new spirit! Why will you die, O house of Israel?' (vv. 21-32).

Before we go further, a word about the authorship of the chapter is in order. Ezekiel 18 is inextricably linked with the issues raised by the initial events of defeat and exile at the hands of the Babylonians; the chapter takes as its point of departure words spoken by the demoralized people (v. 2). This is likely to indicate that the chapter is to be traced back to the prophet himself.[3] Ezekiel 18 is denied to Ezekiel, of course, by those scholars who regard the presence of priestly language as a distinctive mark of later editors.[4] As we suggested in Chapter 2, however, the priestly affinity of much of the book cannot be regarded as a reliable indicator of redactional provenance, since it seems clear that Ezekiel himself was a priest (1.3).[5] The possibility of redactional elaboration (whether by Ezekiel or by later hands) cannot be ruled out and will be considered; we shall, however, attempt to demonstrate that the chapter in fact constitutes a unity.[6]

Our brief sketch of Ezekiel 18 above indicated the concern of the chapter to explain the disaster of exile by emphasizing the responsibility of Israel. Before we embark on a detailed exegesis, we must raise a question which will concern us a good deal, namely the extent to which the presentation of Israel's responsibility in Ezekiel is to be regarded as individualistic in emphasis. The view that Ezekiel 18 is concerned to argue for 'individual responsibility' has been widespread, supported by, for example, Fohrer[7] and von Rad.[8] Eichrodt presented a sophisticated and complex analysis of the chapter which gave an important place to the theme of individualism,[9] whilst a recent example of a strongly individualistic understanding is found in the commentary of Brownlee.[10] Moreover, at the more popular level, it is common to find the view that Ezekiel 18 is about 'individual responsibility' rather less cautiously advanced. Thus Taylor writes, 'What happens ... is not dependent purely on heredity (his father's sins) nor yet on environment (the nation's sins), but is conditioned by personal choice ... This is a thoroughgoing individualism'.[11]

What precisely is meant by 'individual responsibility'? Definition of terms is particularly important here, since ambiguity has sometimes clouded the debate. In what follows, the phrase 'individual responsibility' will be used to mean the moral independence of contemporary individuals; in other words, that particular men and women are judged in isolation from their contemporaries. For an example of insufficient clarity in the discussion of these questions, we may quote A.S. Peake, who wrote of Ezekiel 18, 'Once he had said one generation cannot suffer for the sins of another, it was only a step further to say that one individual cannot suffer for the sins of another'.[12] Peake moves from the statement that the moral independence of generations is being asserted to the assumption that the prophet also insists upon the moral independence of contemporary individuals, without demonstrating that this is justified by the text.

It is by no means clear, however, that Ezekiel 18 does assert 'individual responsibility' in the sense in which we have defined it. Those scholars who claim that Ezekiel 18 asserts the moral independence of contemporary individuals have, we suggest, gone beyond the evidence of the chapter. Far from constituting an argument for 'individual responsibility', the purpose of the chapter is to demonstrate the collective responsibility of the contemporary house of Israel for the national disaster which she is suffering. This is not an uncontroversial reading, however, and so it demands careful demonstration. The remainder of this chapter will be devoted to a detailed exegesis of Ezekiel 18 as an uncompromising statement of the responsibility of the nation before Yahweh. Before we embark on this, however, we must review three major considerations which will shape our exegesis.

Prolegomena to Exegesis

a. In Ezekiel 18 we encounter not an abstract theological discussion, but rather an urgent attempt to convey the true meaning of particular historical events. The 'sour grapes' proverb (18.2) embodies the complaint of the generation suffering the tragedy of defeat and exile, expressing their indignation that the disaster results from the sins of previous generations. Accordingly, Ezekiel's response is concerned with challenging this interpretation. Moreover, it is essential to take account of the fact that the exile was a national crisis, which inevitably affected everyone. It is the 'House of Israel' which Ezekiel addresses (18.25, 29, 31) and his answer to the 'sour grapes' proverb must offer an explanation of the suffering of the nation as a whole.

b. It is essential to draw a distinction between language about criminal law and that relating to divine retribution in order to understand Ezekiel 18, as has been shown by Lindars.[13] Thought proceeds in a quite different way in each of the two cases. In criminal law, when a crime has been committed the culprit is sought and eventually, when he has been declared guilty, punishment is imposed. Such a pattern may be illustrated from Exod. 21.14, 'If a man wilfully attacks another to kill him treacherously, you shall take him from my altar, that he may die'. Or again, we may refer to Num. 15.32-36: here, a man is detained gathering sticks on the sabbath, the case is considered and he is then stoned to death. In such cases we are, strictly speaking, dealing with matters of criminal law, even though there may often, as here, be theological elements in the presentation. With this we may contrast language about divine retribution: this generally starts from the recognition of a particular state of affairs, prosperity or adversity, and then proceeds to attribute this to divine favour or displeasure. For example, 'I have been young, and now am old; yet I have not seen the righteous forsaken or his children begging bread' (Ps. 37.25). Prosperity is here interpreted as divine reward for virtue. On the other hand, misfortune is widely construed as divine punishment for sin, as in the words attributed to Eliphaz in Job 4.8-9, 'Those who plough iniquity and sow trouble reap the same. By the breath of God they perish, and by the blast of his anger they are consumed'.[14]

Ezekiel 18 is clearly concerned with questions about Yahweh's punishment of human sin, that is with divine retribution. Despite their differences, both the prophet and his audience regard the crisis as a punishment of sin by Yahweh; the contested issue is that of whose sins are being punished.[15] The people blame their wicked ancestors; Ezekiel, on the other hand, argues that these events are punishment for the sins of the very people who are now suffering. The fact that there is so much room for disagreement between Ezekiel and his audience derives from the special nature of language about divine retribution. Whereas in criminal law evidence can demonstrate that a particular individual is responsible for a particular crime, it is impossible to demonstrate a direct causal relationship between human sin and divine punishment. This is precisely because the reasoning characteristically goes the other way: adversity is interpreted as punishment for sin and then an attempt is made to identify the sin in question. The search for the guilty party can be very wide-ranging: for example, the Deuteronomistic Historians explain the sufferings of exile as the result of the sins of wicked ancestors such as Manasseh (cf. 2 Kgs 23.26-27). The necessarily tenuous connexion between cause and effect when speaking of sin and God's punishment gives considerable scope for those wishing to 'pass the buck'! So it is that Ezekiel's audience can choose to trace the cause of their sufferings not to their own sins but to those of others.

c. Ezekiel 18 is marked by the frequent use of language drawn from a legal background. This is the third and last of the major considerations which will shape our exegesis. We shall illustrate three distinctive features of this language in turn, namely the test-case format, the statement of judgment and the listing of sins and virtues.[16]

Ezekiel's response to the 'sour grapes' proverb is developed through the presentation of test-cases, each of which illustrates a particular hypothetical situation. Thus, in v. 5 we read, 'If a man is righteous . . . ';[17] in v. 10, 'If he begets a son . . . '; and in v. 14, 'But if this man (in turn) begets a son . . . ' Moreover, in the second half of the chapter we read, in v. 21, 'But if a wicked man turns away from all his sins . . . '[18] In v. 24 we read, 'But when a righteous man turns away from his righteousness . . . ' (v. 26 begins with the same words); and again in v. 27, 'When a wicked man turns away from his wickedness . . . '

Such a format is found elsewhere in Ezekiel. For example, in 14.4 we read, 'Any man of the house of Israel who takes his idols into his heart . . . '[19] Verse 7 begins in a very similar way, and we may also compare v. 9, 'And if the prophet be deceived . . . ' In fact, it was in an article devoted to this section of Ezekiel 14 that Zimmerli demonstrated that such language in Ezekiel is an adaptation of the test-case format of priestly law.[20] For example, at Lev. 20.9 we find, 'Every one who curses his father or his mother shall be put to death' and at Lev. 20.15, 'If a man lies with a beast, he shall be put to death'.[21]

A second feature of legal language found in Ezekiel 18 is the statement of judgment which generally follows each of the hypothetical cases. In its fullest form this consists of two elements: first, a verdict on the behaviour of the person in question; and, second, a declaration about his fate. In v. 9 it is said of the righteous man, 'He is righteous, he shall surely live, says the Lord GOD'.[22] It is important to note that whereas in this first example it is explicitly stated that this is the decision of Yahweh, this is assumed in the examples which follow. In v. 17 we read, 'He shall not die for his father's iniquity; he shall surely live'. Favourable decisions are recorded also in vv. 19, 21, 22, 27 and 28. Conversely, after the other test-cases in Ezekiel 18 unfavourable decisions are declared. Thus it is said of the wicked man in v. 13, 'Shall he then live? He shall not live. He has done all these abominable things; he shall surely die'.[23] In v. 18 we read of the wicked man, 'Behold, he shall die for his iniquity'. In vv. 24 and 26 similar phrases express the unfavourable decision against the formerly righteous man who has turned to sin.

Again, parallel forms of expression are to be found elsewhere in the Old Testament. The declarations of an unfavourable decision which we have just considered are very similar to the pronouncement of the death sentence in the priestly material. This may be illustrated from two verses which we considered earlier: in Lev. 20.9 we read, 'Every one who curses his father or his mother shall be put to death' and again, in v. 15, 'If a man lies with a beast, he shall be put to death'. It seems likely that the negative declarations of Ezekiel 18 represent an adaptation of such priestly language.[24]

If this is correct, it would seem possible that the form of the positive declarations of Ezekiel 18 derives from the priestly statement of acquittal, the counterpart to the pronouncement of the death sentence. We may compare the words of Lev. 18.5, 'You shall therefore keep my statutes and my ordinances, by doing which a man shall live'. (Also worthy of comparison is the priestly declaration over the cleansed leper at Lev. 13.17, 'He is clean'.)[25] However, precise parallels to the phrases which occur in the positive declarations of Ezekiel 18 are not to be found. Certain scholars have argued for an alternative priestly origin for these declarations. Both von Rad and Zimmerli suggested that the phrases 'He is righteous' and 'He shall surely live' have been adapted from a liturgy of entrance at the gates of the Jerusalem Temple, more specifically from declarations of righteousness pronounced over those who had measured up to Yahweh's demands and were thus deemed worthy to enter.[26] Such a ceremony may be reflected in Ps. 118.19-20, 'Open to me the gates of righteousness, that I may enter through them and give thanks to the LORD. This is the gate of the LORD; the righteous shall enter through it.' (Cf. also Pss. 15.1-2; 24.3-4.) Moreover, it may be that a ceremony of entrance to the Temple is reflected in Ezek. 44.5: 'Mark well those who may be admitted to the Temple and all those who are to be excluded from the sanctuary'.[27] It is possible that the positive declarations of Ezekiel 18 had their origin in some such ceremony, although it should be remembered that the existence of such a rite remains a form-critical hypothesis based on the texts we have cited.

We have suggested two possible priestly origins for the positive declarations of Ezekiel 18 (the statement of acquittal and the liturgy of entrance). It is also conceivable that these declarations reflect some legal usage which may not be specifically priestly; we are reminded of the narrative in Genesis 38, in which Judah declares of Tamar: 'she is more righteous than I' (Gen. 38.26).[28] The precise origins of the positive declarations of Ezekiel 18 cannot be demonstrated with certainty. Nevertheless, it seems very probable that they represent the adaptation of some form of legal language.

The third feature of legal language found in Ezekiel 18 is the occurrence of lists of sins and virtues. Verses 5-18 picture a righteous man, his wicked son and righteous grandson; in each of the three parts of this section, the content of righteousness and wickedness is illustrated by the inclusion of a list of sins and virtues. The lists each combine positive and negative statements; thus, for example, the righteous man of vv. 5-9 'does not oppress any one, but restores to the debtor his pledge', whilst the wicked man of vv. 10-13 'commits robbery' and 'does not restore the pledge'.

Similar material is to be found elsewhere in Ezekiel, notably at 22.6-12, 25-29 and 33.15. It is likely that such lists are an adaptation of priestly style: a parallel format may be observed in, for example, Lev. 19.11ff., whilst a number of the sins listed in Ezekiel 18 seem to reflect priestly concerns, for example 'shedding blood' (cf. Gen. 9.6) and 'approaching a woman in her time of impurity' (cf. Lev. 15.24). Moreover, there is a similarity between these lists and those found in Pss. 15.2-5 and 24.4, which are among the Psalms cited by some in support of the hypothesis of a liturgy of entrance to the Temple.[29] Again, though, it proves difficult to pin down the language of Ezekiel 18 exclusively to priestly vocabulary: the reference to the 'oppression of the poor and needy' in v. 12, for example, is reminiscent of Deut. 24.14. Nevertheless, it does seem clear that the lists of sins and virtues in Ezekiel 18 represent yet another feature of legal language.

We have demonstrated that Ezekiel 18 appears to employ three features of legal language: the test-case format, the statement of judgment and the listing of sins and virtues.[30] This is the language of criminal law; and yet here it is not used in its normal context, but is adapted to a rather different purpose. We noted earlier the important distinction between the language of criminal law and that relating to divine retribution.[31] Ezekiel 18 is a discussion of the latter which is nevertheless conducted using language borrowed from the former.[32] Ezekiel's concern is to discuss the causes of a particular historical disaster, the defeat of the nation and the deportations which followed it, but he advances his argument by drawing upon analogies from the realm of criminal law. Recognition of this reapplication of language is the key to the understanding of the chapter.

Exegesis of Ezek. 18.1-20

After a standard formula used to introduce a divine oracle (v. 1), the question is posed: 'What do you mean by repeating this proverb concerning the land of Israel, "The fathers have eaten sour grapes, and the children's teeth are set on edge"?'. The placing of words in the mouths of interlocutors is a characteristic feature of the book of Ezekiel. Sometimes the author caricatures what he regards as the views of his audience, as at 20.32, 'Let us be like the nations, like the tribes of the countries, and worship wood and stone'.[33] Elsewhere, it seems likely that a current proverb is cited; thus, for example, in 12.22 we read 'Son of Man, what is this proverb that you have about the land of Israel, saying, "The days grow long, and every vision comes to naught"?'[34] It is probable that the reference to sour grapes in 18.2 constitutes another case of this. The saying is described as a משל ('proverb') in vv. 2 and 3 and appears to be in the form of a poetic couplet. The same words appear also at Jer. 31.29-30, which would seem to make it all the more likely that we are here dealing with a current proverb.[35] Morgan has suggested that the saying stands in continuity with Wisdom traditions,[36] whilst Sakenfeld has expressed the view that it may owe something to the Decalogue motif of 'visiting the iniquity of the fathers upon the children to the third and fourth generation' (Exod. 20.5).[37] However, the origins of the saying may not be traced with any certainty.

Several times in Ezekiel a saying is used as a device to introduce a debate, quoted only to be rejected. This is the case here in Ezekiel 18, where we read in v. 3, '"As I live", says the Lord GOD, "this proverb shall no more be used by you in Israel"'. Very similar is 12.21-25, where, after the quotation of the proverb concerning the failure of visions, cited above, we read, 'Tell them therefore, "Thus says the Lord GOD, 'I will put an end to this proverb, and they shall no more use it as a proverb in Israel'"'. (Ezek. 33.23-29 follows a similar pattern, though its resemblance to Ezek. 18.2-3 is less close.) The technique of placing words in the mouths of interlocutors may be one of the reasons why one finds such relatively complex reasoning in the book of Ezekiel. Ezekiel 18 is perhaps the best example of this; we shall see the sophisticated way in which the argument is developed, working from what the prophet's audience is held to believe and what such beliefs are said to imply.[38]

The 'sour grapes' proverb of Ezek. 18.2 summarizes the position of the people, which the prophet will procede to counter in the rest of the chapter. They are suffering at the hands of the Babylonians—they are, in their own words, like children whose 'teeth are set on edge'. To whom do the 'children' of the proverb correspond? In other words, who are Ezekiel's specific audience here? We argued earlier that there are good grounds for accepting the witness of the book of Ezekiel itself that the ministry of the prophet took place entirely in Babylonia.[39] If this is correct, then presumably the audience into whose mouths the 'sour grapes' proverb is put are the exiles in Babylonia. The word על in v. 2 should then be understood (with the RSV) to mean 'concerning' rather than 'on' or 'in': the proverb is used by the exiles 'concerning' the fate of 'the land of Israel' (that is, defeat and exile at the hands of the Babylonians) rather than being used by people in the homeland itself. Further, the words לכם ... בישראל in v. 3 (RSV: 'by you in Israel') should be understood to refer to the exiles in Babylonia citing the proverb, rather than to the current inhabitants of the geographical area of Judah.

Ezekiel's hearers are presented as claiming that they are suffering not because of their own deeds but because of the sins of others—'The fathers have eaten sour grapes'. Who are these 'fathers'? The most natural reading is to understand the word to refer literally to the ancestors of those who are now suffering. This seems the more likely since there is contemporary evidence that such ideas were being expressed. Thus, as we noted earlier, the Deuteronomistic Historians, in accounting for the disaster of conquest by the Babylonians, look back to the sins of the notorious king Manasseh and his like: 'Surely this came upon Judah at the command of the LORD, to remove them out of his sight, for the sins of Manasseh' (2 Kgs 24.3). Earlier, in 2 Kgs 22.13, Josiah is portrayed as saying, 'Great is the wrath of the LORD that is kindled against us, because our fathers have not obeyed the words of this book'. Battersby Harford even suggested that Ezekiel 18 is consciously combating the theology of the Deuteronomistic History;[40] be that as it may, these quotations from 2 Kings at least provide evidence that such views were being expressed in Ezekiel's time. Again, in Jer. 15.4, we read 'I will make them a horror to all the kingdoms of the earth because of what Manasseh, the son of Hezekiah, king of Judah, did in Jerusalem' and in Lam. 5.7, 'Our fathers sinned, and are no more; and we bear their iniquities'.

Eichrodt offers an alternative view, suggesting that the 'fathers' of the proverb are the non-exiles who are being blamed by the Jewish community in Babylonia.[41] However, whilst it is true that the prophet's own message is sometimes directed against the inhabitants of Judah (11.14-21; 33.23-29), there seems to be no evidence that the exiles as a whole were blaming their compatriots in the way suggested by Eichrodt. Such a view would, in any case, necessitate a rather forced understanding of the word 'fathers'.

We favour, then, the view that the 'fathers' are ancestors. Daube has offered two possible interpretations of the way in which the ancestors' sins may have been held to affect the descendants in the understanding of those who used the 'sour grapes' proverb.[42] It may be that the exiles are thought to be somehow implicated in the guilt of their forebears, sharing with them in what Daube calls 'Corporate Responsibility', in which case Ezekiel's hearers are resisting the notion that they should be thus involved in guilt resulting from actions which they themselves did not commit. The alternative interpretation offered by Daube is that the exiles are thought of as the 'property' of their forebears; the punishment of the wicked ancestors entails a blight on their property, including their descendants. In this case, the complaint of Ezekiel's audience would be against the suffering of the innocent in the course of the punishment of the wicked ancestors. Daube calls this second model 'Ruler Punishment', comparing our case to material such as 2 Sam. 24, in which the sin of the ruler David is punished by the deaths of seventy thousand Israelites, who are, Daube suggests, regarded as his property. It is perhaps not possible to know for sure in precisely which sense the 'sour grapes' proverb understands the sins of the ancestors to affect the descendants; what does seem clear is that Ezekiel's hearers are pictured attributing their sufferings to the sins of their ancestors and complaining that such a system of justice is unfair (cf. 18.25, 29, 'The way of the Lord is not just').

Zimmerli suggested that the proverb may have been in part a response by the people to the implication of Ezekiel 20 that Israel had been hopelessly rebellious from the beginning of her history.[43] It may indeed be the case that the general picture of a nation sinful since its origin presented in Ezekiel 20 encouraged the pessimism of the proverb. We shall note later, however, that the question posed in Ezek. 20.30, 'Will you defile yourselves after the manner of your fathers?', implies that in ch. 20 as in ch. 18 the prophet understands the present generation to be judged for their own and not their ancestors' deeds.[44]

The 'sour grapes' proverb is more than simply an expression of despair; it is also, as we have we seen, a complaint that Yahweh's system of justice is unfair. And implicit in this is a plea of innocence, a denial of responsibility on the part of those who are suffering. Sakenfeld expresses well the polemical nature of the saying: 'Now the proverb . . . serves as a justification for despair and for transgression'.[45] Ezekiel's audience revel in the fact that the proverb relieves them of responsibility—they have a vested interest in its validity.

Immediately after the prohibition of the 'sour grapes' proverb (v. 3), we read, 'Behold, all souls are mine; the soul of the father as well as the soul of the son is mine' (v. 4). This statement that all souls belong to Yahweh is typical of the radical theocentricity of the book of Ezekiel, in which all things depend on the will of Yahweh.[46] Verse 4 continues, 'the soul that sins shall die': this apparently austere statement is in fact the beginning of Ezekiel's demonstration that the disaster of exile is not meaningless chaos. These words establish the basis upon which Ezekiel's response to the proverb is to be advanced; they enunciate the legal principle that it is the person who is guilty, and not another, who should be punished.[47] We shall see in Chapter 5 that this principle seems to have been the working basis of criminal law in Israel from the earliest times.[48] However, it is important to recognize that in what follows this generally accepted legal principle (which may properly be described as that of 'individual responsibility') is reapplied to a realm of discourse very different from that of criminal law.

Ezekiel reapplies the legal principle that it is the guilty party who should be punished to the discussion of the national crisis of exile.[49] This is done primarily in the long section (vv. 5-18) in which three cases are presented, those of a righteous man, his wicked son and his righteous grandson. As we have seen, these are presented as test-cases in the style of priestly law. Each case concludes with a verdict, reached on the basis of the principle enunciated in v. 4: thus it is said that the righteous man shall live (v. 9), but that his wicked son shall die, despite his father's righteousness (v. 13). These first two cases establish a precedent for the crucial third case, that of the righteous son of a wicked man in vv. 14-17. The key to understanding this section of the chapter is to realize that Ezekiel's audience, to whom he attributes the 'sour grapes' proverb, imagine themselves to be the righteous sons of wicked men. Although a single man is considered in each of the three test-cases, it is the cause of the nation's predicament which is being explored; the proverb blames the sins of previous generations for the sufferings of the present, and accordingly the individuals of the test-cases each represent a generation.

When the principle that 'the soul that sins shall die' (v. 4) is applied to the case of the righteous son of a wicked man, it is clear what the verdict must be: 'He shall not die for his father's iniquity; he shall surely live' (v. 17). If we now relate this test-case to the question Ezekiel is actually addressing, we see that he is asserting that if the present generation were righteous they would not be suffering; since they are suffering, this must be because of their own sins. Thus Ezekiel's hearers cannot be the righteous sons of wicked men, as they suppose themselves to be.

It is easy enough to see how this section of Ezekiel 18, picturing the three men, could be misread as an argument for 'individual responsibility'. However, whilst Ezekiel certainly rejects the idea that the present disaster is a punishment for the sins of previous generations, he is not concerned here with the moral independence of contemporary individuals. He takes for granted the general principle of 'individual responsibility' in the realm of legal practice (and employs it in considering his three hypothetical cases), but the possibility of Yahweh judging individuals in isolation from their contemporaries is not considered. This is because the question at issue is a different one, namely, 'Why is this inevitably communal, national crisis happening?'[50]

The corporate nature of the concerns of Ezek. 18.1-20 has not been taken sufficiently seriously by scholars. The insight that in the book of Ezekiel the language of priestly case law is often reapplied to quite different subject matter owes much to the work of Zimmerli;[51] and yet it may be suggested that even he failed to apply this insight consistently in the case of Ezek. 18.1-20. We noted earlier that Zimmerli favoured the view that the positive declarations of Ezek. 18.9, 17 may have had as their original setting a 'liturgy of entrance', in which righteous individuals were granted admission to the Temple.[52] On this assumption, he wrote, 'Ezekiel, as it were, calls individuals anew to the temple gate and promises them even in exile entrance into life which was once proclaimed in the sanctuary';[53] or again, 'By means of such a series of commandments the prophet seeks to make clear to the inquirers in exile what the will of Yahweh is and how it includes the promise of life for each individual, regardless how his father may have lived'.[54] However, whilst the positive declarations of Ezekiel 18 may quite possibly have their origin in some such 'liturgy of entrance', it is important to recognize that (whatever the specific source of the phrases) this language has now been reapplied to the discussion of a crisis which was inevitably communal and national. To assume that the positive declarations of Ezek. 18.9, 17 may be taken as evidence of an individualistic concern on the part of Ezekiel is to fail to take seriously the reapplication of language which they represent.

We come now to v. 19. Ezekiel portrays his audience as saying, 'Why should not the son suffer for the iniquity of the father?'[55] We noted earlier that the placing of words in the mouths of interlocutors is a common feature of the book;[56] the present verse may be said to be the most subtle and sophisticated case of this literary technique. Ezekiel's audience is pictured as demanding that 'the son' should suffer for the iniquity of 'the father'. These words clearly refer back to the last of the three test-cases, found in vv. 14–17, in which it is said that the righteous son of the wicked man shall live: 'he shall not die for his father's iniquity'. As we noted earlier, Ezekiel's hearers imagine themselves to be the righteous sons of wicked fathers. The words put into their mouths in v. 19 express their objection to the verdict Ezekiel has recorded in this third test-case: they are righteous and yet suffering, so Ezekiel must be mistaken. We have seen that the 'sour grapes' proverb expresses the complaint that they are suffering for the sins of their ancestors, and yet here in v. 19 the same people are pictured as demanding that 'the son' (with whom they identify themselves) *should* suffer for the iniquity of 'the father'! This is indeed paradoxical and can only be explained on the hypothesis that Ezekiel is suggesting that such a demand is implied by his audience's position. They have, as we have shown, a vested interest in the theory embodied in the 'sour grapes' proverb; unless it can be established that one generation suffers for the sins of previous generations, they will have to admit that they are to blame for the current situation. They complain about the injustice of events, but would prefer to go on believing in their own explanation for the disaster rather than admit responsibility. Hence the paradoxical plea of v. 19 that 'the son' should suffer for the iniquity of 'the father'. One might say that this verse, in which Ezekiel's hearers are represented as in effect pleading that they be punished, is a *reductio ad absurdum* of their whole position. So committed are they to the explanation of events given in the 'sour grapes' proverb, that they would, it seems, rather Yahweh be unjust than admit themselves unjust, a theme which will be taken up in v. 25.

In the second half of v. 19, Ezekiel responds to the plea that the righteous son should suffer by affirming that, 'When the son has done what is lawful and right, and has been careful to observe all my statutes, he shall surely live'. In these words, the prophet reiterates and defends the verdict reached in his third test-case (v. 17). By spelling out the demands of justice as he does here (albeit in very summary form), he calls on his hearers to reflect on whether they have indeed 'done what is lawful and right' and 'been careful to observe all my statutes', in other words to consider whether they really are the victims of injustice as their proverb claims. Could it not be that the present sufferings show that they are not 'righteous sons' at all, but are receiving just punishment for their own sins?

Verse 20 reaffirms the basic legal principle of 'individual responsibility' upon which verdicts were reached in the three test-cases. Not surprisingly, therefore, this verse bears similarities to v. 4, in which that principle was first enunciated. Verse 20 begins with the words with which v. 4 ended, 'The soul that sins shall die'. This is spelled out in a way which relates it more specifically to the concerns of the chapter: 'The son shall not suffer for the iniquity of the father, nor the father suffer for the iniquity of the son; the righteousness of the righteous shall be upon himself and the wickedness of the wicked shall be upon himself'. That this verse is a statement of legal principle is the more likely in view of its close similarities to Deut. 24.16, which is unquestionably a legal text. Deut. 24.16 reads, 'The fathers shall not be put to death for the children, nor shall the children be put to death for the fathers; every man shall be put to death for his own sin'.[57] Ezek. 18.20 places the statement that 'the son shall not suffer for the iniquity of the father' before the converse statement (in contrast to the order followed in Deut. 24.16). This is appropriate, since it is the question of whether the innocent son suffers for the sins of the father which really concerns Ezekiel; this is, of course, the subject of the crucial third test-case (vv. 14-17). The words 'nor shall the father suffer for the iniquity of the son' are not directly relevant to the argument Ezekiel is presenting. However, since v. 20 reiterates the legal principle which Ezekiel then applies to his specific concerns, we should not be surprised if the general statement includes words which are not strictly necessary for the particular application at hand.[58]

Deut. 24.16 and Ezek. 18.20 both state the same basic principle of law, namely that no one who is innocent should suffer for the sins of the guilty. It is the other members of the family of the guilty person who are most likely to be included in his punishment, and so these verses specifically mention that the fathers and the sons of the guilty are not to be punished. Fathers and sons are cited here as examples of the thoroughgoing nature of this legal principle of 'individual responsibility'. It is important to be clear about the difference between vv. 2 and 20 of Ezekiel 18 with regard to the use of the words 'father' and 'son'. In v. 2, the proverb speaks of Yahweh's punishment of sin through his activity in history: 'the fathers' are the previous generations who are being blamed for the sufferings of 'the children', who are the present generation. Verse 20, on the other hand, is a statement of legal principle: 'the father' and 'the son' of the wicked are cited here as examples of closely related contemporaries who might suffer for the iniquity of the wicked; the legal principle of 'individual responsibility' states that even these are not to be punished.

The legal statement of Deut. 24.16 is one of a series of laws of a humanitarian nature which appear in Deuteronomy 24-25.[59] The concern of the verse is to protect the innocent; they must not be punished for the sins of the wicked. This is the presupposition also of the legal principle upon which Ezekiel's test-cases are decided; and yet he uses this humanitarian rule to provide the key to the proper understanding of suffering which is already happening. The legal principle which is cited in Deut. 24.16 and in Ezek. 18.4, 20 was intended to prevent any undeserved suffering of the innocent which might happen in the future; Ezekiel's broader purpose in Ezekiel 18 is to explain the deserved suffering of the wicked which is already happening.

The way in which Yahweh's punishment of sin is understood in Ezekiel 18 may be contrasted with the handling of the same issue in certain passages of the deuteronomistic literature. We have seen that Deut. 24.16 states that in the operation of the criminal law one person must not be punished for the sins of another; and yet, when considering the question of Yahweh's punishment of sin through his activity in history, the Deuteronomistic Historians explain the Exile as punishment for the sins of previous generations and above all of Manasseh (2 Kgs 23.26; 24.3).[60] A comparison of these deuteronomistic texts might suggest that Yahweh is not felt to have been as fair in his dealings with his people in history as they are with one another in matters of law. Ezekiel 18, on the other hand, by rejecting the notion that the disaster is a punishment for the sins of previous generations, seeks to demonstrate that Yahweh's activity in history is every bit as just as the demands of legal practice: the present generation suffers for its own sins.

Exegesis of Ezek. 18.21-32

With v. 21, a new section of the chapter begins. Up to this point, Ezekiel has been concerned solely with the question of whose sins are being punished in the present events of exile; he has been attempting to persuade his hearers of their responsibility. He has not completed that task and will return to it, but for the moment he turns to consider a different but closely related question, namely that of repentance. Responsibility implies the possibility of repentance; he argues (again by analogy to particular cases) that repentance is always possible and that Yahweh always wants his people to repent.

In v. 21 it is said that if a wicked man repents, 'he shall surely live; he shall not die'. Verse 22 underlines the fact that none of the repentant sinner's past transgressions will be remembered against him. The opposite case is described in v. 24: if a righteous man turns to sin, 'he shall die'; none of his previous righteous deeds will be remembered. In vv. 26-28 both cases are reiterated; v. 26 deals with the apostasy of the righteous and vv. 27-28 with the repentance of the wicked. The consistent message in this section is that what matters is present orientation; the past is forgotten. Righteous and wicked are judged as they are now: there is no 'treasury of merit', as Sakenfeld puts it,[61] but conversely none of the sins of the past will be remembered against the penitent. The prophet continues to address the corporate situation of exiled Israel; having demonstrated that one generation is not condemned for the sins of previous generations, he now goes on to argue that if the nation repents, even its own past behaviour will not be an obstacle to choosing 'life'.[62]

This section deals with the dual themes of repentance and apostasy, but it is clearly the possibility and value of repentance which dominates. Not only is this theme handled at greater length but the section is arranged in a chiastic fashion, so as to give prominence to the positive theme of repentance. The section opens (vv. 21-22) and closes (vv. 27-28) with the case of the man who turns from evil, rather than with its negative counterpart, which is dealt with in vv. 24 and 26. This positive emphasis is further highlighted in v. 23 (the words of which are echoed also in the final verse of the chapter): '"Have I any pleasure in the death of the wicked", says the Lord GOD, "and not rather that he should turn from his way and live?"'

The verses of Ezekiel 18 which we are now considering represent a shift from the question of whose sins are being punished to that of repentance. Not only is the change in focus at v. 21 somewhat marked; a further complexity is that in vv. 25, 29 and 30a we apparently return to the issue of responsibility. It seems strange, at first sight, to find repentance discussed before Ezekiel has completed the argument for his interpretation of the disaster. However, this is yet another example of the sophisticated way in which he advances his case, introducing the theme of repentance before he has said his last word on the question of whose sins are being punished. The subtlety of the chapter is seen in the way that here at v. 21, before he has finished persuading his hearers of their blame, Ezekiel boldly anticipates their acceptance of responsibility and tells of the attractive possibility of a fresh start. In this way he not only broaches the theme of repentance but also hopes to move his audience a little closer to admitting their responsibility.

We have referred in passing to vv. 25 and 29, which must now be given closer attention. Verse 25 reads: 'Yet you say, "The way of the Lord is not just". Hear now, O house of Israel: Is my way not just? Is it not your ways that are not just?' Verse 29 is virtually identical. Both occur among verses dealing with repentance, and yet seem to be concerned primarily not with the possibility of repentance, but rather with the same question as that addressed in vv. 1-20, namely whether Ezekiel's hearers are in fact, as they claim, suffering for the sins of their ancestors. The words 'Is it not your ways that are not just?', addressed to Israel in both v. 25 and v. 29, clearly indicate that Ezekiel's audience has not yet acknowledged responsibility for the present events. Accordingly, it seems that their words, 'The way of the Lord is not just', express precisely the same complaint as is articulated in the 'sour grapes' proverb of v. 2, namely that Yahweh is punishing the present generation unjustly. Despite their setting, then, vv. 25 and 29 are concerned essentially not with the possibility of repentance, but rather with the question of whose sins are being punished in the present disaster. By such an interweaving of the themes of responsibility and repentance, Ezekiel attempts to manoeuvre his audience into the position Yahweh demands of them.[63]

Verses 25 and 29 provide further examples of the technique of placing words in the mouth of the audience being addressed, so as to show them the implications of what they are saying and persuade them to alter their position. These two verses state that Ezekiel's hearers are challenging the justice of Yahweh; this has been implicit in the discussion from the start of the chapter, but it is now made explicit for the first time. The very words 'The way of the Lord is not just' have a shocking presumption about them, and even by summarizing his audience's position in this way the prophet has dealt a blow against it. In response Ezekiel asks, in the name of Yahweh, 'Is my way not just?' and then he puts directly the question which was posed indirectly by the whole of the first section (vv. 1-20): 'Is it not your ways that are not just?' This explicit challenge represents the culmination of that elaborate argument based on the adaptation of case law. We saw when considering the paradoxical v. 19 that Ezekiel was implying that his hearers would rather believe they are punished unjustly than admit responsibility. Now, in vv. 25 and 29, he suggests that they would rather Yahweh be unjust than admit themselves unjust.[64] These verses in fact present a stark choice: either it is the house of Israel which is unjust, or Yahweh himself—which is the more reasonable assumption? Ezekiel demands of his audience a complete *volte-face*; what they need to question is not Yahweh's justice, but the basic premise of their whole position, namely the arrogant assumption of their own innocence. Once this premise falls, Ezekiel's own line of argument follows.

Verse 30a, introduced by the word לכן ('Therefore'), summarizes

Ezekiel's response to the 'sour grapes' proverb: '"Therefore I will judge you, O house of Israel, every one according to his ways", says the Lord GOD'. Here Ezekiel addresses the nation, the house of Israel, and rejects his audience's interpretation of the national crisis, namely that the sins of previous generations are being punished. The words איש כדרכיו (translated in the RSV, 'every one according to his ways') are not to be understood to imply that Yahweh will punish individuals in isolation from their contemporaries. Rather, they are to be seen as a third and final reference to the legal principle (enunciated earlier, in vv. 4 and 20) whereby it is the guilty party who is to be punished. We might paraphrase thus: 'Therefore I will judge you, O house of Israel, by analogy to the legal principle whereby each individual is punished for his own crime'. Applied to the question at issue in Ezekiel 18, as we have shown, this means that the present generation is being punished for its own sins alone.

The final words of the chapter (vv. 30b-32) focus on the challenge to repentance. 'Get yourselves a new heart and a new spirit! Why will you die, O house of Israel?' (v. 31); 'Turn and live' (v. 32). These words make explicit the challenge to repentance which is clearly implied in vv. 21-24 and 26-28.

We have completed our exegesis of Ezekiel 18. Having demonstrated the corporate concerns of the first half of the chapter, we have assumed that the challenge to repentance in the second half is addressed to the community as a whole. But is this assumption correct, or is the repentance of independent individuals envisaged? When considering the earlier section of the chapter (vv. 1-20) it was possible to show that the nation as a collective unit was the subject of discussion; with vv. 21-32, however, it is more difficult to decide, for a number of reasons. First, whereas the consideration of responsibility in vv. 1-20 pertains to a given historical situation which was inevitably corporate (namely defeat and exile), the issue of repentance addressed in vv. 21ff. concerns an open opportunity, which could, theoretically, be either a collective or an individual experience. Second, although in vv. 21ff., as in vv. 1-20, we find the use of the test-case format and of legal declarations, an important difference is to be observed.[65] Whereas in vv. 1-20 the three test-cases were discussed as though actual legal cases, from which a theological analogy was then drawn, in the present section the distinction between legal and theological discourse seems to be less rigorously maintained. Thus, whilst it would seem to be universally true of legal practice that a man who commits a crime is held responsible, regardless of his former righteousness (cf. vv. 24, 26), the statement that when a wicked man repents his past transgressions will not be held against him (vv. 21-22, 27-28) is more surprising! Despite the use of legal terminology, it is clear that here we are already dealing with a statement about how Yahweh himself acts. (This is also suggested by the inclusion in the midst of this section of the words, '"Have I any pleasure in the death of the wicked", says the Lord GOD, "and not rather that he should turn from his way and live?"'[18.23].)[66] So when in these verses reference is made to an individual penitent, it is not clear whether this is simply because the test-case format characteristically operates in terms of particular cases, or because Ezekiel is indeed concerned with the repentance of independent individuals. It is conceivable, then, that the two halves of the chapter differ significantly in this regard. Greenberg, for example, asserts that at v. 21 the focus shifts 'from intergenerational moral autonomy to the liberation of the individual from the burden of his own past'.[67]

There are, however, good reasons for believing that in vv. 21ff. Ezekiel is in fact envisaging the corporate repentance of the nation as a whole. First, Ezekiel's argument to persuade his hearers of their responsibility is not complete at v. 20; he returns to it in vv. 25, 29 and 30a. The references to repentance in vv. 21-24 and 26-28 are thus sandwiched between material which attempts to persuade the present generation of its responsibility for the inevitably corporate disaster. Thus it seems likely that in these verses Ezekiel is concerned for the repentance of that same generation as a collective unit. Second, in the last verses of the chapter, where the challenge to repentance implied in vv. 21-24 and 26-28 is made explicit, we read: 'Why will you die, O house of Israel?' (18.31). This address to the house of Israel (cf. Ezek. 18.25, 29) confirms that it is the nation as a whole which is being challenged to repent. Moreover, the same verse calls upon Israel to get 'a new heart and a new spirit'—a corporate image indeed![68]

We conclude, then, that throughout the chapter the unit of responsibility envisaged by Ezekiel is the nation as a whole. In vv. 1-20 it is the present generation of Israel whom the prophet shows to be responsible for the disaster of defeat and exile and in vv. 21ff. it is that same community whom he exhorts to 'turn, and live'. Although the distinction between legal and theological discourse is less rigorously maintained in Ezek. 18.21ff. than in the first part of the chapter, it is again the case that the citing of individuals is due to the legal convention of dealing with particular cases. Whilst it is of course true that national repentance would necessarily involve change within particular individuals, it is no part of the purpose of Ezekiel here to argue for the repentance of individuals in isolation from the corporate people of God.[69]

Would Repentance Avert Disaster?

How is this call to repentance in Ezekiel 18 related to the imminence of the judgment which is anticipated throughout chs. 1-24?

A comment on the unity of Ezekiel 18 is called for at this point. We have shown that the themes of responsibility and repentance are subtly interwoven and that the two halves of the chapter form an integrated whole. This leads us to oppose the view of those scholars who regard the section of the chapter primarily concerned with repentance, namely 18.21ff., as a later addition.[70] Ezekiel 18 is an integral unit; we must make sense of it as a whole, including the call to repentance.

We must also consider the probable dating of Ezekiel 18 and the period of the prophet's activity from which it is likely to derive. We know that his ministry began in about 593, but does Ezekiel 18 address a situation before or after the final collapse of Jerusalem in 587? In literary terms, the chapter is clearly placed before the fall of the city, news of which is brought by a fugitive in 33.21-22. Zimmerli, however, argued that it responds to the situation immediately after 587. Together with 3.16b-21 and 33.1-20, Ezekiel 18 represented for him a new phase of the prophet's activity after the destruction of the city, offering the prospect of a fresh start through repentance. (In Zimmerli's view, Ezekiel 18 came to be inserted earlier in the book in the course of the redactional process.) The final disaster has happened; repentance is now called for as the means of securing a new beginning.[71]

There are, however, good reasons to believe that Ezekiel 18 belongs to the period before 587. Zimmerli took עַל in 18.2 to mean 'in', giving the sense 'What do you mean that you repeat this proverb in the land of Israel?'; the 'sour grapes' proverb was thus understood to be used by the community in Palestine in the aftermath of the fall of Jerusalem in 587.[72] (Zimmerli advanced this view in spite of the fact that he believed Ezekiel's immediate audience to be the exiled community.)[73] In contrast to this, we have argued that על in Ezek. 18.2 means 'concerning' and that the proverb is used by the exiled community.[74] If the proverb is indeed used by the exiles of 597, then the position of Ezekiel 18 within the first half of the book seems very natural: at some point relatively soon after commencing his ministry in 593, the prophet addressed the major question of the cause of the disaster, which he and his immediate audience had been experiencing to the full since 597.

The position of Ezekiel 18 within the book is important and, in the absence of clear indications that this literary setting is contradicted by historical evidence, it should be respected. It is true that this chapter could be seen as interrupting the sequence of Ezekiel 17 and 19 (which share much in both theme and style), but Zimmerli's explanation for the alleged insertion of ch. 18 could equally well be taken as an argument in favour of the authenticity of its present position. He wrote, 'The insertion of ch. 18 at this point may belong together with the fact that ch. 17, as 19, shows the judgement on a succession of kings. Ch. 18, on the other hand, seeks to destroy any fatalistic misunderstanding of the course of judgement'.[75] Zimmerli certainly failed to demonstrate that Ezekiel 18 must be a 'late prophetic saying' inserted 'into the first half of the book';[76] in particular, his argument that 'In the didactic elaboration of ch. 18 we can see again an element of the later phase of the prophet's preaching' involves a significant element of circularity.[77]

There can be no denying that the fall of Jerusalem constitutes the fulcrum of the book of Ezekiel; the year 587 ushers in the time of new beginnings,[78] and it was partly for this reason that Zimmerli wished to date Ezekiel 18 after the final disaster.[79] However, the challenge to repentance in the chapter cannot be taken as evidence of a setting after 587; for, as we shall see, when Ezekiel comes to speak of hope for the future, all is dependent on the gift of Yahweh and is contrary to what Israel deserves (e.g. Ezek. 36.32, 'It is not for your sake that I will act, says the Lord GOD; let that be known to you. Be ashamed and confounded for your ways, O house of Israel').[80]

We must, then, make sense of Ezekiel 18 as coming from before the fall of Jerusalem. This being so, how are we to understand the call to repentance? Is it implied that repentance would avert the final disaster? Surely not; exile has, after all, already claimed Ezekiel and his immediate audience, and the final judgment upon Jerusalem itself is imminent.[81] We have seen that Ezekiel 18 operates on the assumption that the crisis is already being suffered—in the words of the proverb, the children's teeth are already set on edge. The 'life' to which the chapter calls the house of Israel clearly cannot mean exemption from the disaster. But how, then, are the references to repentance to be understood?

The motif serves two functions. The first is to underline Israel's responsibility for the inevitable punishment. The call to repentance in chs. 1–24, reiterated in ch. 33,[82] does not anticipate a national conversion in the brief interim before the final disaster, nor is it implied that such penitence would reverse the tide of punishment. Rather, by emphasizing the demand of Yahweh, the call to repentance underlines the fact that Israel has had every warning and is wholly to blame for the crisis which is even now engulfing her.[83] Heaton is correct when he writes, 'The formal disputation on responsibility in 18.1-32, which has been thought to offer the possibility of avoiding judgement by penitence, is probably simply intended to affirm that the exiles are suffering for their own sins and not for those of their fathers'.[84] The words 'Why will you die, O house of Israel?' (Ezek. 18.31) are, then, words of the deepest pathos: Israel is dying as the prophet speaks—and the purpose of the chapter is to show that this is the just act of Yahweh.

But the repentance motif is by no means only a rhetorical device to emphasize responsibility; it has a second function too. We read in Ezek. 18.23, '"Have I any pleasure in the death of the wicked", says the Lord GOD, "and not rather that he should turn from his way and live?"' and again in 18.32, '"I have no pleasure in the death of any one", says the Lord GOD'. The disaster may not now be avoidable, but (though he has certainly ordained it) this is not what Yahweh would wish for Israel. Even in Ezekiel 18, where the call to repentance serves primarily to highlight the nation's responsibility for the disaster, there is revealed also the yearning of Yahweh for the obedience of his people. As we shall see, Ezekiel's God will not in the end allow the sin of Israel to be the last word. Beyond the disaster— and not before—the prophet looks to a new beginning for his people, in which 'life' will consist in the fullness of relationship with God, in contrast to the 'death' of estrangement from him.[85] But this new beginning is as yet barely hinted at in the call to the dying Israel to 'turn and live'; when the new day actually dawns, it will in no way depend upon Israel's own repentance, indeed it will appear in spite of the behaviour of the nation.

This understanding of the place of the call to repentance is not uncontroversial, and so, before closing this chapter, it is appropriate to show briefly how our proposal accounts for certain other evidence which might be thought to point in a different direction. Attention must be given here to the 'watchman' motif of 3.16-21 and 33.1-9. For Zimmerli, this expressed a call to repentance after the final disaster of 587;[86] again, we believe that the placing of this motif in the period before the announcement of the fall should be taken more seriously.[87] But if the watchman motif belongs before the fall, does it not seem to imply that repentance would avert the disaster?

Wilson helps us see the proper significance of the watchman motif.[88] He notes that the language used to define the watchman's office is not quite appropriate to the image, since for the most part it is legal rather than military terms that are used. Ezek. 33.1-6 introduces the watchman image in a general, hypothetical style: 'If I bring the sword upon a land, and the people of the land take a man from among them, and make him their watchman . . . ' (33.2); in this section, military language is certainly employed (e.g. 33.3, 'If he sees the sword coming upon the land and blows the trumpet and warns the people. . . ').[89] However, when the role of watchman is personalized as the prophet's task (33.7-9; cf. 3.16-21), it is legal language that is used (e.g. 33.8, 'If I say to the wicked, "O wicked man, you shall surely die". . . '). As Wilson shows, 'The prophet's job is not to announce impending military danger, but to deliver to the accused a legal decision which Yahweh has already given'.[90] Though (like the call to repentance in Ezekiel 18) the watchman motif witnesses also to Yahweh's yearning for the obedience of his people, its immediate function is to deliver to Israel the sentence of death.

The motif of the dumbness of the prophet is also relevant here, for Wilson has demonstrated that this too is related to the inevitability of the oncoming disaster. Ezekiel is said to be made dumb by Yahweh immediately after his call (3.22-27); and the dumbness is said to last until the news of the fall of Jerusalem in 587 reaches him (33.21-22;

cf. 24.25-27). This raises many exegetical problems; in particular, there have been numerous attempts to explain the curious phenomenon that between these two occasions the prophet preaches his tirade of judgment upon Israel.[91] Wilson finds the key to the prophet's dumbness in the words of Ezek. 3.26 which state that the prophet is not to be a איש מוכיח for the people. The RSV translates the phrase 'and (you shall be) unable to reprove them', but Wilson argues persuasively that איש מוכיח means a legal mediator for the people in the dispute between Yahweh and Israel.[92] The sense would then be that, like Jeremiah (cf. Jer. 7.16), Ezekiel is forbidden to intercede for the people. The prophet can deliver Yahweh's judgments to the people, for when Yahweh speaks to his people through the prophet his mouth will be opened (3.27), but communication cannot move in the opposite direction. 'No longer can the people argue with Yahweh through the prophet. The time for a fair trial has past.'[93] From the time of his call to the fall of Jerusalem, the prophet can only speak Yahweh's word of judgment against the city and the people.

We have seen, then, that the watchman image essentially amounts to a report of the death sentence already decided by Yahweh and that the dumbness motif is a way of underlining the inevitability of the disaster. Such a reading coheres with the recurrent insistence in the account of the prophet's call (especially Ezek. 2.1-7; 3.4-11) that his audience are an obdurate people, 'impudent and stubborn' (2.4). They are 'a rebellious house' (a refrain repeated six times here),[94] for whom the only appropriate message is the imminence of absolute judgment. The prospects of repentance are clearly bleak: 'The house of Israel will not listen to you; for they are not willing to listen to me; because all of the house of Israel are of a hard forehead and of a stubborn heart' (Ezek. 3.7). Indeed, we are reminded of the thankless task of Isaiah, called to 'make the heart of this people fat' (Isa. 6.10); Ezekiel is told: 'Behold, I have made your face hard against their faces, and your forehead hard against their foreheads' (Ezek. 3.8). We find further evidence of deep pessimism about Israel's ability to respond in the reviews of her history found in Ezekiel 16, 20 and 23. Israel has had every warning and can have no excuse; judgment is now fixed: 'When this comes—and come it will!—then they will know that a prophet has been among them' (Ezek. 33.33).[95]

We may now summarize our findings in this chapter. We have seen that Ezekiel 18 places a heavy stress on the responsibility of Israel for the exilic crisis. We have demonstrated, moreover, that this is an emphasis on the collective responsibility of the present generation for its own situation; they cannot blame past generations. Both the explanation of the current disaster and the call to repentance are addressed to the corporate 'House of Israel'. Finally, we have argued that the chapter is to be read in the light of the situation before the fall of Jerusalem in 587 and that the immediate function of the call to repentance is to underline Israel's responsibility for her fate.

Chapter 4

THE RESPONSIBILITY OF ISRAEL: II

Although Ezekiel 18 contains the most elaborate statement of the responsibility of Israel to be found in the book, this is the consistent theme of the whole of chs. 1-24. In the present chapter, we shall consider (somewhat more briefly) a number of other passages which are of particular importance for an understanding of the responsibility of Israel as presented in Ezekiel.[1]

Exegesis of Ezekiel 9

The format of this chapter of Ezekiel is very different from that of Ezekiel 18. There we found a closely reasoned logical argument involving the adoption and reapplication of legal language; Ezekiel 9, on the other hand, is couched in the form of a vision. Nevertheless, despite these differences, the two passages are comparable in the strong emphasis which they place on the responsibility of Israel.

In Ezekiel 9, a man 'clothed in linen, with a writing case at his side' is told by Yahweh, 'Go through the city, through Jerusalem, and put a mark upon the foreheads of the men who sigh and groan over all the abominations that are committed in it' (9.3-4).[2] After the man clothed in linen has been sent on his mission, six other men, described earlier as 'executioners of the city, each with his destroying weapon in his hand' (9.1), are told, 'Pass through the city after him, and smite; your eye shall not spare and you shall show no pity; slay old men outright, young men and maidens, little children and women, but touch no one upon whom is the mark. And begin at my sanctuary' (9.5-6). And so the man clothed in linen and the six executioners go about their allotted tasks.

Garscha, who attributes only about thirty verses of the whole book to the prophet, assigns ch. 9 to a secondary stratum.[3] However, Hölscher, even though he attributed only one seventh of the book to

Ezekiel, regarded the bulk of ch. 9 as primary,[4] as indeed do the great majority of commentators.[5] As in ch. 18, the close link with the initial crisis of conquest is a likely indication that ch. 9 comes from the prophet Ezekiel himself.

It is made quite clear in Ezekiel 9 that Israel's punishment is absolutely deserved. This is the just act of a powerful God against his sinful people: 'The guilt of the house of Israel and Judah is exceedingly great; the land is full of blood, and the city full of injustice' (9.9). Both the general and the more immediate context of Ezekiel 9 point to the imminence and thoroughness of judgment as the primary theme of the chapter. The general setting is the long first section of the book, chs. 1–24, characterized by the insistent declaration of judgment. The more immediate context is the account, in chs. 8–11, of a visionary journey: Ezekiel is 'lifted up between earth and heaven' by the Spirit, and brought 'in visions of God' to Jerusalem (8.3). The prophet is first shown a series of examples of the abominations practised by the community in Jerusalem (8.5-17); this account provides the basis for the judgment which follows. When, in Ezek. 9.9, Yahweh justifies the severe punishment described in our chapter, reference is made back to the words of the elders in 8.12, 'The LORD does not see us, the LORD has forsaken the land'. The last verse of ch. 8 sets the scene for the slaughter of the people: 'Therefore I will deal in wrath; my eye will not spare, nor will I have pity; and though they cry in my ears with a loud voice, I will not hear them' (8.18). Zimmerli argued persuasively that the sequence of subject matter in chs. 8 and 9 reflects the form of prophetic declarations in the context of Holy War (cf. 1 Kgs 20.28).[6] He saw ch. 8 (the abominations in the Temple) as corresponding to the motivation clause in such declarations, whilst ch. 9 was seen as corresponding to the announcement of judgment. Be that as it may, the sequence certainly highlights the emphasis of Ezekiel 9 upon the imminence of judgment.

When considering Ezekiel 18, we argued that there are no good grounds for believing that the chapter represents an argument for 'individual responsibility' or indeed reflects a particular concern for the individual. However, in the motif of the marking of the foreheads of the righteous in ch. 9 an element of individualism is clearly evident. It seems to be envisaged that if any are to be found who 'sigh and groan over all the abominations that are committed', then these individuals are to be spared in the general punishment. This motif has certainly contributed to the popular notion that 'individual responsibility' is an important part of the message of Ezekiel.[7] It is important, though, to consider the marking of the foreheads of the righteous in its wider context and to reflect further upon the purpose of the passage in which it occurs.

A careful reading of Ezekiel 9 reveals the extent to which the motif of the marking of the foreheads of the righteous is subordinated to the theme of the thorough punishment of the wicked. It is only those who, by 'sighing and groaning', positively dissociate themselves from the abominations which are committed that are to be spared (9.4). Absolutely everyone else is to be smitten, not only the ringleaders nor even only the actively wicked. Verse 6 gives an exhaustive list of the categories of people who are to be slain: 'old men . . . , young men and maidens, little children and women'. This list, including, as it does, categories which one might have expected to be exempt, seems to be designed to convey a sense of the inclusive nature of the coming judgment. We may compare similar lists in Ps. 148.11-12; Joel 3.1-2 (Eng. 2.28-29); Deut. 29.9-10 (Eng. 29.10-11). Particularly close to the present example are Jer. 6.11, which says of the wrath of Yahweh, 'Pour it out upon the children in the street, and upon the gatherings of young men also; both husband and wife shall be taken, the old folk and the very aged' and also 1 Sam. 15.3, 'Now go and smite Amalek, and utterly destroy all that they have; do not spare them, but kill both man and woman, infant and suckling, ox and sheep, camel and ass'. Ezekiel is determined to convey the fact that the impending punishment will be absolutely thorough.

Indeed, there seems to be no direct interest in the possibility that there may be some righteous to be spared. When the prophet asks, in 9.8, 'Ah Lord GOD! wilt thou destroy all that remains of Israel in the outpouring of thy wrath upon Jerusalem?', the answer given by Yahweh appears to be in the affirmative: 'The guilt of the house of Israel and Judah is exceedingly great; the land is full of blood, and the city full of injustice; for they say, "The LORD has forsaken the land, and the LORD does not see". As for me, my eye will not spare, nor will I have pity, but I will requite their deeds upon their heads' (9.9-10). The theme of neither sparing nor pitying is a recurrent one, found in the verse which precedes our chapter (8.18), in the middle of the chapter (9.5) and here again at the end (9.10).

The final verse of the chapter reports that the man clothed in linen returns, saying, 'I have done as thou didst command me'. The fact that this one man was to mark individually the foreheads of any righteous led one to expect that they were likely to be few, but now that the man clothed in linen has returned, we are not even told whether he in fact found any deserving the mark on the forehead.[8] As we have said, the exchange in 9.8-10 implies that there was none to be found. We are reminded of the familiar theme of the call narratives, 'All the house of Israel are of a hard forehead and of a stubborn heart' (Ezek. 3.7). And indeed we may compare also Ezek. 22.30, 'I sought for a man among them who should build up the wall and stand in the breach before me for the land, that I should not destroy it; but I found none'. However, it would be a mistake to press for an answer to the question whether the man clothed in linen actually found any who sighed and groaned over the abominations. The instruction to mark any righteous occurs, after all, within an account of a vision; we should not attempt to pursue the motif further than is appropriate.[9] The important point is precisely that we are not told whether any deserving the mark on the forehead were found; this confirms that the central concern is not with the possibility of exemption from punishment for any righteous. What we do know is that, now the man clothed in linen has completed his task, all hope of escape for the guilty is past. We heard in v. 5 that the executioners were to pass through the city after him, and we read in vv. 7 and 8 that they were already smiting. In Ezekiel 10, even the man clothed in linen turns destroyer, scattering burning coals over the city (10.2, 7).

We have seen the very considerable extent to which the motif of the marking of the foreheads of the righteous is subordinated to the primary theme of the thoroughness of the coming punishment of the wicked. What is the positive role of the marking motif in the chapter? This may be said to consist in three elements. First, the instruction to mark, and thereby exempt, any active righteous makes it clear that the merciless slaughter is in fact a just act of judgment. Second, the very minimal definition of those who are to receive the sign (not all except the actively wicked, but only those 'who sigh and groan over all the abominations that are committed') emphasizes the thorough-going nature of the impending punishment. Third, the marking of any righteous means that there can now be no hope of escape for the guilty.

What may be said, then, about the place of individualism in Ezekiel 9? It is certainly the case that an element of individualism is to be recognized in the motif of the marking of the foreheads of the righteous. On the other hand, the passage can in no sense be said to constitute an argument for, or defence of, the notion of 'individual responsibility'. As we have seen, the marking motif plays a decidedly subordinate role within the chapter. Moreover, within this same chapter, alongside this motif, we find material which represents a rather more collective notion of responsibility. The inclusion of little children in the punishment recalls the emphasis on family solidarity and collective retribution which is a feature of many Old Testament narratives (e.g. Josh. 7.24-25; Num. 16.32).[10] We may also note the collective emphasis of 9.9: 'The guilt of the house of Israel and of Judah is exceedingly great; the land is full of blood, and the city full of injustice'.[11] As Kaufmann wrote of Ezekiel 9, 'collective and individual retribution are spoken of in the same breath'.[12] If we recall the historical setting of Ezekiel's ministry, namely the subjugation of Judah by Babylonia, such complexities are readily understandable. Though the prophet might well feel some concern for the fate of the righteous in a general punishment, the nature of this great catastrophe was such that, in one way or another, all were inevitably involved.

The motif of the marking of foreheads almost certainly takes for granted the notion that ideally the righteous should be spared in a general punishment. As we shall see later, the principle of individual responsibility seems to have been an important feature of criminal law from early times.[13] Ezekiel 9, of course, deals not with criminal law but with divine activity in human affairs; even in this context, however, there is reason to believe that concern for the individual was nothing new. The sparing of the righteous is a recurrent motif in the Pentateuch; for example, we find reference to the deliverance of righteous Noah (Gen. 6.5-8), or again, we hear the plea of Abraham, 'Far be it from thee to do such a thing, to slay the righteous with the wicked!' (Gen. 18.25). Of course, the dating of these narratives and of the traditions which they represent is a very complex matter.[14] It is conceivable that they did not appear in writing until the time of the Exile, but it is hard to believe that the theme of the sparing of the righteous does not go back to much earlier tradition. It is, then, most unlikely that the motif of the marking of the righteous in Ezekiel 9 is to be regarded as in any sense an innovation.[15]

Before leaving Ezekiel 9, we may observe that there is such an emphasis on the imminence and absoluteness of judgment here that all talk of repentance is eclipsed. Ackroyd describes the chapter as an 'expression of the urgency with which the prophet makes his appeal',[16] but, as we have argued, the motif of the marking of any righteous serves rather to spell out to the sinful nation the fact that there can now be absolutely no hope of escape.

Ezekiel 14

This chapter falls into two parts, 14.1-11 and 14.12-23. Although both seem to reflect the influence of the priestly case law format and also manifest a strong emphasis on Israel's responsibility for her fate, there is otherwise little continuity in content and it seems reasonable to treat the two sections independently.

Exegesis of Ezek. 14.1-11

This section is introduced by the motif of elders coming to Ezekiel (14.1; cf. 8.1; 20.1). They have come to 'inquire' of God (that is, they seek a favourable oracle from the prophet), but Yahweh declares that these men are guilty of idolatry and that their inquiry is presumptuous and unacceptable (14.3; cf. 20.3, 31). And so judgment is pronounced upon the idolater: 'I the LORD will answer him myself; and I will set my face against that man, I will make him a sign and a byword and cut him off from the midst of my people' (14.7-8). Moreover, a word of warning is added for any prophet who presumes to speak a word on behalf of Yahweh without authority: 'I will stretch out my hand against him, and will destroy him from the midst of my people Israel' (14.9).

As we shall see, this passage bears the marks of priestly language; not surprisingly, then, a number of scholars contend that it derives from a secondary stratum.[17] However, as we argued in Chapter 2, there are no conclusive grounds for believing that such language is evidence of the work of redactors rather than a feature of the style of Ezekiel himself;[18] indeed, it was to these very verses that Zimmerli devoted an important study of the distinctive style of the prophet.[19] The fact that Ezek. 14.1-11 shares with 8.1ff. and 20.1ff. the introductory motif of inquiry by elders would seem to strengthen the case for regarding the passage as primary, in the absence of clear evidence that this is a redactional formula. Moreover, the grounding of this section in the immediate historical situation of the Exile is another pointer in this direction.[20]

Some scholars excise parts of the passage as secondary additions (for example, Fohrer seeks to remove vv. 3b, 6 and 7 as glosses and vv. 9-11 as an appendix).[21] Such attempts to abbreviate the passage are based primarily on the presence of certain repetitions (e.g. compare vv. 4 and 7). As we have seen, however, Carley and Boadt have warned of the difficulties in applying this criterion to questions of authorship in the book of Ezekiel, since repetition may well have been an important feature of the style of the prophet himself.[22] There is in fact no compelling reason to doubt that Ezek. 14.1-11 constitutes a single unit.[23]

We must consider next the language used in this passage. Ezek. 14.1-11 employs a striking mixture of formulae which are typical of prophetic address (e.g. 14.6, 'Therefore say to the house of Israel, "Thus says the Lord GOD, . . . "') and others which have affinities to the priestly writings, very similar to those we found in Ezekiel 18.[24] Thus the statement of how Yahweh deals with idolatry is couched in terms of a discussion of a particular legal case, 'Any man of the house of Israel who . . . ' (14.4, 7; cf. Lev. 17.8).[25] That the language found in Ezek. 14.1-11 is indebted to that of priestly law was demonstrated at length by Zimmerli, who also traced the development of the phrases which have been adopted.[26] The fate which is to befall the condemned idolater is expressed in another priestly phrase, 'I will cut him off from the midst of my people' (14.8; cf. Lev. 17.10).[27] These words seem to imply not that the legal death penalty is to be imposed by human agency, but rather that the guilty party will suffer a direct blow from Yahweh himself.[28] The phrase 'they shall bear their punishment', used in v. 10, seems similarly to refer to Yahweh himself dealing a punitive blow against the offender.[29] In such a case, the role of the community is simply to exclude the doomed sinner from the circle of fellowship; in this respect, these phrases may be seen to be related to the practice of excommunication.[30]

As in the other passages we have considered, here in 14.1-11 we find a strong emphasis on responsibility. It is stated in v. 5 that the house of Israel are 'all estranged from me through their idols'. As we have seen, in v. 10 it is said that both the idolatrous inquirer and the prophet who gives oracles without divine authority 'shall bear their punishment'; this phrase conveys unambiguously the weight of responsibility which the sinner carries. That Israel's fate is the result of her flagrant sins is again, then, stated without equivocation.

To what extent is it the responsibility of the individual which is envisaged here? We read in vv. 8-9 of Yahweh cutting off both the idolatrous inquirer and the deceived prophet from the midst of his people Israel. An individualistic motif can, it seems, be found here, but we must look more closely, giving particular attention to the nature of the language used. We have seen that although the priestly formulae used here refer primarily to the infliction of a punitive blow from Yahweh, they seem also to be related to the practice of excommunication from the religious community of Israel. We may note here a paradoxical feature of all language of excommunication, namely that it involves a strong sense both of individual responsibility and also of the vital importance of the community: the guilty individual is singled out for punishment, but this is for the very purpose of preserving the social unit. A similar ambivalence marks Ezek. 14.1-11, where language about the exclusion of the sinner is closely related to concern for the ultimate preservation of the community. In vv. 4-5, Yahweh answers the idolatrous inquirer in order to 'lay hold of the hearts of the house of Israel'. In v. 8, the idolatrous inquirer is cut off 'from the midst of my people' and in v. 9 the deceived prophet is destroyed 'from the midst of my people Israel'. Finally, we read in v. 11 that the punishment of the inquirer and the prophet are to the end that 'the house of Israel may go no more astray from me . . . but that they may be my people and I may be their God'. Thus it would seem that the element of individualism in 14.1-11 serves the more collective purpose of safeguarding the assembly of Yahweh.

However, it seems likely that even this is to overstate the place of individualism in the passage. We read in 14.5 that the house of Israel are 'all' estranged from Yahweh through their idols.[31] This is difficult to relate to the notion of the exclusion of individual idolaters from the community, and would seem to imply that the whole house of Israel, as a collective group, is judged wicked and deserving of punishment. How are we to explain this? In his important study of 14.1-11, Zimmerli demonstrated that a distinctive feature of the style of the prophet Ezekiel is that at times, notably when employing the

format of priestly case law, he reapplies language which originally
dealt with individual legal cases to collective groups and above all to
the nation of Israel.[32] He argued that the 'cutting off' of the
idolatrous inquirer is to be explained in terms of the teaching format
of the prophet, whose real concern is not with individuals but rather
with the national apostasy of the community of Israel as a whole,
who are 'all' estranged from Yahweh through their idols:

> If we do not regard this forceful turning of a saying originally
> referring to an individual to the basic problem of "Israel", we shall
> not grasp the real intention of the oracle . . . The divine saying does
> not restrict itself with this threat of judgement to individual men,
> but shows immediately the deeper truth that this holy wrath has in
> mind "Israel" when speaking about the individual sinner.[33]

If this is correct, it is nothing less than the 'cutting off' of the nation
as a whole which is envisaged; Ezekiel is again seen to be less
individualistic than he at first appears.

In 14.1-11, as in ch. 18, we find a call to repentance. In fact, 14.6
contains the first explicit case of this in the book: 'Therefore say to
the house of Israel, "Thus says the Lord GOD, 'Repent and turn
away from your idols; and turn away your faces from all your
abominations'"'. This call to repentance comes as something of a
surprise after vv. 3-5, which seem to anticipate a declaration of
absolute judgment, and indeed after the preceding chapters with
their strong emphasis on imminent cataclysm. How is this to be
explained?

As in ch. 18, the repentance motif serves two functions. If the
'cutting off' of the nation as a whole is indeed anticipated in 14.1-11,
then again the role of the call to repentance would seem to be in the
first instance rhetorical, serving to underline Israel's responsibility
for the inevitable disaster.[34] Israel is under final judgment; repentance
now will not avert the collapse of Jerusalem. The inevitability of the
disaster is highlighted by the refusal of the inquiries of the elders; as
Wilson demonstrates, the prophet's response here is thoroughly
consistent with the command in Ezek. 3.26 that he should not be a
mediator. 'Ezekiel is not allowed to intercede for the people in order
to remove the judgement. They are told only to turn, and there is no
indication that this turning will prevent the destruction of the
city'.[35]

But the repentance theme is not simply a device to highlight responsibility. As we have seen before (with regard to ch. 18), the call also testifies to an earnest desire on the part of Yahweh for the obedience of his people. He cannot, it seems, allow the 'cutting off' of Israel to be the last word; his ultimate concern is expressed in 14.11: 'that the house of Israel may go no more astray from me'. The call to repentance in 14.6 offers just a hint of the possibility of a new future.[36] Yet no new beginning can be envisaged until after the judgment is complete—and then it will depend not upon Israel's own response but upon the obedience which Yahweh himself will grant as gift (cf. 36.26-27). Moreover, as with the judgment (14.5, 'the house of Israel . . . are all estranged from me through their idols'), so too with the prospect of a new future, the entire proceeding relates to the people of Israel as a whole, 'that they may be my people and I may be their God' (14.11).

Exegesis of Ezek. 14.12-23

This section of ch. 14 begins by describing the manner in which Yahweh deals with a land which sins against him. After a standard introductory formula in v. 12, vv. 13-20 are couched in the test-case format which we have found in a number of other passages.[37] These verses appear to lay down a general principle according to which Yahweh deals with any land which sins against him. Verse 13 begins, 'Son of man, when a land sins against me by acting faithlessly . . . ' There follows reference to four forms of punishment which he may send upon such a land: famine (v. 13), wild beasts (v. 15), a sword (v. 17) and pestilence (v. 19).[38] In each case, it is said that even if Noah, Daniel and Job (three men of exemplary righteousness) were present in the land, they would save only their own lives (vv. 14, 16, 18, 20).[39] Verses 16, 18 and 20 elaborate upon this to say that they would not deliver even their own sons and daughters. Verse 21 then relates this general principle specifically to the fate of Jerusalem in particular, 'How much more when I send upon Jerusalem my four sore acts of judgment, sword, famine, evil beasts and pestilence, to cut off from it man and beast!'[40] Finally, vv. 22-23 deal with the case of some chance survivors.

In the present case, as in others we have considered, a number of scholars regard the use of the test-case format as a feature of a secondary stratum.[41] As we have argued before, however, it is by no

means clear that the presence of such language should be attributed
to the work of redactors rather than to the style of the prophet
himself.[42] Given the close relation of the subject matter to the
immediate context of conquest by the Babylonians, there is no
compelling reason to deny vv. 12-21 to Ezekiel.[43] More problematic,
however, is the question whether vv. 22-23 are an addition to the
passage; this matter will be considered in the course of our
exegesis.

As in all the passages which we have considered so far, the
responsibility of Israel for her fate is strongly emphasized in 14.12-
23. This is implicit in the test-case material (v. 13, 'When a land sins
against me by acting faithlessly . . . '), and explicit in v. 23, 'You shall
know that I have not done without cause all that I have done'. This is
another of the passages in Ezekiel which have often been understood
to be strongly individualistic. For example, Stalker writes, 'Thus, the
ancient principle of solidarity . . . is here repudiated by Ezekiel';[44] or
again, Taylor comments, 'Salvation will be on a purely individual
basis'.[45] We must consider more closely the understanding of
responsibility represented here.

The first point to note is that it seems to be assumed that Noah,
Daniel and Job would deliver their lives by their righteousness if they
were present; in other words, the basic ideal that the righteous
should be spared in a general punishment seems to be taken for
granted here, as in Ezekiel 9, rather than advanced as something
new.[46] It is indeed possible that vv. 13-14 are intended actually to
assert (rather than to assume) that Noah, Daniel and Job would save
at least themselves, since the word לבדם ('alone', 'only'), which is
found in vv. 16 and 18, is not found here; moreover, there is in v. 14
no reference to the fact that the three righteous would save neither
sons nor daughters, as is stated in vv. 16, 18 and 20. Thus the
purpose of vv. 13-14 could conceivably be to establish the basic
principle that at least the righteous would be spared, before the
subsequent verses make the point that they would deliver no one
else. However, it is much more probable that the four cases, famine
(vv. 13-14), wild beasts (vv. 15-16), the sword (vv. 17-18) and
pestilence (vv. 19-20), are intended to be parallel with each other,
and that, as in the other three cases, vv. 13-14 should be understood
to mean that the three hypothetical righteous would save '*but* their
own lives' (as the RSV translation indicates). This seems the more

likely since v. 20 (which, like v. 14, lacks the word לברם ['alone', 'only']) undoubtedly has this sense, as is shown by the reference to neither son nor daughter being spared. And so, as we suggested earlier, it seems that the sparing of the righteous is taken for granted throughout 14.12-20; we do not find here the enunciation of a new principle.

Nevertheless, although 14.12-20 is concerned with an old principle rather than a new one, it is certainly the case that the passage asserts that this old principle is to be operated with unprecedented rigour. This is the distinctive feature of the four cases related here and it must be acknowledged as a strongly individualistic theme. The rigour with which the principle of individual responsibility is to be applied is expressed most clearly in the word לברם in vv. 16 and 18, 'they *alone* would be delivered'. The statement that not even sons and daughters are to be spared on account of the righteous (vv. 16, 18, 20) spells out the implications of this word. Sons and daughters, being among the closest relatives, represent those one would think most likely to be spared, if any one at all were to be spared with the righteous. This is very similar to 9.6, where even children who do not bear the mark on the forehead are to be slain.[47]

It is particularly noteworthy that 14.12-20 appears to represent a conscious departure from current tradition about Noah. In its present form, the story of the Flood in the book of Genesis is probably exilic, though it is very likely that it contains earlier elements. There, Noah's close family are spared (Gen. 6.18; 7.1, 7), even though it seems to be Noah alone who had found favour with God (Gen. 6.8, 9; 7.1).[48] In Ezekiel 14, on the other hand, it is asserted that such generosity cannot be presumed upon—if Noah were here now he would deliver neither son nor daughter. The old principle of individual responsibility is indeed to be operated with unprecedented rigour.

It is essential, however, to ask why this is so; what is the basic purpose of this passage? This is perhaps best seen by brief comparison with some other narratives in the Old Testament. Many passages are marked by a solicitude for the fate of the righteous in a general punishment; indeed, it may well be that this was a primary impulse behind the development of the notion of individual responsibility.[49] We have already mentioned the sparing of righteous Noah from the Flood; another example is provided by the Passover narrative, in which we find a similar concern that the righteous should not share the same fate as the wicked.[50] A further case is the account of Abraham pleading for Sodom in Gen. 18.22ff., to which we have referred a number of times. The major focus of the passage is indicated by v. 25: 'Far be it from thee to do such a thing, to slay the righteous with the wicked, so that the righteous fare as the wicked!' Indeed, so prominent is this preoccupation that it is envisaged that the whole city should be spared if even as few as ten righteous may be found there (v. 32). Daube coined the term 'Communal Merit' to describe the principle according to which this might happen.[51] All three of these passages have the sparing of the righteous as a primary focus; in contrast, the basic concern of Ezek. 14.12ff. is significantly different. The prophet anticipates an imminent judgment which will 'cut off man and beast' (14.13, 17, 19, 21). His purpose is to stress the thoroughness of judgment; there will certainly be no place for 'Communal Merit' this time, not even on the basis of family solidarity.

It is important to recognize that we are dealing here with rhetoric. Ezekiel does not envisage segregation between paragons of virtue and their unrighteous offspring actually taking place; rather, the motif of the three hypothetical righteous is a forceful way of saying to the wicked that justice will be thorough and absolute. The format in which Ezek. 14.12ff. is presented must not be allowed to obscure this fact. Let us examine the implications of this more closely.

As we have seen, vv. 12-20 are couched in the style of priestly case law (e.g. 14.13, 'When a land ... '). After these statements about what happens when Yahweh punishes a land, we come to v. 21. After a standard formula introducing the divine oracle, we find the phrase אַף כִּי. This generally has a comparative sense, meaning 'how much more' or 'how much less' according to context.[52] In Ezek. 15.5, the only other case of its use in the book, it is used to mean 'how much less'; the present context demands the translation 'how much more'. We seem, then, to have in vv. 12-20 a general statement applicable to any land, which is only related specifically to Jerusalem at v. 21: 'How much more when I send upon Jerusalem ... '[53] Thus, at first sight, it would appear that the rigour of Yahweh's application of the principle of individual responsibility when punishing lands is presented as a general rule.

However, we may question whether Ezekiel's purpose is in fact so general. The Old Testament prophets seem characteristically to have been concerned not with abstract theorizing but rather with addressing the people of Yahweh in concrete situations. In the light of this, it seems probable that the theoretical appearance of Ezek. 14.12-20 is to be attributed to Ezekiel's use of the test-case format as a teaching technique rather than to any intention to establish a general theory of responsibility. This has implications for our assessment of the importance of individualism here. 14.12ff. undoubtedly exhibits significant elements of individualism; however, it is only because of the test-case format that the rigorous application of the principle of individual responsibility appears general and theoretical.[54] The purpose of Ezekiel here is an *ad hoc* one; he addresses a specific and desperate situation. We are in fact dealing with an example of prophetic hyperbole: the sins of Israel are so great (the situation is even worse, it is implied, than at the time of the Flood) that an overwhelming punishment is now imminent, so thorough that the most righteous people who can be imagined would not be able to deliver even their closest relatives.[55]

Verses 22-23 remain to be considered. At first sight, these last verses of the chapter seem to conflict with what has gone before, for they contain two surprises. First, they refer to the survival of a residue or remnant (פלטה) which does not deserve to survive. Second, they speak of these survivors leading out sons and daughters. This has led some to regard vv. 22-23 as a secondary addition.[56] However, we shall argue that they not only have an integral place within 14.12-23 but actually clarify the meaning of the passage.[57]

As we have noted, the remnant spoken of in vv. 22-23 does not deserve to survive; these people are not in the same category as the three hypothetical righteous of vv. 12-20. Rather they are chance left-overs, like the 'two legs or a piece of an ear' mentioned in Amos 3.12 or the 'two or three berries in the top of the highest bough' of Isa. 17.6.[58] Being survivors by chance only, they are not delivered by the righteousness of any one else, and so their appearance does not, strictly speaking, contradict what has been asserted in vv. 12-21. As for the survival of sons and daughters, this too is best understood as a matter of their own chance survival rather than of family solidarity; if sons and daughters cannot share in the benefits of their parents' righteousness at 14.16, 18 and 20, it seems unlikely that they profit from their parents' sheer luck here in 14.22-23. These verses are, then, not actually incompatible with what has gone before.

And yet they do come as something of a surprise after 14.12-21. What is their purpose? We may note three points. First, the primary intention of vv. 22-23 is revealed in the words, 'When you see their ways and their doings... you shall know that I have not done without cause all that I have done'. In other words, the survival of a few sinners will provide evidence of the justice of the general punishment.[59] This is a further example of Ezekiel's characteristic concern to vindicate Yahweh's name and actions;[60] it also underlines the responsibility of Israel for her fate, which we have seen to be the consistent theme of chs. 1-24.

Second, it is of importance that vv. 22-23 strengthen the case for viewing the whole of 14.12ff. as concerned more with the concrete realities of Ezekiel's day than with any abstract theology of responsibility. Although vv. 22-23 are not, strictly speaking, incompatible with vv. 12-21, it must be said that vv. 12-21 do raise the expectation that absolutely no one but the righteous will survive, and this expectation is certainly contradicted by vv. 22-23. If vv. 12ff. were really intended to advance a definitive doctrine, the place of vv. 22-23 would be very difficult to explain, as they would appear to undermine the purpose of the preceding verses. As it is, however, vv. 22-23 confirm our insight that Ezekiel is not promulgating a general theory of responsibility but rather addressing a specific and desperate situation.

Third, we may note that vv. 22-23 take it for granted that any survivors will be undeserving ones (in other words, that there will be no Noahs, Daniels or Jobs), another indication that 14.12ff. is to be understood as an example of hyperbole rather than as an anticipation of actual segregation. We are reminded of 3.7, 'all the house of Israel are of a hard forehead and of a stubborn heart'; of 9.11, where the return of the man clothed in linen is reported without any indication as to whether any deserving the mark on the forehead were to be found; and of 22.30, where Yahweh looks for a man 'to build up the wall and stand in the breach', but finds none. It is clear that Ezekiel regards his people as sinful virtually 'to a man' and anticipates an imminent punishment which will be well-nigh total. Moreover, the assumption that any survivors will be by chance rather than desert underlines the fact that we find in 14.12-23 no call to repentance. In this respect, as in others which we have noted, 14.12-23 is very close to ch. 9, for in both passages the theme of repentance is eclipsed completely by an overriding emphasis on the imminence of absolute judgment.

The Responsibility of Israel

We must now draw together the threads of our discussion of this theme.

1. We have seen that Ezekiel 9, 14, and 18 all assert unequivocally that the events of defeat and exile are Yahweh's just punishment of Israel's sins. In this respect, the passages which we have studied in detail may be said to be typical of chs. 1–24 as a whole, dominated by the theme of the absolute responsibility of Israel for the punishment which is engulfing her.

2. We have seen that the expression of this responsibility is somewhat less individualistic than has often been suggested. We have argued that ch. 18 is to be understood as an attempt to explain the national disaster as punishment of the present generation of Israel— and that it is in no sense concerned with the moral independence of individuals. We have acknowledged individualistic motifs in both ch. 9 and 14.12-23, but have found these to be subordinate to a more collective primary theme, namely the imminent onset of the thorough judgment of the nation. Moreover, we have seen that 14.1-11 seems to envisage the 'cutting off' of the idolatrous nation as a whole, rather than merely the punishment of individual idolaters.

Our intention has not been to deny altogether an individualistic element in the statement of Israel's responsibility in Ezekiel, but rather to show that this is less prominent than has generally been claimed and that, where it does occur, it is not presented polemically or as an innovation. If further evidence is needed that Ezekiel is not resolutely committed to the principle of individual responsibility, we may point to some remarkable words found towards the end of the major section constituted by chs. 1–24:

> Say to the land of Israel, 'Thus says the LORD, "Behold, I am against you, and will draw forth my sword out of its sheath, and will cut off from you both righteous and wicked. Because I will cut off from you both righteous and wicked, therefore my sword shall go out of its sheath against all flesh from south to north"' (Ezek. 21.8, 9 [Eng. 21.3, 4]).[61]

These words would seem to have scant regard for any with a mark on the forehead, little respect even for any Noahs, Daniels or Jobs. They clearly pose a problem for any scholar wishing to present Ezekiel as a great individualist; thus, for example, Irwin claimed that the passage we have quoted from ch. 21 must come from early in the prophet's ministry, before he had reached the full maturity of his individualistic view.[62] But such special pleading is unnecessary, for Ezekiel's concerns are in no way systematic; rather his preaching employs a range of motifs, some more individualistic and others more collective, to further his primary purpose of stressing the imminent and thorough judgment of Israel by Yahweh.

3. We have found that in some passages of judgment all talk of repentance is eclipsed (e.g. 9; 14.12-23) and we have argued that even where a call to repentance is found (e.g. 14.1-11; 18) it serves primarily as a rhetorical device, underlining the responsibility of Israel for the now inevitable disaster. Again, the words of 21.8, 9 (Eng. 3, 4) would seem to confirm our interpretation: the sword of Yahweh is about to 'go out of its sheath against all flesh from south to north'. No distinction is to be made between righteous and wicked; the nation as a whole is under judgment and there is no suggestion that repentance would avert the disaster.

Our study of selected passages from Ezekiel 1-24 has demonstrated that Ezekiel's concerns centre neither upon individualism nor even upon repentance. Rather, his overriding purpose is to declare the impending judgment and Israel's absolute responsibility for it. This emphasis is nowhere clearer than in the final chapter of this long section of the book:

> 'Because I would have cleansed you and you were not cleansed from your filthiness, you shall not be cleansed any more till I have satisfied my fury upon you. I the LORD have spoken; it shall come to pass, I will do it; I will not go back, I will not spare, I will not repent; according to your ways and your doings I will judge you', says the Lord GOD (Ezek. 24.13-14).

Chapter 5

COLLECTIVE AND INDIVIDUAL RESPONSIBILITY
IN THE OLD TESTAMENT

We have argued that it is by no means to be assumed that 'individual responsibility' is a distinctive concern of the book of Ezekiel. We have suggested that even where elements of individualism are to be found they seem to be taken for granted rather than argued for polemically. We have seen, moreover, that such elements of individualism as do appear must be set alongside statements such as that of Ezek. 21.8, 9 (Eng. 21.3, 4), 'I will cut off from you both righteous and wicked'. The purpose of the present chapter is to attempt (albeit briefly) to set Ezekiel within the broader Old Testament picture and to consider the extent to which the complexities we have found within Ezekiel are typical of the Old Testament as a whole. The range of material available for study is, of course, vast and our treatment is inevitably selective. It is hoped, however, that an understanding of some of the major issues and difficulties inherent in the discussion of responsibility in the Old Testament as a whole will give us a clearer perspective on the presentation of Israel's responsibility in Ezekiel.

The developmental hypothesis

Discussion of questions relating to responsibility in ancient Israel has long been influenced by the view that there took place during the course of the history of ancient Israel a gradual but steady shift from a tendency to think of responsibility in collective terms to an increasingly individualistic emphasis. The way in which Ezekiel has been read has at times been coloured by this broader hypothesis. This 'developmental' view gained ground among the liberal scholars of the nineteenth century, and is to be found in its classic form in our own century in the work of F. Baumgärtel.[1] A position which is (despite disclaimers) not dissimilar is adopted by Eichrodt,[2] whilst comparable presentations have become commonplace in more popular works.[3]

We may sketch the alleged development briefly. The understanding of responsibility in the early period has been seen as typified by the story of Achan in Joshua 7, in which Achan's whole family and all of his possessions are destroyed with him when he is punished for his sin. Particular attention has been devoted to the period of defeat and deportation in the sixth century, when the cohesion of the national unit was seriously weakened; this has often been characterized as the time of a crucial breakthrough to a clear notion of individual responsibility. Especially relevant to our concerns is the claim that the prophets of this period, and particularly Ezekiel, were innovating in introducing a hitherto unprecedented emphasis on the individual.[4] The period after the Exile has often been seen as the time when some of the theological implications of this allegedly new-found individualism were worked out. Thus both the exploration of the problem of undeserved suffering in the book of Job and also the emergence of the belief in personal resurrection reflected in the Apocalyptic literature have at various times been seen as conditioned by an increased emphasis on the importance of the individual.[5]

We have indicated that it is by no means clear that Ezekiel was concerned to stress individual responsibility. What, then, may be said of the broader view that a gradual development in Israel's thinking about responsibility can be traced?

Important issues of method

A number of significant methodological questions are raised by this discussion. Failure to take full account of these has, we suggest, led to unnecessary confusion in the debate. We next, therefore, review five of these major issues in turn.[6]

1. The word 'responsibility' itself raises numerous difficulties. Some scholars have tried to explain many Old Testament passages as examples of 'collective responsibility'. Yet, is 'responsibility' always the appropriate word to use? We must heed the warning of Porter, who writes that 'the term *responsibility* for the relation of the group to the crime of one of its members has to be used with some caution'.[7] In fact, the relation of the group to the crime in such cases may depend on a number of factors other than 'responsibility'. Here

are three examples of passages which are often understood in terms
of 'collective responsibility', but which are perhaps better understood
in other ways: first, the story of 1 Samuel 14, in which a divine oracle
is withheld because of Jonathan's sin in eating honey after his father
has sworn that no one should eat food on the day of battle. Porter
argues that it may be more accurate to say that the people suffer the
consequences of Jonathan's sin rather than that they actually share
in his responsibility for contravening Saul's oath. Second, the
episode recounted in Num. 17.11ff. (Eng. 16.46ff.), in which plague is
described as spreading rapidly—and indiscriminately—through the
camp, as a consequence of the sinful murmuring of the people. Aaron
is sent with his censer to stand between the dead and the living and
stem the apparently rampant advance of the punitive consequences
of sin. Here we may be helped by Koch's emphasis on the fact that
sin is often presented in the Old Testament as an infectious power
which, once let loose, is very difficult to contain.[8] In such cases,
precise definitions of 'responsibility' are not to be sought. Third, we
read in 2 Samuel 24 that pestilence is sent upon Israel after David's
census of the people. Here too, as Daube has pointed out, talk of
shared 'responsibility' may be inappropriate. He suggests that the
disease is sent upon Israel not because all Israelites are held to share
David's responsibility but because they are seen as his property—it is
David who is being punished by the death of his people.[9]

2. Much depends on the kind of material with which we are
dealing. As an example of this, we may recall the distinction made
earlier between language about criminal law and that concerning
God's punishment of human sin.[10] In criminal law, as we shall see,
the basic principle of individual responsibility seems to have been
established in Israel from very early times.[11] On the other hand,
because of the special nature of language about God's punishment of
human sin, the latter area was more often marked by notions of
collective punishment than was the realm of criminal law. As we
have argued, ideas about God's punishment of human sin generally
start with the recognition of a particular state of affairs (adverse
circumstances, such as the prospect of military defeat) and then
proceed to attribute this state of affairs to divine displeasure.
Moreover, because it is not easy to show a direct causal relationship
between sin and divine punishment (precisely because the reasoning
characteristically goes the other way, from adversity to talk of sins

being punished), the tendency is often to take a broad view, which lends itself to language of collective responsibility. Indeed, this may even involve talk of present hardship being the result of the sins of earlier generations (as in 2 Kgs 23.26, where it is said that, in spite of the virtues of Josiah, disaster will still come upon Judah, because of the sins of the earlier king Manasseh). Thus the degree of emphasis placed on individual responsibility or collective responsibility may depend as much on the subject matter of the material with which we are dealing as on the period from which it comes.[12]

3. A further difficulty is presented by the fact that we do not find anywhere in the Old Testament a systematic theory of responsibility. This observation holds true with regard to both narrative and law. Various understandings of responsibility are reflected in narrative, to be sure, but always indirectly, in the course of telling a good story. The legal material too is characteristically concerned with specific cases rather than with general theoretical principles. Our biblical texts, then, are not to be made to yield abstract 'theologies of responsibility'; their concern is rarely, if ever, systematic or doctrinal. This renders attempts to trace a development in Israel's thought about responsibility very problematic.

4. Material often combines collective and individualistic elements. We may illustrate this by reference to two important passages. The first of these is Joshua 7, in which Achan steals articles devoted to Yahweh. The chapter is often cited in discussions of responsibility because of the striking vv. 24-25, where not only Achan but also 'his sons and daughters, his oxen and asses and sheep, and his tent, and all that he had' are destroyed.[13] However, we may note a further complexity presented by the earlier vv. 16-18. Joshua attempts to identify the guilty party by gradually narrowing down the area of responsibility (presumably by sacred lot) from Israel to the tribe of Judah, to the family of the Zerahites, and eventually to Achan. It is clearly here regarded as important and just to isolate the cause of Israel's trouble in order to deal with it. The story of Achan may thus be said to contain certain individualistic elements as well as the more collective features we have noted.[14]

A comparable complexity marks Genesis 18. Here Abraham pleads with Yahweh that he should not slay the righteous of Sodom along with the wicked. Gen. 18.25 is a clear statement of the view that it would be inappropriate for Yahweh to act in such a way: 'Far be it from thee to do such a thing, to slay the righteous with the wicked, so that the righteous fare as the wicked ... shall not the Judge of all the earth do right?'[15] In this may be found a concern for the individual, a recognition that it may at times be necessary to deal with units smaller than the group if justice is to be done. However, the solution which is envisaged is that if ten righteous be found, the whole city should be spared, righteous and wicked alike (18.32). This is a strongly collective notion, for which Daube coined the term 'Communal Merit'.[16] Thus again we find individual and collective elements side by side as part of a rather complex picture.[17] Indeed, such an ambivalence is a feature of many Old Testament passages.[18] Material which is so complex internally does not lend itself to being placed easily within any simple developmental model of the emergence of individualism in ancient Israel.

5. A further difficulty faced by any developmental hypothesis is that of dating. Even if passages with a straightforward line on responsibility were to be found, these would have to be datable with some degree of certainty if they were to lend support to a hypothesis of the kind we have been considering. Such certainty is, of course, rarely attainable. Indeed, in certain areas, including Pentateuchal studies, such scholarly consensus as had emerged has been considerably eroded over recent years.[19]

The developmental hypothesis challenged

The cumulative weight of the methodological considerations we have reviewed tends to undermine the viability of a view which envisages a steady growth of individualism in Israel. But our challenge can be sharpened further if we focus upon the individualistic elements which may be discerned in relatively early material and, conversely, the collective elements to be found in relatively late material. We must, of course, remain aware here of the difficulty inherent in dating all material highlighted above.

There seem to have been important elements of individualism in Israelite thinking about responsibility from early times. The general principle of 'individual responsibility' (that it is the guilty party who should be punished) seems to have been a feature of criminal law from a particularly early date. Porter, with reference to the so-called 'Book of the Covenant' in Exodus 20–23 and also to the laws of

Hammurabi, writes: 'The idea of individual responsibility, as far as the law is concerned, is seen to be at least as primary and as early as group responsibility, and this, not only in Israel, but throughout the entire early Semitic world'.[20] We may compare the words of Mayes with regard to the legal statement of Deut. 24.16, 'The fathers shall not be put to death for the children, nor shall the children be put to death for the fathers; every man shall be put to death for his own sin'. On grounds of form, Mayes regards this as an older law quoted by the compilers of Deuteronomy, and states that 'It affirms a principle which is by no means a late phenomenon in Israelite history'.[21] It will be remembered that we argued in Chapter 3 that in Ezekiel 18 the prophet appeals to an established legal principle of 'individual responsibility' (see especially 18.4, 20), which he then applies to the discussion of a very different matter, namely the suffering of the nation Israel.[22]

We suggested earlier that material concerning God's punishment of human sin is more likely to speak of collective responsibility than are texts relating to criminal law. Nevertheless, even the former quite often exhibits an explicit awareness of the problem presented by the suffering of those who are, strictly speaking, innocent. There is evidence of this even in narratives for which a case for early dating can be made; thus, for example, we have already noted Gen. 18.25, 'Far be it from thee to do such a thing, to slay the righteous with the wicked'. If it be objected that the passage from which this comes is not demonstrably early, we may point to the Flood story of Genesis 6–9, which may well have a basis in pre-Israelite tradition.[23] Here the righteous individual Noah is spared in a general punishment (albeit taking his family with him). The difficulties of dating make all such discussion problematic; nevertheless, we may at least assert that neither in criminal law texts nor in material concerning God's punishment of human sin are there to be found any good grounds for regarding individualism as an exclusively or even a distinctively late phenomenon.[24]

Conversely, it must be stressed that strongly collective elements are to be found in the later Old Testament period (for example, Dan. 6.24, where the wives and children of Daniel's accusers are included in punishment, and Esth. 9.7-10, where the ten sons of the villain Haman are slain), and indeed in the New Testament (for example, Mt. 23.35-36, where punishment for all the righteous blood shed from Abel to Zechariah the son of Barachiah is to come upon the present generation of the scribes and the Pharisees). In all periods and in all strata of the literature we seem to find an awareness of the tension between the individual and the group. There is no good reason to doubt that throughout the history of ancient Israel the complexities of the relationship between the one and the many were fully experienced and reflected in language.

Can we trace any development?

We do not deny that certain developments in the understanding of responsibility may be discerned in the biblical material. However, it is important to acknowledge that there seem to be developments both in the direction of an increased emphasis on individual responsibility and also in the opposite direction, towards a more collective emphasis. We may briefly illustrate these two divergent trends.

A sensitivity to the anomaly of undeserved suffering does seem to have had an influence at times in modifying an earlier willingness to think in terms of collective units. Thus Daube plausibly argues that the ceremony to be performed by elders of the city nearest to which a dead body has been found (Deut. 21) may be a modification of a practice whereby the inhabitants of the city would actually be punished for the murder.[25] Moreover, it may well be that the engagement with the problem of undeserved suffering in the book of Job and also the emergence of a belief in personal resurrection (reflected, it seems, in Dan. 12.2) are related to an increased concern for the life of the individual and to the wish to vindicate the justice of God in relation to that particular life. The likelihood that certain developments of this kind took place may readily be acknowledged. What must be resisted, however, is any tendency to generalize from such specific developments and to postulate a simple, one-way development towards increased individualism.

Sometimes there may have been developments in the opposite direction to that usually envisaged. For example, it may be argued that an important innovation of the eighth-century prophet Amos was to address his message of judgment not simply to particular individuals but to the nation of Israel as a whole, giving fresh use to certain forms of prophetic address previously applied to individuals.[26] We ought not to assume without question that all developments in the area of language about responsibility were in the direction of an increased emphasis on the individual.

The evidence concerning collective and individual responsibility in the Old Testament (of which we have considered only a representative fraction) is clearly highly complex. It may be that a model from New Testament studies may help us to express the diversity which we find. Robinson and Koester have spoken of a variety of different 'trajectories' in the New Testament, by which is meant independent, often divergent, developments which are not to be regarded as mutually exclusive and which may indeed exist simultaneously.[27] The individualizing trend which may be discerned in certain post-exilic literature should be thought of as just one 'trajectory' in a complex overall situation which does not fall into any one simple pattern. We should be very wary of speaking of 'the thought of Israel' as though Israel were at any time a monolithic unity. It is very probable that there was at all times a rich diversity within the theological thought of the disparate group known as Israel.[28]

We may now summarize the major points at which this short survey of the broader Old Testament picture sheds light on our study of Ezekiel.

1. Seen in this wider perspective, some of the complexities which characterize the understanding of responsibility in the book of Ezekiel become less puzzling. The variation between more individualistic elements (for example, the motif of the marking of the foreheads of the righteous in ch. 9) and more collective elements (such as the reference to the cutting off of both 'righteous and wicked' in 21.8, 9 [Eng. 21.3, 4]) may be seen as typical of the diversity which marked language relating to responsibility in all periods.
2. The absence from Ezekiel of any sense that individualistic elements are being advanced as innovations is readily understandable in the light of the fact that notions of individual responsibility seem to have played a part in thought about responsibility in Israel from early times.
3. The view that the contribution of Ezekiel marked a crucial stage in the evolution of individualism in Israel not only misrepresents the evidence concerning Ezekiel but also

attempts to impose an excessively simple pattern upon language about collective and individual responsibility in the Old Testament as a whole.

Chapter 6

THE RADICAL THEOCENTRICITY OF EZEKIEL

Our concern so far has been to explore the ways in which the responsibility of Israel is understood in the book of Ezekiel. We must now turn to consider how the activity of Yahweh is presented. We shall pursue this inquiry by investigating a range of formulae and motifs, all of which serve to highlight the extent to which the focus of the book is consistently upon Yahweh himself.

'*I am Yahweh*'

'I will make you a perpetual desolation and your cities shall not be inhabited. Then you will know that I am the LORD.' These words, addressed to Edom in Ezek. 35.9, represent just one example of a formula which occurs in Ezekiel some fifty-four times in its basic form and over twenty more times with minor variations. The basic pattern consists of a statement that Yahweh will punish (or deliver) Israel (or the nations), followed by the words וידעתם (וידעו) כי אני יהוה 'and you (or they) shall know that I am Yahweh' (RSV: 'The LORD'). It is generally the case that the group for whom knowledge of Yahweh is anticipated is the same as that which is said to be the object of Yahweh's punishment or deliverance. However, this is not always the case; in fact a wide range of permutations is to be found.[1] The consistent factor is that the formula is always associated with the account of an action of Yahweh.

In the great majority of cases, the formula is appended to a reference to Yahweh acting to punish. It occurs some twenty times as part of a statement that the *nations* will know that 'I am Yahweh' when Yahweh punishes them; the example with which we began, taken from Ezek. 35.9, belongs to this category.[2] Not surprisingly, these references all fall, without exception, within chs. 25-32, 35 and

38–39, that is to say within the sections of the book devoted to the theme of judgment upon the nations. In a further twenty or so cases it is stated that *Israel* will know that 'I am Yahweh' when Yahweh punishes her.[3] For example, Ezek. 11.10: 'You shall fall by the sword; I will judge you at the border of Israel; and you shall know that I am the LORD'. This use of the formula occurs almost exclusively within chs. 1–24, the section of the book devoted to the theme of judgment upon Israel.

These two categories account for almost all the cases relating to punishment; a much rarer application does occur, however, in which it is said that Israel will know that 'I am Yahweh' when Yahweh punishes the nations.[4] In Ezek. 39.21-22 we read: '. . . all the nations shall see my judgment which I have executed, and my hand which I have laid on them. The house of Israel shall know that I am the LORD their God, from that day forward'. On the other hand, there seems to be no case in which it is said that the nations will come to know that 'I am Yahweh' when Yahweh punishes Israel.[5]

Turning now to the considerably smaller number of cases in which the formula is appended to declarations of Yahweh's deliverance, we find that these almost all state that Israel will know that 'I am Yahweh' when she herself is delivered. For example, in Ezek. 36.11, the mountains of Israel are told: 'I will cause you to be inhabited as in your former times, and will do more good to you than ever before. Then you will know that I am the LORD'. There are about a dozen such cases,[6] most of them occurring in the more hopeful section of the book which follows the announcement of the fall of Jerusalem in ch. 33, although closely related cases are to be found earlier in the book, as in 16.62 and 20.20, 42, 44. There seems to be no case of the formula being used in connexion with a reference to Yahweh delivering the nations.[7] The few remaining cases relating to deliverance speak of the nations knowing that 'I am Yahweh' when Yahweh delivers Israel.[8] An example of this is to be found in 36.23, where Israel is told: 'the nations will know that I am the LORD . . . when through you I vindicate my holiness before their eyes'. Our formula has, then, a broad range of application, Yahweh revealing his essential nature in both judgment and deliverance.[9]

Before exploring the background and significance of this formula, we must consider whether it is likely to derive from Ezekiel himself. Hölscher believed that this prosaic phrase could not possibly come

THE NATIONS WILL KNOW THAT 'I AM YAHWEH' WHEN...

(A) Yahweh punishes the nations

25.5, 7, 11, 17; 26.6; 28.22, 23; 29.6, 9, 16; 30.8, 19, 25, 26; 32.15; 35.4, 9, 15; 38.23; 39.6.

(Variations: 25.14; 35.12)

(B) Yahweh delivers the nations

(C) Yahweh punishes Israel

(D) Yahweh delivers Israel
36.23; 39.7

(Variations: 17.24; 36.36; 37.28)

ISRAEL WILL KNOW THAT 'I AM YAHWEH' WHEN...

(E) Yahweh punishes the nations

28.26b; 39.22

(F) Yahweh delivers the nations

(G) Yahweh punishes Israel

6.7, 10, 13, 14; 7.4, 27; 11.10, 12; 12.15, 16, 20; 20.26; 22.16; 23.49; 24.24, 27; 39.28a

(Variations: 5.13; 7.9; 13.9, 21, 23; 14.8; 17.21)

(H) Yahweh delivers Israel

16.62; 20.42, 44; 28.24, 26a; 29.21; 34.27; 36.11, 38; 37.6, 13; 39.28b

(Variations: 20.20; 34.30)

from the prophet (whom he viewed as above all a poet), and so regarded all occurrences as secondary.[10] S. Herrmann believes that Ezekiel preached no message of hope, and so views as redactional all the cases of our formula used in association with references to the deliverance of Israel.[11] Both Hölscher and Herrmann, however, brought particular presuppositions about Ezekiel to their discussion of this question.[12] A consideration of each occurrence in its context suggests that, although a proportion may be redactional (e.g. 16.62; 28.26), nevertheless a wide range of cases in all the major categories have a good claim to be regarded as primary material (e.g. 11.10; 35.9; 36.11).[13] In fact, this formula would seem to provide an example of the phenomenon we described in Chapter 2, whereby a number of features of the prophet's style appear to have been taken up and employed in secondary strata.[14]

Even among those scholars who regard the bulk of the occurrences of the formula as primary, opinions differ concerning its significance within the style and theology of Ezekiel. Fohrer regards it as merely 'an interpretive formula that has been appended to other literary types'.[15] But Zimmerli was surely correct in observing that in most cases it is integrally related to the contexts in which it occurs and in contending that it constitutes a central and distinctive feature of the style and theology of the prophet.[16]

What of the background of the formula? The words 'I am Yahweh' occur in many different parts of the Old Testament (for example, Exod. 6.2;[17] 20.2;[18] Lev. 19.12;[19] Deut. 5.6; Ps. 81.11 (Eng. 10); Isa. 45.5;[20] Jer. 9.23 (Eng. 24); 24.7). In view of the extent of this range, it would seem inappropriate to attempt to relate Ezekiel's use of the particular words 'I am Yahweh' exclusively to any one background.

It may be of more value to consider the formula as a whole: 'and you (or they) shall know that I am Yahweh'. There are two parts of the Old Testament where similar expressions occur, namely the books of Kings and the book of Exodus. In 1 Kgs 20.28, a man of God tells the king of Israel: 'Thus says the LORD, "Because the Syrians have said, 'The LORD is a god of the hills but he is not a god of the valleys', therefore I will give all this great multitude into your hand, and you shall know that I am the LORD"' (1 Kgs 20.13 is very similar).[21] Zimmerli emphasized the importance of this background, highlighting in particular the close similarity between the verses in 1 Kings 20 and the oracles against the nations in Ezekiel 25.[22] He suggested that the formula which we have been considering had its origin in the oracles of institutional prophets against foreign nations, a proposal which found some support also in the work of von Rad on the Holy War.[23] Carley has more recently argued for the same conclusion, this being an important element in his thesis that Ezekiel had especially close affinities with pre-classical prophecy.[24]

Fohrer, on the other hand, has been critical of the attempt to find the origin of Ezekiel's formula in the Deuteronomistic History: 'The occurrence of this formula twice in anecdotal prophetical utterances does not provide a broad enough basis for the assumption that centuries later Ezekiel made use of an early literary type'.[25] Fohrer goes so far as to suggest that 1 Kgs 20.13, 28 (Zimmerli's primary examples) were inserted by the last deuteronomistic redactor of the books of Kings on the basis of Ezekiel's words.[26] He looks rather to an alternative background, namely the account of the confrontation between Moses and Pharaoh in the book of Exodus. For example, in Exod. 7.17, we read: 'Thus says the LORD, "By this you shall know that I am the LORD; behold I will strike the water that is in the Nile"'.[27]

In spite of the disagreements between Zimmerli and Fohrer with regard to the precise background of our formula, their views have one important feature in common, namely the belief that it had its origin in oracles against the nations. We saw earlier that the use of the formula in Ezekiel falls into three main categories.[28] If it did indeed originate in oracles against the nations, then one of these categories is readily explained, namely that in which the nations come to know that 'I am Yahweh' when Yahweh punishes them.[29] Moreover, another is closely related, namely that which speaks of Israel coming to know that 'I am Yahweh' when Yahweh delivers her.[30] The motif of the deliverance of Israel is often associated with that of the punishment of the nations; it is not difficult to see how a formula used initially of Yahweh's punishment of the nations might become extended to be used of Yahweh's deliverance of Israel.[31]

What, however, are we to make of the remaining major application of the formula in Ezekiel, namely that which states that Israel will come to know that 'I am Yahweh' when Yahweh punishes her?[32] A particularly striking case is found in Ezek. 11.9-10, where the house of Israel is told: 'I will give you into the hands of the foreigners ... and you shall know that I am the LORD'. How can such a use be explained if, as seems probable, our formula had its origin in oracles against the nations? We appear to have here a paradoxical inversion of an established form, of a kind which is not unknown elsewhere in the prophetic literature.[33] We may compare Amos 1–2, where oracles against various foreign nations are followed by a similar oracle directed against Israel herself (Amos 2.6ff.), or again Jer. 21.5-6, where, in a bold overturning of the tradition of Holy War, Yahweh is portrayed as saying that he himself will fight against Jerusalem. It seems likely that, by means of a similar dramatic inversion, the use of our formula has, at some point, been broadened to include oracles against Israel.[34]

What, then, are the theological implications of the formula? We have seen that it is invariably connected with the account of an action of Yahweh. The use of the verb ידע followed by כי finds a close parallel in phrases such as that in Gen. 42.34, 'Bring your youngest brother to me; then I shall know that you are not spies but honest men'. In this instance proof or evidence of the truth is being sought. Similarly, in our formula, Yahweh's activity in punishment or deliverance is cited as evidence of a truth which would seem to be Ezekiel's central concern.[35] Although the formula does not generally begin with an explicit purpose clause,[36] the notion of purpose is nonetheless prominent. The actions of Yahweh are, it appears, deliberately directed toward the end that it may be known that 'I am Yahweh'.

This is a somewhat cryptic message; indeed, it is normally presented without elaboration.[37] This gives our formula a certain aura of mystery, which serves to highlight the theocentricity of Ezekiel's presentation. Moreover, the concern that it should be known that 'I am Yahweh' is at times so pressing that the specific recipients of this revelation fade into relative obscurity and it becomes unclear precisely who is being addressed—in such cases we are forcefully reminded that the focus is upon the God who is known rather than upon those by whom he is known.[38]

Even when it is quite clear who is being addressed the theocentric focus is unambiguous. Thus, for example, when reference is made to the nations coming to know that 'I am Yahweh', there are clear indications that the purpose is to highlight the revelation of Yahweh rather than to offer a positive vision of the role of the nations. Reventlow has argued otherwise, claiming to find in our formula evidence of a concern that the nations should give allegiance to Yahweh.[39] Some scholars have agreed, even comparing this alleged feature of Ezekiel with the universalism which is often attributed to Deutero-Isaiah.[40] However, close examination of the function served by the statement that the nations will know that 'I am Yahweh' casts considerable doubt upon Reventlow's hypothesis.[41] We have seen that in no case is it said that the nations will know that 'I am Yahweh' when Yahweh delivers them[42] or when he punishes Israel.[43] The vast majority of cases speak of the nations coming to know that 'I am Yahweh' when they are punished.[44] This would seem to count against Reventlow's view, for the examples in this category suggest that the nations are to be 'taught a lesson' in the negative sense, rather than that they will turn in allegiance to Yahweh. Thus in Ezek. 25.17 we read: 'I will execute great vengeance upon them with wrathful chastisements. Then they will know that I am the LORD, when I lay my vengeance upon them'. In none of these cases do we find real evidence that the nations are morally chastened or inclined to repentance. There remains only the small number of verses in which it is said that the nations will know that 'I am Yahweh' when Yahweh delivers Israel.[45] This group of texts might be thought more likely to lend support to Reventlow's position. However, as we have seen, deliverance for Israel is invariably related to judgment upon the nations.[46] Moreover, evidence of repentance on the part of the nations is again lacking. It would seem, then, that the use of the 'I am Yahweh' formula lends no support to the view that there is in Ezekiel a positive hope that the nations will turn in allegiance to the God of Israel; rather, reference to the nations here is a rhetorical device, serving to highlight the central concern, which is the revelation of Yahweh.

'In the sight of the nations'

We have challenged Reventlow's attempt to show that the 'I am Yahweh' formula is to be associated with a positive hope that the nations will turn to Yahweh. Another important formula which he considers in this connexion is the phrase 'in the sight of the nations' (לעיני הגוים) or 'in their sight' (לעיניהם). Closely related are the expressions 'among the nations' (בגוים) and 'among them' (בתוכם). As an example of the use of these phrases, we may cite a verse which also features the 'I am Yahweh' formula, namely Ezek. 36.23: 'I will vindicate the holiness of my great name, which has been profaned among the nations (בגוים), and which you have profaned among them (בתוכם); and the nations will know that I am the LORD ... when through you I vindicate my holiness before their eyes (לעיניהם)'. The formula 'in the sight of the nations' (לעיני הגוים) is found in 5.8; 20.9, 14, 22, 41; 22.16; 28.25; 38.23; 39.27; related expressions occur at 5.14, 15; 36.21, 22, 23; 39.21. Occasionally these phrases are employed of Israel, punished by Yahweh and the object of reproach before the nations (5.8, 14, 15; cf. 16.41), but more characteristically they are used of Yahweh himself as witnessed by the nations, as in 36.23 quoted above. Some texts speak of the profanation of Yahweh's name in the sight of the nations (20.9, 14, 22; 36.21, 22, 23; cf. 22.16), whilst others look forward to his self-vindication in their sight (20.41; 28.25; 36.23; 38.23; 39.21, 27).[47]

Reventlow's understanding of the formula 'in the sight of the nations' (and related variants) rests on the view that it is based on language used of witnesses in legal cases. We read in Jer. 32.12: 'I gave the deed of purchase to Baruch ... in the presence of (לעיני) Hanamel my cousin, in the presence of (לעיני) the witnesses (העדים) who signed the deed of purchase, and in the presence of (לעיני) all the Jews who were sitting in the court of the guard' (cf. also Gen. 23.18). The witnesses in such cases are essentially those who observe and see justice done. However, an important part of Reventlow's case is that he understands these witnesses to be more than merely detached bystanders; he argues that, in ancient Israel, they would be very fully involved and would have to consider their own position in the light of the events they witnessed. Reventlow understands the language of Ezekiel in a closely analogous way: when Yahweh 'vindicates his holiness before the eyes of the nations' (as in Ezek. 36.23), we are to think of the nations as considering their own position and giving positive assent to Yahweh.[48]

Again, however, it is by no means clear that Reventlow is correct. To begin with, it is not to be assumed that the formula in Ezekiel is dependent on such legal usage. The phrase לעיני is used in many non-legal contexts (for example, Gen. 42.24; 47.19; Exod. 4.30). Moreover, whilst it may well be that in ancient Israel legal witnesses were thought of as being personally involved in the proceedings,[49] it must be said that Reventlow fails to demonstrate that this feature of ancient Israelite legal practice (if such it be) is mirrored in the way the role of the nations is understood in Ezekiel. The references to the nations in the cases we are considering are very bare and give no indication of any positive interest in their response for its own sake. For example, in Ezek. 36.20ff. the emphasis is overwhelmingly upon the restoration of Israel and the vindication of Yahweh which it represents, rather than upon the nations. This passage provides the clearest illustration of the theocentric focus of the material in Ezekiel which speaks of the profanation and vindication of Yahweh's name in the sight of the nations; the concern is not with the nations knowing or witnessing Yahweh so much as with Yahweh being known and witnessed. The nations seem to be at most a backdrop to the promised vindication of Yahweh: 'It is not for your sake, O house of Israel, that I am about to act, but for the sake of my holy name, which you have profaned among the nations' (36.22).[50]

We suggest, then, that the reference to the nations as witnesses in such cases is essentially rhetorical. We may compare such phrases as 'I call heaven and earth to witness against you this day' (Deut. 30.19) or, again, 'Hear, O heavens, and give ear, O earth; for the LORD has spoken: "Sons have I reared and brought up, but they have rebelled against me"' (Isa. 1.2).[51] Whilst it is possible that such expressions had their origin in language which invoked the gods to maintain a treaty,[52] in their biblical use they are stylized rhetorical phrases; heaven and earth are not really expected to respond. In the absence of any clear evidence of a hope that the nations will respond positively to Yahweh, it seems reasonable to understand the words 'in the sight of the nations' in Ezekiel as a similar rhetorical expression.[53]

As in our consideration of the 'I am Yahweh' formula, so here too we have found abundant evidence of the radical theocentricity of Ezekiel. The overriding concern is that Yahweh should be known as he is: 'So I will show my greatness and my holiness and make myself known in the eyes of many nations. Then they will know that I am the LORD' (38.23).

'For the sake of my name'

It has become increasingly clear during the course of this study that in the book of Ezekiel the focus of attention is invariably Yahweh himself. We have already seen evidence that this emphasis marks not only the material which threatens judgment upon Israel but also that which speaks of hope of restoration. The time has come now to explore the latter theme more directly and in particular to consider the primary motivation of Yahweh's deliverance of Israel, as presented in the book. We shall review in turn a number of possible reasons why Yahweh might act to save his people.

1. Is it in order to punish the nations that Yahweh delivers Israel? As we have seen, there is in Ezekiel neither an expectation that Yahweh will favour the nations nor any hope that they will ultimately give allegiance to him. However, the possibility that Yahweh acts primarily in order to punish the nations for their wickedness deserves attention, not least because such a notion is to be found elsewhere in the Old Testament. We may compare Deut. 9.4-5, which emphasizes that Yahweh is to favour Israel not because she deserves it but 'because of the wickedness of these nations'.

This concern plays a significant part in Ezekiel too. Chapters 25–32 and 35 contain a series of oracles against foreign nations, which are marked by a ferocity comparable to that directed against Israel in 1–24. The oracle against the Philistines in 25.15-17 may be taken as typical: 'Because the Philistines acted revengefully . . . I will execute great vengeance upon them with wrathful chastisements. Then they will know that I am the LORD'. The sin of hubris features particularly prominently, whether the personal arrogance of the prince of Tyre (28.2ff.) or of the Pharaoh of Egypt (32.2) or the national presumption of Edom (25.12ff.; 35.10ff.). Again, chs. 38–39 speak of the vanquishing of Gog, who appears to symbolize the nations' opposition to Yahweh. Thus the theme of the wickedness of the nations and their punishment by Yahweh certainly has its place in Ezekiel. However, though this is a significant concern, at no point does it appear to constitute in itself the primary motive of Yahweh's actions.

2. Is it, then, because Israel deserves favour that Yahweh delivers her? A reading of Ezekiel 1–24 makes it abundantly clear that the fate which has befallen Israel represents punishment for her many sins. There are numerous references to Israel being treated precisely as she deserves (for example, 7.27: 'According to their way I will do to them, and according to their own judgments I will judge them'). Moreover, we have seen that a feature of at least some of the material

in chs. 1–24 (such as 18 and 14.1-11) is a challenge to repentance: 'Get yourselves a new heart and a new spirit ... turn, and live' (18.31-32). All of this might lead one to expect that if restoration were ever to come, it would have to be because Israel had earned it by her righteousness.

However, when the prospect of restoration does appear in Ezekiel, this is not what we find at all. On the contrary, 'Thus says the Lord GOD: "It is not for your sake, O house of Israel, that I am about to act"' (36.22). The motif of shame for past sins underlines the fact that deliverance is undeserved; later in the same chapter we read: 'Then you will remember your evil ways, and your deeds that were not good; and you will loathe yourselves for your iniquities and your abominable deeds' (36.31).[54] Admittedly, it is said that Israel will be cleansed (36.25), given a 'new heart' and a 'new spirit' (36.26), and made to walk according to Yahweh's statutes (36.27), but all of this is a promise for the future, part and parcel of the gift of restoration, and certainly not a condition upon which it depends. As for the call to repentance, we have argued that this is primarily a rhetorical device to emphasize the responsibility of Israel for the disaster of defeat and exile.[55]

It must be acknowledged that the Old Testament as a whole is marked by reluctance to speak of divine favour as deserved. Even in Deuteronomy, a book characterized by moral exhortation with rewards promised for right conduct, the notion that the blessings enjoyed by Israel are merited is corrected (Deut. 7.7-8; 9.4-5).[56] But it is in Ezekiel that the conviction that divine favour is undeserved is articulated more consistently than anywhere else in the Old Testament: '"It is not for your sake that I will act", says the Lord GOD, "let that be known to you. Be ashamed and confounded for your ways, O house of Israel"' (36.32). We may assert with confidence that the reward of Israel's right conduct is not to be numbered among the motives for Yahweh's deliverance of Israel, as this is presented in Ezekiel.

3. Is it, then, out of love for Israel that Yahweh acts to deliver her? A contrast between deserved favour and undeserved love can be found in Deut. 7.7-8: 'It was not because you were more in number than any other people ... but it is because the LORD loves you'. Again, in Hosea we find Yahweh's love for Israel compared not only to a man's love for an unfaithful woman (3.1), but also to a father's love for a child (11.1).

The closest parallel to such language in Ezekiel is found in ch. 16, which relates the story of the foundling girl, representing Jerusalem. Yahweh passes by the girl, and declares her to be 'at the age for love' (16.8). The verse continues: 'I spread my skirt over you, and covered your nakedness; yea, I plighted my troth to you and entered into a covenant with you'. The relationship between Yahweh and his people is here expressed in terms of marriage. It should be noted, however, that all the phrases used in this verse appear to be either legal or sexual; we do not find here much evidence of real warmth of affection.[57] Moreover, the reference is to the original election of Israel, from which she subsequently fell away, rather than to a promise of restoration.[58] Elsewhere in Ezekiel we find little, if any, indication of Yahweh's love for his people. Chapter 23 tells of two women, Oholah and Oholibah, who represent Samaria and Jerusalem respectively. The language of warmth and affection is absent here too; we read simply: 'They became mine, and they bore sons and daughters' (23.4). Moreover, as in the previous case, restoration is not envisaged. Finally, we note ch. 24, in which the destruction of the sanctuary at Jerusalem is compared to Ezekiel's loss of his beloved wife (24.16). One might expect in this context some reference to Yahweh's affection for Israel, but again it is not to be found. In 24.21, Yahweh declares: 'Behold, I will profane my sanctuary, the pride of your power, the delight of your eyes, and the desire of your soul'; but at no point is the sanctuary spoken of as loved by Yahweh himself.

Ezekiel's God is not presented as a loving god. We note, for example, that neither the root אהב ('love') nor the root חסד ('steadfast love, kindness') is ever used in Ezekiel in connexion with Yahweh. Vocabulary relating to the emotions is not eschewed altogether—Yahweh's anger and jealousy are emphasized, especially in chs. 1–24 (e.g. 5.13). However, love and affection do not appear to be prominent features of his character; there is an element of the austere and the remote about Ezekiel's God. We shall not, it seems, find in the love of Yahweh the basic reason for his restoration of Israel.

4. We have considered, albeit briefly, a number of possible motives for Yahweh's deliverance of Israel, as this is presented in Ezekiel. All three we have rejected as ultimately unsatisfactory: the notion that restoration derives from Yahweh's punishment of the nations, that it constitutes a reward for a deserving Israel, and that it represents

essentially an expression of Yahweh's love for his people. To discover the primary motivation of this dramatic initiative we must turn instead to another characteristic formula, that which speaks of Yahweh acting for the sake of his 'name'. Ezek. 36.22 provides a typical example: 'It is not for your sake, O house of Israel, that I am about to act, but for the sake of my holy name, which you have profaned among the nations to which you came'.

There are fourteen references to the divine 'name' (שם) in Ezekiel.[59] On five occasions reference is made to Yahweh 'acting' (עשה) for the sake of his name (20.9, 14, 22, 44; 36.22). He is also said to 'have concern for' (חמל על) his name (36.21), to 'vindicate the holiness of' (קרש) his name (36.23), to 'make known' (ירע) his name (39.7), and to 'be jealous for' (קנא ל) his name (39.25). It is of particular importance, as we shall see, that the verb with which the divine 'name' most frequently appears is 'to profane' (חלל). Profanation of the 'name' is mentioned on no less than nine occasions (20.9, 14, 22, 39; 36.20, 21, 22, 23; 39.7).[60] Reference to Yahweh's 'name' takes a variety of forms: four times we find the simple 'my name' (שמי) (20.9, 14, 22, 44); rather more often (nine times) the form adopted is 'my holy name' (שם קרשי) (20.39; 36.20, 21, 22; 39.7 (twice); 39.25; 43.7, 8); finally, there occurs just once the form 'my great name' (שמי הגרול) (36.23).

The word שם is used in a broad range of senses in the Old Testament.[61] Although a 'name' can be simply a label of identification (as in the names of the rivers in Gen. 2.11-14), it frequently amounts to an expression of the essential nature of its bearer (for example, Ps. 9.10: 'Those who know thy name put their trust in thee, for thou, O LORD, hast not forsaken those who seek thee'). In this sense, the 'name' of a person can mean his character as revealed in his actions; this is exemplified in a recurrent motif of the book of Amos, in which the refrain 'the LORD is his name' is repeated after references to Yahweh's creative activity (Amos 4.13; 5.8-9; 9.5-6). On occasion, Yahweh is entreated to act according to his revealed character, as in Ps. 109.21: 'But thou, O GOD my Lord, deal on my behalf for thy name's sake; because thy steadfast love is good, deliver me!' The Psalmist here seems to call on Yahweh to behave in keeping with his reputation for steadfast love. Elsewhere the notion of 'reputation' is even more prominent, as in Josh. 7.9, where Yahweh is asked: 'What wilt thou do for thy great name?'[62] It is in the light of references such as these that we are to understand שם as found in the Ezekiel material which we are considering.

A high proportion of the cases of the word in Ezekiel occur in two significant passages.[63] The first of these is ch. 20, which presents a survey of Israel's long history of sin, as an illustration of the wayward inclinations of this nation. Three times it is said that Yahweh had resolved to punish his people as they deserved, but on each occasion he withheld his hand (20.9, 14, 22). Yahweh's restraint is explained in all three cases (with only minor variations) in the words: 'But I acted for the sake of my name, that it should not be profaned in the sight of the nations, in whose sight I had brought them out'. Whereas this passage takes the form of an historical retrospect, the other, more central to our purposes, looks forward to Yahweh's imminent deliverance of Israel. This second passage is Ezek. 36.20ff.; we read that when the people of Israel were exiled among the nations, they profaned Yahweh's 'holy name', for men said of them, 'These are the people of the LORD, and yet they had to go out of his land' (36.20). As a result, Yahweh had concern for his 'name', declaring 'It is not for your sake, O house of Israel, that I am about to act, but for the sake of my holy name' (36.22). In the following verse, we read that Yahweh is to 'vindicate the holiness of' his 'great name, which has been profaned among the nations'. Both of these passages, then, speak of the profanation of the 'name' of Yahweh and state that it is for the sake of this 'name' that Yahweh acts to spare an undeserving Israel. In both it would seem that the primary purpose of Yahweh's activity is the vindication of his reputation.

What aspect of Yahweh's reputation is particularly in mind? The profanation of the divine 'name' appears to consist essentially in the casting of doubt upon Yahweh's power and effectiveness. The words which the nations utter in 36.20, 'These are the people of the LORD, and yet they had to go out of his land', amount to a charge that Yahweh was too weak to prevent other nations (aided presumably by their gods) from exiling his people. The nations express similar opinions elsewhere in Ezekiel too, as in 25.8 and 35.10. That it is essentially the power of Yahweh which is questioned by the nations is confirmed by the fact that it is the restoration of Israel which will ultimately vindicate his 'name' in their eyes. The nations have misinterpreted Israel's defeat as a sign of Yahweh's weakness.[64] He must now (even at the cost of waiving the rigour of his judgment) act to correct this misconception and vindicate his reputation as a powerful god.[65]

A number of scholars have been at pains to argue that we should not think of Ezekiel's God as 'merely concerned for his reputation'.[66] Carley writes: 'When the prophet speaks of Yahweh acting "for the sake of his name" he was alluding not to divine self-interest, but to the necessity of Yahweh vindicating his character as a God of compassion and forgiveness, as well as of uncompromising wrath against the impenitent'.[67] However, these scholars tend to paint Ezekiel's God in rather more congenial colours than does the book itself. They underestimate the radical nature of Ezekiel's theocentricity and by so doing in fact diminish the grandeur of his portrayal of Yahweh. As we have seen, the ultimate motive of Yahweh's activity is found in his desire to vindicate his 'name', the primary content of which is, it seems, not his reputation as a compassionate, forgiving or even a just god, but rather his reputation as a powerful deity. It would not be inaccurate to say that in Ezekiel Yahweh does indeed in a sense act out of 'divine self-interest'.[68]

'I will vindicate my holiness'

Before concluding the present chapter, we may touch briefly upon one further feature of the language of Ezekiel which gives clear expression to this God-centred emphasis. This is the theme of the holiness of Yahweh. We have observed that the 'name' of Yahweh often appears in the fuller form 'holy name' (שם קדש).[69] We have also noted that in Ezek. 36.23a Yahweh is spoken of as 'vindicating the holiness of' or 'sanctifying' (וקדשתי) his 'great name'. It would seem, then, that there is in Ezekiel an association between the word שם and words of the root קרש. In addition to the nine occasions when the noun קֹדֶשׁ is used with שם, the verb קרש is frequently employed in closely related contexts.

The verb קרש is used most often in Ezekiel in the Niphal form, with the sense of 'to vindicate one's holiness' or 'to sanctify oneself', as in 36.23b, 'The nations will know that I am the LORD ... when through you I vindicate my holiness before their eyes'.[70] The Hithpael form of the verb is used once in the same sense (38.23). It is the Piel form which is employed at 36.23a, 'I will vindicate the holiness of my great name'.[71]

We find in the use of the verb קרשׁ in Ezekiel a strongly theocentric focus. This is underlined by the fact that the subject is invariably Yahweh himself (the verb generally having a reflexive sense: 'I will vindicate my holiness', 'I will sanctify myself'). Procksch expressed the sense well: 'What is indicated is not so much entry into a state of holiness as the expression of the essence of divine holiness'.[72]

The emphasis on the holiness of Yahweh in Ezekiel is not without parallel elsewhere. Indeed the theme of divine holiness in the Old Testament is a rich and far-ranging one, which cannot be examined in detail here.[73] There are particularly close affinities between Ezekiel and the Holiness Code (Lev. 17–26), as has been demonstrated by Reventlow.[74] It seems likely that Ezekiel's use of the root קרשׁ owes something also to previous prophetic usage, notably that of Isaiah of Jerusalem, as has been argued by Bettenzoli.[75] Nevertheless, as Muilenburg wrote, 'Ezekiel's awareness of the divine holiness is more awesome, more sublime and majestic, more cosmic and "tremendous" than that of his prophetic predecessors'.[76]

The motif of divine holiness in Ezekiel gains particular force from the fact that it forms part of a network of interrelated themes. To a remarkable degree, language pertaining to the holiness of Yahweh occurs together with and shares the emphases of the other motifs we have considered in this chapter. We have already commented upon the link between Yahweh's 'holiness' and his 'name'. We may note also that the phrase 'in the sight of the nations' or a related formula is almost always to be found where the verb קרשׁ is used in Ezekiel. Moreover, every such case occurs in conjunction with the 'I am Yahweh' formula (or a variation upon it).[77] Furthermore, as in certain other contexts we have noted, so also in those passages in which the verb קרשׁ is used, the theme of the vindication of Yahweh's power is usually prominent; some cases concern the restoration of Israel (as in 36.23), others primarily the punishment of the nations (for example, 28.22). 'So I will show my greatness and my holiness and make myself known in the eyes of many nations. Then they will know that I am the LORD' (38.23).[78]

We have seen, then, that a range of formulae and motifs in Ezekiel serve to highlight the extent to which the focus of the book is consistently upon Yahweh himself: 'I am Yahweh', 'In the sight of the nations', 'For the sake of my name' and 'I will vindicate my holiness'.[79] In the use of each we have found evidence of a distinctive emphasis on the absolute centrality of Yahweh and his self-manifestation, a radical theocentricity which is of an order difficult to parallel anywhere in the Old Testament.

Chapter 7

A NEW HEART AND A NEW SPIRIT

In the previous chapter we saw the extent to which in the book of Ezekiel the focus is consistently upon Yahweh himself. We now turn to investigate the point at which this radically theocentric emphasis impinges upon the question of Israel's response to Yahweh, namely the remarkable motif of the divine gift of a 'new heart' and a 'new spirit'.

In Ezekiel 36 we read that Yahweh is to act to restore Israel for the purpose of vindicating the holiness of his 'name', which has been profaned among the nations. As we have seen, the demands of strict justice are to be waived, for Israel does not deserve such favour (36.22, 32). We are told in v. 25 that Yahweh will 'sprinkle clean water' upon his people and cleanse them of all those things which have made them unworthy. The words which follow, in vv. 26 and 27, are indeed striking: 'A new heart I will give you, and a new spirit I will put within you; and I will take out of your flesh the heart of stone and give you a heart of flesh. And I will put my spirit within you, and cause you to walk in my statutes and be careful to observe my ordinances'. Very similar words occur in the context of the long Jerusalem vision of Ezekiel 8–11. In an oracle which speaks of the restoration of the exiles, we read: 'I will give them one heart, and put a new spirit within them; I will take the stony heart out of their flesh and give them a heart of flesh, that they may walk in my statutes and keep my ordinances and obey them' (11.19-20).

We have seen that the primary motivation for Yahweh's activity as presented in Ezekiel is to be found in a concern for divine self-vindication. It would appear to be as a consequence of this that the people of Israel are to receive as a gift that which they had never been able to muster for themselves, namely the ability to respond to and obey Yahweh's will. Let us consider more closely the notion of the giving of a 'new heart' and a 'new spirit', examining each of these phrases in turn.

A New Heart

The Hebrew noun לב has been described as 'the most important word in the vocabulary of Old Testament anthropology'.[1] Only rarely do we find the word used in relation to God;[2] the vast majority of cases (over 800, in fact) relate to human beings. Of the two forms of the word (לֵב and לֵבָב), the shorter is much the commoner and it is this form which is overwhelmingly predominant in Ezekiel, where it occurs in thirty of the thirty-five cases in which the word is used. The spelling seems in fact to be a matter of stylistic preference rather than of semantic difference.[3]

The word is employed in a wide range of senses. It is used of the physical organ which beats in the breast (as in Jer. 4.19: 'Oh, the walls of my heart! My heart is beating wildly'). The image of the replacement of the heart of stone with a heart of flesh in Ezek. 11.19 and 36.26 would seem to reflect this physical sense. The word is also used, as in the common metaphorical use of 'heart' in English, of the emotions (for example, 1 Sam. 2.1: 'My heart exults in the LORD'). The lover speaks to the לב of the beloved (cf. Isa. 40.2). The word is used of the emotions only occasionally in Ezekiel: at 36.5, Edom is said to have plundered Judah 'with wholehearted joy' (בשמחת כל-לבב), whilst a number of times hearts are said to 'melt' in fear at the prospect of judgment.[4]

Much more common than either the 'physical' or the 'emotional' sense, however, is the use of לב to mean the rational faculty; in fact, this accounts for the largest number of cases in the Old Testament as a whole. For example, in 1 Kgs 5.9 (Eng. 4.29) it is reported that 'God gave Solomon wisdom and understanding beyond measure, and largeness of לב like the sand on the seashore', and Exod. 36.1 speaks of 'every man wise in heart (חכם-לב) in whom the LORD has put ability and intelligence'. There are a number of instances of this 'rational' sense in Ezekiel; in 38.10, we read: 'On that day, thoughts will come into your לב (RSV: 'mind')'.[5]

Of particular relevance to our present concerns, however, is the use of the word as a designation of the locus of the moral will. In 1

Sam. 24.6 (Eng. 24.5) we read that 'the לב of David smote him, because he had cut off Saul's skirt'. In Joel 2.13 Israel is challenged to repent with the words 'Rend your hearts and not your garments'. This 'moral' sense is particularly predominant in Ezekiel: the heart of Israel is said to be 'wanton' (6.9), and it is into their hearts (על־לבם) that the elders of Israel take their idols (14.3; cf. 20.16). At the beginning of his ministry, Ezekiel is warned that the people of Israel are חזקי־לב (2.4) and קשי־לב (3.7), both phrases meaning 'stubborn hearted'.[6] It is this unresponsive and insensitive 'heart of stone' which is now to be replaced (11.19; 36.26).[7]

There is a further nuance of the word לב which sheds light on the Ezekiel texts which concern us. It is used at times to mean reality as distinct from outward appearance. When Samuel is looking for the future king, he is told: 'man looks on the outward appearance (לעינים), but the LORD looks on the heart (ללבב)' (1 Sam. 16.7). There is a similar contrast also in one of the examples quoted above, namely Joel 2.13, 'Rend your hearts and not your garments', and with this we may compare Ezek. 33.31: 'With their lips they show much love, but their heart is set on their gain'. It is a serious matter, then, when Israel takes her idols right into her heart (Ezek. 14.3); and, conversely, to replace the heart (as is envisaged in Ezek. 11.19 and 36.26) is to effect as profound a change as is possible.[8]

In the Ezekiel texts which at present concern us (11.19-20 and 36.26-27), then, two important senses of לב converge, the heart as the locus of the moral will and as the symbol of inner reality as distinct from mere outward appearance.

A New Spirit

The noun רוח is used very frequently of God as well as of man; for this reason, Lys spoke of it as a 'theo-anthropological' term.[9] This word too is used in a wide range of senses. In almost a third of the 389 instances in the Old Testament, it refers to the wind, particularly as a mighty force at Yahweh's disposal. Thus in Ezek. 13.11, 13, the 'stormy wind' (רוח־סערות) is spoken of as an instrument of divine wrath, and in 37.9 we find reference to the 'four winds'. In a closely related sense, רוח is used of the God-given breath of life. The meaning here is very similar to that of another noun, נשמה; the two words are used in parallel in Isa. 42.5: 'Thus says God, the

LORD, . . . who gives breath (נשמה) to the people upon (the earth) and spirit (רוח) to those who walk in it'. In Ezek. 37.9, 10, 'the breath' (הרוח) is summoned to vivify the dry bones. The word is also used in a more general sense of the dynamic power of Yahweh, inspiring Judges (as in Judg. 3.10) and kings (1 Sam. 16.13). It is the spirit of Yahweh which comes upon prophets, such as Balaam (Num. 24.2). This sense is particularly common in Ezekiel, as in 11.5: 'And the Spirit of the LORD fell upon me, and he said to me, "Say, 'Thus says the LORD . . .'"'[10] It is רוח (generally without the article) which enters into Ezekiel and makes him stand (2.2; 3.24), which snatches him up and transports him (3.12, 14; 8.3; 11.1, 24a; 43.5; cf. 11.24b).[11] Some relatively late Old Testament passages look forward to an eschatological outpouring of the רוח of Yahweh: 'And it shall come to pass afterward, that I will pour out my spirit on all flesh' (Joel 3.1 [Eng. 2.28]; cf. Isa. 61.1). Perhaps it is partly against the background of such a development that we are to read Ezek. 36.27, 'I will put my spirit (רוחי) within you'[12] and also 37.14, 'I will put my spirit within you, and you shall live'.[13]

Three further senses of the word remain to be considered, all of them used of human beings. רוח is spoken of as the medium both of understanding (as in Ezek. 11.5: 'So you think, O house of Israel; for I know the things that come into your רוח [RSV: 'mind']')[14] and of feeling (for example, Ezek. 3.14: 'I went in bitterness in the heat of my רוח [RSV: 'spirit']').[15] However, of the various senses in which the word is used of human beings, the most relevant to our inquiry is that in which it refers to the moral will, both in a positive and in a negative sense. Thus the רוח can be 'steadfast' and 'willing' (Ps. 51.12, 14 [Eng. 51.10, 12]) or it can be 'a spirit of harlotry' (Hos. 5.4). It is in the light of such expressions that we are to understand the 'new spirit' (רוח חדשה) of Ezek. 11.19 and 36.26.[16]

In the texts which are our present concern, then, we find the word רוח used in two basic senses. In the expression 'I will put a new spirit within them/you' in 11.19 and 36.26, it is used in one of its 'anthropological' senses, to refer to 'the moral will', whilst in the phrase 'I will put my spirit within you' in 36.27 the sense is specifically theological: 'the dynamic power of Yahweh'. However, these senses converge, as becomes clear in 36.26-27, where the two expressions, 'I will put a new spirit within you' and 'I will put my spirit within you', are quite clearly intended to refer to the same reality, namely the renewal of the moral will of the house of Israel by the outpouring of the dynamic power of Yahweh.

The use of רוח of the will is very similar to what we described as the 'moral' sense of the word לב.[17] Indeed, it seems that the 'new heart'[18] and the 'new spirit' both refer primarily to the gift of a renewed capacity to respond to Yahweh in obedience. This is the more likely in view of the words which follow the promise in both 11.19-20 and 36.26-27. In 11.20 the purpose of the gift is defined as being 'that they may walk in my statutes and keep my ordinances and obey them', whilst in 36.27 we read, 'I will cause you to walk in my statutes and be careful to observe my ordinances'. It is probably unwise to attempt to distinguish between the aspects of obedient moral response represented by the 'new heart' and the 'new spirit' as does Wolff, who relates the former to 'the pure guidings of the conscience' and the latter to 'the steadfast power of the will to act accordingly'.[19] We should rather regard the two expressions as essentially synonymous, each conveying both these aspects of the promised renewal.[20]

Covenant Renewed

A number of scholars emphasize that the gift of the 'new heart' and 'new spirit' in Ezekiel 11 and 36 is to be viewed in terms of the 'covenant' model of the relationship between Yahweh and Israel. Immediately after the promise of the ability to respond we find, in both of the passages under review, the assurance that 'they/you shall be my people, and I will be their/your God' (11.20; 36.28). Similar words occur elsewhere in Ezekiel at 14.11; 34.30-31; 37.23, 27.[21] In the Old Testament as a whole, this formula frequently occurs in the same context as the word ברית ('covenant'), as in Exod. 6.7; Lev. 26.12; Deut. 29.12 (Eng. 29.13); Jer. 11.4; 31.33; 32.38. Within Ezekiel, we find these words juxtaposed to ברית at 34.30-31 (cf. 34.24) and 37.23, 27. It seems, therefore, that they represent a formula associated with the realm of 'covenant' language.[22]

Commenting on this formula, von Rad wrote: 'This puts it beyond all doubt that Ezekiel is speaking of a saving appointment of Yahweh analogous to the making of the old covenant'.[23] It was in the light of the same formula that Zimmerli interpreted the difficult verse Ezek. 11.16, 'I have been a sanctuary to them for a while (or 'in small measure') in the countries where they have gone'.[24] He suggested that these words are based on part of our formula, namely, 'I will be their God'. He argued that 11.16 refers to a limited (albeit gracious) relationship between Yahweh and his people in exile; 11.20, however, offers the promise of a renewal of the full reality of the 'covenant' relationship, expressed in the words of the complete formulation: 'They shall be my people, and I will be their God'.[25]

Renewal as a Corporate Experience

When investigating the way in which Israel's responsibility is presented in Ezekiel, we argued that the place of 'individual responsibility' has often been exaggerated and that, for the most part, the house of Israel is punished as a collective group. When similar questions are raised in connexion with the hopeful material in the book, what do we find?

Some have sought to interpret the promise of a 'new heart' and a 'new spirit' in a particularly individualistic way. Thus Eichrodt, writing of the giving of the spirit, argued that 'it is a misinterpretation to associate it with the people as a whole', preferring to see here 'a direct connection between the covenant God and every single member of his people'.[26] He wished to stress that 'the spirit of God permeates each individual member of the people of God so as to carry out an inward transformation'. 'Here', Eichrodt claimed, 'we see the new importance of the individual member of the people'.[27]

However, the text of Ezekiel itself gives little justification for such an individualistic reading. First, we may consider the audience addressed in each of the two passages which concern us. The promise of restoration declared in Ezek. 11.14-21 is for the exiled community as distinct from those in Jerusalem;[28] significantly, however, 11.15 defines the exiles in the very corporate phrase 'the whole house of Israel, all of them' (כל־בית ישראל כלה). Turning to ch. 36, we find that the prelude to the promise is presented in terms of the 'house of Israel' (36.17, 21) and indeed that the declaration itself is addressed to the 'house of Israel' (36.22, 32). Second, we have seen that 'heart' (לב), 'spirit' (רוח) and 'flesh' (בשר) are all terms used of aspects of the human being;[29] thus the replacement of the 'heart' and the giving of a 'new spirit' are indeed strongly 'corporate' images.[30] One distinctive feature of the verses in ch. 11 may highlight this collective emphasis:

it is possible that the phrase 'one heart' (לב אחד) in 11.19 reflects the hopes for the reunification of the people which are found, for example, in 37.22.[31] Third, the formula 'they/you shall be my people, and I will be their/your God' (11.20; 36.28), to which reference has already been made, underlines the essentially collective nature of the promise.

It must be said that to hold that the renewal affects the people of Israel as a whole is not necessarily, as Eichrodt implied, to interpret it merely in terms of 'the outward regulation of obedient conduct'.[32] Nor, of course, is it to deny that particular individuals are involved in the renewal of the nation. Our concern is rather to protect these passages from distortion by anachronistic individualizing interpretation. Such an understanding is confirmed by the collective emphasis of the hopeful sections of Ezekiel as a whole. Thus, for example, the 'dry bones' of ch. 37 are said to be 'the whole house of Israel' (37.11), and the promise of new life there is addressed by Yahweh to 'my people' (עמי) (37.12, 13). That this passage refers not to individual resurrection but to the corporate renewal of Israel is, of course, generally recognized.[33] Ezek. 37.15ff. looks forward to the reunification of Judah and Israel; v. 22 emphasizes that they shall no longer be two nations but 'one nation' under 'one king', whilst v. 24 speaks of the promised king as 'one shepherd' over the people (cf. 34.23). The final verses of ch. 37 (37.26-28) envisage the restored community gathered around the sanctuary, a theme which is explored at length in the last nine chapters of the book (40–48; cf. 20.40-44). This strongly collective picture of the promised restoration as presented in Ezekiel complements our earlier demonstration that the material dealing with judgment is much less individualistic than has often been assumed.

The Setting and Authorship of the Two Passages

Ezek. 11.19-20

As we have noted, the book of Ezekiel is characterized by a greater degree of systematic organization than any other prophetic book. The report of the fall of Jerusalem in 587 (33.21-22) represents the turning point between the preceding material, which is overwhelmingly concerned with judgment (both upon Israel and upon the nations), and that which follows, which is devoted largely to promises of favour for Israel. For the most part, this pattern has a consistency which suggests that at some point a deliberate editorial systematization has been imposed upon the book. There are, however, a small number of exceptions to the overall pattern. 11.14-21 is one such, a short hopeful section standing isolated in the midst of material concerning judgment upon Israel.[34]

Ezek. 11.14-21 occurs within the account of the great vision of chs. 8-11, which describes the abominations in the Temple and the onset of judgment. In 11.5-12, Ezekiel delivers an oracle of judgment against the complacent leaders of Jerusalem. In v. 13 we are told that one of these, Pelatiah, drops dead during the prophet's tirade. At this, Ezekiel cries, 'Ah Lord GOD! Wilt thou make a full end of the remnant of Israel?' The section which is our particular concern, 11.14-21, follows immediately after these words. As in other cases which we have noted (particularly ch. 18), a divine oracle is preceded by words which are placed in the mouths of those whose position the prophet is to contradict. The inhabitants of Jerusalem are portrayed as saying: 'They have gone far from the LORD; to us this land is given for a possession' (11.15). It is in response to this arrogant presumption that the prophet declares that the favour of Yahweh is to be granted to the exiles.

There are indications that 11.14-21 was originally a self-contained unit and not integrally related to its setting. The preceding section, 11.1-13, seems to stand awkwardly in its present context, in a number of respects. It is odd to find Ezekiel addressing twenty-five men outside the Temple after the references to the six executioners in 9.2, 7 and to the man clothed in linen scattering burning coals in 10.2, 7. Moreover, the sin with which the elders are charged at 11.6, which seems to be the murder of the innocent, is rather different from the cultic sins which are recounted in ch. 8. Finally, 11.1ff. interrupts the account of the departure of the glory of Yahweh, which is said in 10.19 to be at the east gate of the Temple. Thus it may well be that 11.1-13 was introduced into its present position some time after the composition of the basic account of the Temple vision.

Not only does 11.1-13 seem somewhat out of place; there is the further complexity that the connexion between the address to the leaders of Jerusalem in 11.1ff. and the hopeful oracle to the exiles in 11.14-21 appears somewhat tenuous. Although the two passages share the theme of the arrogant presumption of the leaders of

Jerusalem, there are significant differences, chief among which is that 11.1ff. is entirely focused upon Jerusalem and makes no reference to those already in exile. The shared theme of the presumption of the Jerusalem community should perhaps, then, be regarded as the factor which prompted the attachment of the self-contained section 11.14-21 to 11.1-13, rather than as evidence of an original link between these two passages.

However, though 11.14-21 seems to constitute a self-contained unit, there is reason to believe that this is early material. As we have noted, 11.15 pictures a complacent Jerusalem community; these people imagine that their lot is much better than that of the exiles. This best fits a setting in the period between 597 and 587, before the fall of Jerusalem, for after the destruction of the city and Temple no such sharp contrast could be drawn.[35] If these verses do envisage the situation before 587, it would seem reasonable to believe that they derive from Ezekiel himself, though this is not to rule out the possibility of some redactional elaboration.[36] This self-contained unit presumably found a place in the first part of the book, despite its hopeful content, because it was apparent that it reflected the situation which obtained before the final disaster.[37]

Ezek. 36.26-27
In sharp contrast to the isolation of 11.14-21 in the midst of material of a very different tone, 36.26-27 stands in a section which largely concerns the promised restoration. Chapters 34–37 paint a vivid picture of hope for the future.[38] The exiles will return to the land (34.13; 36.24; 37.12), cities will be rebuilt (36.10, 33ff.), nature itself will be renewed (34.25ff.; 36.8-9, 29-30). Judah and Israel will be united again (37.15ff.), there will be a restored Davidic monarchy (34.23-24; 37.22, 24-25) and Yahweh will set his sanctuary in the midst of his people for evermore (37.26ff.). It is within this broad setting that the promise of the renewal of Israel's will through the outpouring of Yahweh's spirit is announced in 36.26-27.[39]

Ezekiel 36 itself begins with a command to the prophet to address the mountains of Israel. A word of assurance is given, reversing the condemnation enunciated in ch. 6. The nations which had oppressed Israel shall themselves suffer reproach. As for Yahweh's own people, 'I will cause you to be inhabited as in your former times, and will do more good to you than ever before' (36.11). With v. 16 a new section begins, and this forms the immediate context of our verses. The section is cast in narrative form, first reviewing the past and then looking to the imminent future. Yahweh had scattered Israel among the nations because of her many wicked sins (vv. 17-19). This, as we have seen, had led the nations to interpret the fate of Israel as evidence of the weakness of Yahweh, whose 'name' was thereby profaned (vv. 20-21). At this point, the focus of the passage shifts to the prospect of a new divine initiative: Yahweh resolves to act to vindicate his 'name' (vv. 22-23). To this end, he is to gather his people from all the nations and bring them back to their own land (v. 24), cleansing them of all their uncleannesses (v. 25).[40] It is now that the gift of the 'new heart' and the 'new spirit' and the outpouring of the spirit of God are announced (vv. 26-27), and the 'covenant' formula reaffirmed (v. 28). The verses which follow give further details of the restoration, particularly its more physical aspects, and underline the fact that it is in spite of rather than because of Israel's behaviour that all this is to happen (vv. 29-32). Two shorter sections, each with its own introductory formula, fill out the picture (vv. 33-36 and 37-38).

What of the question of authorship? S. Herrmann has suggested that the deliverance oracles in the book are to be attributed to redactors active later in the exilic period. For Herrmann the hopeful nature of this material is itself, it seems, an indication that it does not derive from Ezekiel.[41] However, such a position, as we suggested earlier, tends to beg the question of the content of the prophet's teaching.[42] Indeed, at least two telling theological arguments can be advanced in favour of attributing a message of hope to Ezekiel himself. We saw earlier that the theme of restoration is intimately related to the emphasis on the need for Yahweh to vindicate his 'name'.[43] There are indications that this motif of the vindication of the 'name' is a feature of Ezekiel's own theology.[44] If this is so, there would seem to be a strong probability that the restoration theme itself is integral rather than extraneous. Raitt offers another theological argument, based on the presence of strikingly rigorous elements within the oracles of restoration in Ezekiel (e.g. 36.22-23, 31-32; 37.23). He notes a 'remarkable combination of unconditional promises of deliverance together with a vivid awareness of the validity and profoundly serious implications of the judgment'.[45] As Raitt argues, this interpenetration of grace and rigour is most reasonably accounted for on the hypothesis that the themes of judgment and hope come from the one prophet, wrestling to 'make sense of the movement of God's initiative toward salvation without ignoring the reality and justice of the judgment God brought on Judah'.[46]

Theological arguments call for care, however, if circularity is to be avoided, and they are best not advanced in isolation from other criteria. If we consider style, certain aspects of ch. 36 do in fact suggest authorship by Ezekiel. The vocabulary and motifs of the chapter exhibit numerous features characteristic of what appears to be 'primary' material in the book. For example, the address 'Son of man' (36.1, 16; cf. 2.1; 3.1, 3, 4), reference to Yahweh's wrath (חמה) and jealousy (קנאה) (36.5-6, 18; cf. 5.13; 8.18), and the placing of words in the mouths of interlocutors (36.20, 35; cf. 12.22; 18.2). These stylistic features, taken with the two theological considerations touched upon above, would seem to constitute a strong case for the primary provenance of Ezekiel 36. The matter is not quite so simple, however. To demonstrate continuity of style is not to prove that one has isolated the *ipsissima verba* of the prophet. We have seen that even where features originate with the prophet they may become the common currency of the redactional tradition.[47] We cannot, therefore, discount the possibility of redactional elaboration. Thus, for example, there are indications that the two sections at end of the chapter (vv. 33-36 and 37-38) may well be secondary additions.[48]

The probability, then, is that 36.16ff., including the verses which particularly concern us (36.26-27), contain a theme which is Ezekiel's own, in words which are largely his but which may also have been elaborated by disciples.[49] However, this question cannot be left without consideration of a further important issue, for there are here striking affinities with certain other Old Testament literature, of which some account must be given.

Affinities with other literature

Since the question of the literary relations of Ezekiel is a vast one, we must confine ourselves to a brief consideration of that material which relates most directly to Ezek. 11.19-20 and 36.26-27.[50]

A number of passages in the book of Jeremiah exhibit significant similarities to these verses of Ezekiel; of these, we note the three most striking. Jeremiah 24 recounts the vision of the two baskets of figs, one of good figs and the other of bad. The good are identified with the exiles, and are contrasted with the bad which represent King Zedekiah and those who live in Judah and Egypt. This is similar to the contrast between the two communities in Ezek. 11.14-21. The return of the exiles is promised in Jer. 24.6, after which we read: 'I will give them a heart (לב) to know that I am the LORD; and they shall be my people and I will be their God, for they shall return to me with their whole heart' (24.7). The reference to the gift of a 'heart' and the occurrence of the 'covenant' formula, which occurs in both Ezek. 11.20 and 36.28, are particularly noteworthy.[51]

In Jeremiah 32, following the account of Jeremiah's purchase of a field in Anathoth, there is another passage relevant to our concerns. 32.37 looks forward to the return of the exiles to the land; then, in the next verse, we find the familiar formula, 'they shall be my people, and I will be their God'. A further promise follows: 'I will give them one heart and one way, that they may fear me for ever, for their own good and the good of their children after them' (32.39). We have already commented upon the occurrence of the phrase 'one heart' in this verse as in Ezek. 11.19.[52] Jer. 32.40 goes on to say: 'I will put the fear of me in their hearts'. One further similarity to Ezekiel 34–37 is to found in these verses, namely the reference to the making of an 'everlasting covenant' in Jer. 32.40 (cf. Ezek. 37.26).

One further passage should be mentioned in this context: Jer. 31.31-34. The theme of the 'new covenant' of Jer. 31.31 echoes that of the 'new heart' and 'new spirit' of Ezekiel.[53] In v. 33, we read the remarkable words: 'I will put my law within them and write it upon their hearts'. The similarity of this declaration to the gift promised in Ezek. 11.19-20 and 36.26-27 is obvious. The reference to the תורה ('law', or perhaps more accurately 'teaching') of Yahweh in Jer. 31.33 may be compared to the words of Ezek. 11.20, which define the purpose of Yahweh's gift to Israel as being 'that they may walk in my statutes and keep my ordinances and obey them', and also the very similar words of Ezek. 36.27. Furthermore, in Jer. 31.33 the 'covenant' formula, 'I will be their God, and they shall be my people', reappears.[54]

Von Rad regarded the parallels between Ezek. 36.26-27 and Jer. 31.31ff. and 32.37ff. as so significant that he wrote: 'one feels that Ezekiel must somehow have had Jeremiah's prophecies in front of

him'.[55] There are in fact many points of similarity between the books
of Jeremiah and Ezekiel, extending well beyond the passages which
are our immediate concern,[56] and it is widely believed that Ezekiel
was aware of much in the Jeremiah tradition. Some scholars
maintain that this included actual dependence on written material,[57]
whilst others prefer to speak simply of oral influence.[58]

We cannot, however, overlook the fact that the three passages in
Jeremiah which bear the closest resemblance to Ezek. 11.19-20 and
36.26-27 are among those Jeremianic prose passages in which
deuteronomistic influence seems most apparent.[59] This raises the
broad question of deuteronomistic influence in Ezekiel, and in
particular in the texts which especially concern us. Most scholars
acknowledge that the book of Ezekiel bears some marks of the style
and concerns of the book of Deuteronomy.[60] For example, the
centralization of sacrificial worship seems to be reflected in a number
of places, such as Ezek. 6.13 and 18.6. Turning to the Ezekiel texts
which are our immediate concern, we find that much of the wording
of Ezek. 11.14-21 is very close to Deuteronomy: the reference to the
'scattering' of Israel in 11.16 recalls Deut. 4.27, whilst the 'gathering'
promised in the following verse is reminiscent of Deut. 30.3-5. The
description of obedience in Ezek. 11.20 closely resembles the
language of Deut. 26.16-19. In Ezekiel 36 too we find further marked
affinities with Deuteronomy; for example, the description of the
renewal of nature in Ezek. 36.29-30 employs a number of words
particularly characteristic of Deuteronomy (e.g. דגן 'grain').

However, there are two respects in which our texts are most
significantly paralleled by Deuteronomy and the wider deuteronomistic
literature. These are, indeed, two of the features shared with the
Jeremiah texts we reviewed earlier. They are the 'covenant' formula,
'You shall be my people, and I will be your God', and the motif of the
'heart' as the place of moral response to Yahweh. We must give
further attention to each of these.

We touched upon the formula earlier and indicated the grounds for
associating it with a 'covenant' background.[61] Whilst 'covenant'
language is not especially prominent in the book of Ezekiel,[62] there
are two passages in which the words 'You shall be my people, and I
will be your God' (or a variation) are used in the same context as the
word ברית ('covenant'). The first of these is in ch. 34, where in v. 24
there occurs the single-sided formula, 'I, the LORD, will be their

God'. In the following verse, in connexion with a reference to the banishment of wild beasts, we find the promise of a 'covenant of peace' (ברית שלום) (cf. Isa. 54.9-10). The final two verses of the same chapter (34.30-31) contain an extended version of the full double-sided formula. The other passage, which again promises restoration, is in ch. 37. The double-sided formula occurs here in both vv. 23 and 27: 'I will be their God, and they shall be my people' (37.27). In v. 26, we find another reference to a 'covenant of peace', this time equated with an 'everlasting covenant' (ברית עולם) (cf. Isa. 55.3; Jer. 32.40; 50.5; Ezek. 16.60).[63]

It is important to note that most of the instances of the formula 'You shall be my people, and I will be your God' in the Old Testament appear to fall within literature of the late seventh and the sixth centuries, and predominantly within material related to Deuteronomy.[64] Indeed a growing body of scholarly opinion holds that the use of the word ברית as a central theological category may itself be a product of this general period of Israel's history, and indeed primarily a mark of the deuteronomistic movement. Nicholson writes: 'It is fair to regard 'covenant' as a theological theory about God's relationship with Israel which, though first formulated in earlier times, came into its own at the hands of the Deuteronomic circles in the years leading up to the Exile'.[65]

The use of the motif of the 'heart' as the place of moral response to Yahweh provides another notable parallel to the deuteronomistic literature.[66] In the famous words of Deut. 6.4-5, Israel is commanded to love Yahweh 'with all your heart' (בכל-לבבך), as well as 'with all your soul, and with all your might'.[67] The word לבב ('heart') is frequently used in Deuteronomy in connexion with obedience to Yahweh, often with the verb שמע ('to hear', 'to obey'); for example, Deut. 30.2: 'Obey his voice in all that I command you this day, with all your heart . . . ' The words of the law are sometimes spoken of as being in or upon the 'heart', as in Deut. 6.6; 30.14. Indeed, the notion of the 'heart' as the place of moral response is particularly characteristic of Deuteronomy and the wider deuteronomistic literature.[68]

In addition to this general feature, we may note also more specific parallels to the gift promised in Ezek. 11.19-20 and 36.26-27. In Deut. 30.6, we find the remarkable statement that Yahweh will circumcise the 'heart' of Israel, so that she will be able to fulfil the command (of Deut. 6.4-5) to love Yahweh with all her 'heart'. This promise would seem to take us beyond the moral exhortation and challenge which characterize the bulk of Deuteronomy (note especially Deut. 10.16: 'Circumcise therefore the foreskin of your heart, and be no longer stubborn') to a recognition of Israel's need for Yahweh to enable the response which he demands. It is probable that Deuteronomy 30 comes from the exilic period;[69] we may perhaps discern here a deuteronomistic theology 'come of age' under the shock of Babylonian conquest and deportation, events which appeared to demonstrate the inability of Israel to live up to the demands of Yahweh. It may be that such a development is reflected also at those points in the Deuteronomistic History where the 'heart' is mentioned in connexion with Yahweh granting a new ability to do his will (for example, 1 Sam. 10.9: 'When he turned his back to leave Samuel, God gave him another heart'; cf. 1 Kgs 8.58). The moral renewal of Israel promised in Ezekiel is so similar to this material that the probability that Ezekiel 11 and 36 reflect deuteronomistic influence must be regarded as strong.

It would be a mistake, however, to view this development of a theology of 'grace' during the exilic period as an exclusively deuteronomistic phenomenon.[70] Such themes are too widely evidenced for that to be the case. Among the Psalms which are likely to be exilic (recognizing that dating is difficult), we may note especially Psalm 51: 'Create in me a clean heart, O God, and put a new and right spirit within me' (Ps. 51.12 [Eng. 10]; cf. 79.8-9). Comparable hopes are a feature of Deutero-Isaiah (cf. Isa. 43.25; 44.3; 48.9-11). Furthermore, the Priestly strand of the Pentateuch, if such may be isolated, is particularly marked by unconditional promises (e.g. Gen. 9.8-17).[71] It is doubtful whether all of these are to be accounted for on the hypothesis of a complex web of dependence, whether oral or written. Rather, it is probable that they are (for the most part) independent responses to the same situation, albeit made in the light of much shared history and tradition. The experience of defeat and exile was indeed a traumatic one for Israel as a whole, demanding a radical re-evaluation of theological assumptions. It would seem that many came to feel that if there were to be a future it would have to depend entirely upon Yahweh rather than upon the merits of Israel. Nevertheless, the point remains that the particular form in which these developments are expressed in Ezekiel owes much to deuteronomistic influence.

The Contribution of Ezekiel

We have suggested that Ezek. 11.19-20 and 36.26-27 reflect deuteronomistic influence in a number of ways, of which two are particularly important, namely the 'covenant' formula and the motif of the 'heart' as the locus of the moral will. Were these deuteronomistic features mediated entirely by Jeremianic material or were they absorbed more directly? What connexion, if any, is there between these deuteronomistic features and Ezekiel himself? Can we discern the distinctive contribution of the prophet? Such questions threaten to take us into the realm of speculation, but some cautious exploration is in order.

S. Herrmann posits a deuteronomistic school tradition, responsible for the hopeful material in both Jeremiah and Ezekiel. He distinguishes sharply between the work of the prophet Ezekiel and a deuteronomistic elaboration of the book, arguing that Ezekiel 34–37, for example, came into being in Palestine later in the exilic period.[72] However, this view may be criticized on a number of grounds. Chapters 34–37, with their strong emphasis on the theme of return from exile (e.g. 36.24; 37.12), read most naturally as the product of the exiled community in Babylonia, hoping for restoration. Moreover, we have seen that the closely related material in Ezek. 11.14-21 appears to reflect conditions peculiar to the period 597-587.[73] Above all, however, Herrmann's hypothesis fails to do justice to those elements in this material which may be said to reflect the style and theology of Ezekiel himself. Two important features may be postulated as constituting the distinctive contribution of Ezekiel.

The noun רוח ('spirit') is an important feature of both Ezek. 36.26-27 and 11.19. If לב ('heart') is characteristic of deuteronomistic material, the same can certainly not be said of רוח. The word is conspicuously rare in Deuteronomy, where it occurs just twice (2.30 and 34.9). By contrast, it occurs frequently in Ezekiel (51 times) in a wide range of senses.[74] The sparse occurrence of the word in Deuteronomy (and also, incidentally, in Jeremiah) may be due to the fact that it had unwelcome associations with false prophecy. On the other hand, its frequent use in Ezekiel is just one of a number of affinities with more primitive prophecy which are a feature characteristic of Ezekiel.[75]

The second feature is the radical theocentricity which we have seen to characterize Ezekiel.[76] The setting of the promise of a 'new heart' and 'new spirit' in Ezek. 36.26-27 is significant here. We have seen that Yahweh restores his undeserving people in order to demonstrate his power and thereby vindicate his profaned 'name'. However, Israel's long history of sin (cf. Ezek. 16, 20 and 23) had shown her inability to live up to the demands placed upon her. And so Yahweh is now to act to preclude the possibility of a repeated pattern of sin and consequent profanation of the divine 'name'. Thus the divine gift of a 'new heart' and a 'new spirit' to Israel is primarily a means of protecting the 'name' of Yahweh from ever again being profaned. The radical theocentricity of this conception stands out clearly in comparison with the account of the divine promise of the 'circumcision of the heart' in Deut. 30.1-10, which is couched in much more 'affectionate' terms. In that passage, Yahweh is spoken of as 'having compassion' (רחם) upon his people (Deut. 30.3) and 'taking delight' (שׂושׂ) in prospering them (30.9). Here, then, we find a second important respect in which our texts reflect the characteristic style and theology of Ezekiel himself.

How are we to account for the presence in Ezek. 11.19-20 and 36.26-27 of features which seem to be distinctive of Ezekiel alongside those which seem to reflect deuteronomistic influence? We have seen that the material in chs. 34–37 seems to have undergone some elaboration in the redactional tradition. It is possible that the present form of our text results from a deuteronomistic redaction of a basic core of Ezekiel material. It may be, though, that the relationship between the prophet and the deuteronomistic elements in these verses is even closer than such a description would suggest, and that Ezekiel was himself subject to deuteronomistic influences which have left their mark here.[77] Though this cannot be demonstrated, it is by no means implausible; it seems that Ezekiel was resident in Jerusalem (presumably the primary location of deuteronomistic activity) during the latter part of the seventh century, prior to his deportation in 597, and it may in any case be that deuteronomistic preachers were active among the exiles in Babylonia.[78]

We may offer, then, the following conjecture as to the process which shaped our texts. Whilst still in Jerusalem, Ezekiel imbibed at least some of the concerns and style of the deuteronomistic movement. These elements were reinforced both through an awareness of the Jeremiah tradition and through the influence of deuteronomists active in Babylonian exile. The form of expression of the promise of renewal in Ezekiel thus came to owe much to the deuteronomistic movement (which may well have continued to exercise an influence upon the redactional tradition after Ezekiel's time). Nevertheless, Ezekiel has also left his personal stamp on the expression of the promise, not only in his use of 'spirit' language, but also in the radical theocentricity of his presentation.[79]

Chapter 8

DIVINE INITIATIVE AND HUMAN RESPONSE IN EZEKIEL

In the light of this study, what can we conclude about the relationship between divine initiative and human response in Ezekiel? As we have seen, the book is marked by strong tensions, of which none is more dramatic than that between the challenge to Israel to get a 'new heart' and a 'new spirit' in 18.31 and the promise that a 'new heart' and a 'new spirit' will be given to Israel in 36.26-27. These texts represent the twin poles of the book: on the one hand, a strong insistence upon Israel's responsibility before her God and, on the other, a remarkable assurance that Yahweh will enable his recalcitrant people to obey him.

The first part of the book (chs. 1-24) places consistent emphasis upon the responsibility of Israel for the disaster of defeat and exile. Israel is to be treated precisely as she deserves (e.g. 7.27: 'According to their way I will do to them, and according to their own judgments I will judge them'). There is to be neither mercy nor pity (e.g. 8.18: 'I will deal in wrath; my eye will not spare, nor will I have pity; and though they cry in my ears with a loud voice, I will not hear them'). Chapter 18 exemplifies this marked stress on the responsibility of Israel for her fate: the disaster is presented as the fully deserved punishment of a wicked people by its just and powerful God. We have seen that the chapter is concerned to demonstrate that it is the sins of the present generation (and not previous generations) that are being punished. In chs. 9 and 14 too we find an unqualified assertion of Israel's responsibility and a conviction that the wholesale judgment of the nation is imminent.

Thus chs. 1-24 consistently emphasize the responsibility of Israel. Indeed, even the call to repentance, where it occurs, serves this end. At the culmination of ch. 18 we find the striking words 'Get yourselves a new heart and a new spirit!' (18.31), and yet, as we have seen, this is to be understood as primarily a rhetorical device highlighting the fact of Israel's responsibility. A call to repentance is found also in 14.1-11, but this, like the similar motif in ch. 18, is primarily intended to underline Israel's responsibility for the disaster which is engulfing her. In ch. 9 and 14.12-23 the imminence of judgment is stressed to such an extent that reference to repentance is eclipsed altogether.

In stark contrast to the stress on responsibility in the first half of the book, when we turn to the hopeful material (which comes, of course, predominantly in its second half), we find Israel described as the undeserving recipient of favour. In fact it is stated explicitly that the promised restoration is to take place *in spite of* Israel's unworthiness (e.g. 36.31-32: 'Then you will remember your evil ways, and your deeds that were not good; and you will loathe yourselves for your iniquities and your abominable deeds. It is not for your sake that I will act, says the Lord GOD; let that be known to you. Be ashamed and confounded for your ways, O house of Israel'). It is promised that Israel will change her ways, but only through the gift of Yahweh: 'A new heart I will give you, and a new spirit I will put within you' (36.26; cf. 11.19). Israel's obedience will be the result rather than the cause of deliverance, part and parcel of the restoration and certainly not a condition upon which it depends.

How are these two poles of the theology of Ezekiel to be related? The key to this question is surely to be found in the radical theocentricity of Ezekiel, which we explored in detail in Chapter 6. The strong emphasis on the responsibility of Israel before Yahweh itself constitutes an expression of this. We see this above all in the frequent use of the 'I am Yahweh' formula in the context of judgment upon Israel (e.g. 6.7: 'The slain shall fall in the midst of you, and you shall know that I am the LORD'). It is exemplified also in the recurrent references to the wrath, fury and jealousy of Yahweh, which are poured out upon sinful Israel (e.g. 5.13: 'Thus shall my anger spend itself, and I will vent my fury upon them and satisfy myself; and they shall know that I, the LORD, have spoken in my jealousy, when I spend my fury upon them'). Furthermore, ch. 18 provides us with one of the key statements linking Israel's responsibility with the God-centred focus of the book: 'Behold, all souls are mine; the soul of the father as well as the soul of the son is mine: the soul that sins shall die' (18.4).

When Ezekiel and his tradition come to speak of hope for the future, this too is presented in a distinctively theocentric way. The 'I am Yahweh' formula is here again a very important one (e.g. 36.11: 'I will do more good to you than ever before. Then you will know that I am the LORD'). Israel's restoration is, as we have seen, totally undeserved and there is, moreover, little evidence to suggest that Yahweh acts out of love for Israel. The concern to punish the nations does play an important part, but even this is subordinated to the primary motive of Yahweh's action, which is seen to be the vindication of his 'name'.

The nations had misunderstood the defeat of Israel, construing it as a sign of Yahweh's weakness rather than his powerful and righteous punishment of his own people. Yahweh acts to vindicate his profaned 'name' and thereby his reputation as a powerful God 'in the sight of the nations' (36.23). Even this latter formula, far from revealing any positive concern for foreigners, constitutes rather another rhetorical device, the real concern of which focuses upon Yahweh, to whose self-vindication the nations bear witness. It is in such a context that we read of the gift of a 'new heart' and a 'new spirit' (36.26-27; cf. 11.19), the primary purpose of which is to preclude the otherwise inevitable danger of Yahweh having to punish his people again, with the renewed risk of the profanation of his 'name' which that would bring.

Thus whilst there might appear to be a stark contrast between the emphasis on Israel's responsibility and the gift of the ability to respond, an underlying continuity is to be found in the radically theocentric basis of both.

The point at which Yahweh's initiative and Israel's response are most crucially related is, of course, in the motif of the giving of a 'new heart' and a 'new spirit'. Israel's response is so important (for the reasons indicated above) that Yahweh himself promises to make it possible. This paradoxical conception raises the question of how far the responsibility of Israel remains intact.[1] Echoes of the theme of Israel's responsibility do remain, even in ch. 36: Israel is to 'be careful to observe my ordinances' (36.27), and she is to loathe herself for her iniquities and her abominable deeds (36.31). Ultimately, however, since obedience is guaranteed, it would seem that the responsibility of Israel has been subsumed in the overriding initiative of Yahweh.

This certainly stands in marked contrast to the thrust of the first half of the book, with its absolute insistence on the responsibility of the nation for the disaster of exile. However, the disjunction between 18.31 and 36.26-27 is not quite so marked as might first appear, if we remember that the words 'Get yourselves a new heart and a new spirit!' (18.31; cf. 14.6) demand a particular interpretation in their context. The primary purpose of this rhetorical device is, as we have seen, to highlight responsibility for the crisis which has engulfed the nation rather than to issue a realistic call to repentance which might avert disaster and thereby secure the future.

We earlier identified two poles in the theology of Ezekiel, the responsibility of Israel and the gift of Yahweh. If one pole had to gain predominance, it was perhaps inevitable, given the radical theocentricity of Ezekiel, that it should be that of divine initiative. After all, at times even the presentation of judgment in Ezekiel is so God-centred that Israel's responsibility is apparently subsumed. This is seen in the reference to the punishment of the prophet whom Yahweh himself has deceived (14.9-10), and even in the bizarre verses which speak of Yahweh giving to his sinful people 'statutes that were not good and ordinances by which they could not have life'. Even such things as these can, it seems, be traced to this paradoxical God—'I did it that they might know that I am the LORD' (20.25-26). This trend is all the more marked in the material relating to deliverance. If in 20.25-26 Yahweh enables sin that he might be known, in 36.26-27 he enables obedience, for the sake of his 'name'.

Thus divine initiative has enabled human response, even if responsibility, in the fullest sense of the word, has not been altogether preserved. If the conception of the gift of obedience appears to strain logic, it is as well to remember that this is an attempt to give adequate expression to a tension which ultimately defies resolution and that it represents but one stage of a complex debate about 'grace' and 'responsibility' which has been a feature of the Judaeo-Christian tradition throughout the centuries.

It is in this area and not that of 'individualism' where the major contribution of Ezekiel is to be sought. We considered the question of individualism in relation to both judgment and deliverance. In our exegesis of ch. 18, we found the language of priestly case law reapplied to provide a rationale for the national calamity, and concluded that the chapter could in no sense be regarded as a defence of 'individual responsibility'. We identified certain individualistic motifs in chs. 9 and 14, but found these to be subordinate to the conviction that the thoroughgoing judgment of Israel as a collective unit is imminent. Indeed, the theme of 'individualism' does not seem to be nearly as prominent in Ezekiel as has widely been held. On the contrary, the primary task of the prophet seems to be to articulate a national judgment which will 'cut off both righteous and wicked' (21.8-9 [Eng. 21.3-4]). When restoration is finally announced, once again it is the 'house of Israel' as a collective unit which is addressed. As we have seen, both in its own terms and in relation to the Old Testament as a whole, Ezekiel has been misrepresented in this respect.

The major contribution of Ezekiel consists in the fact that here everything rests ultimately upon the mysterious nature of the God who acts that it might be known that 'I am Yahweh'. If at times Ezekiel's portrayal of his God strikes us as somewhat uncongenial and forbidding, this should not blind us to the profundity and the grandeur of his theological presentation. Nor should we underestimate the significance of the motif of the gift of a 'new heart' and a 'new spirit' which is itself grounded in this theological position. It is true that some have viewed the development of a theology of 'grace' in the exilic age as a retreat from the real prophetic task of ethical proclamation, to the 'internalization' of religion.[2] However, in the opinion of this writer, the insight that humankind is ultimately impotent without God remains one of the central truths about human existence. The extent of the debt of subsequent tradition to the theological developments of the exilic age—and not least to Ezekiel—has yet to be fully explored and acknowledged. The theme of the freely given 'grace' of God, accepting the unworthy and granting the gift of obedience, is one which Church and Synagogue hold in common. A serious recognition of this shared heritage could have profound implications for Jewish-Christian dialogue.

NOTES

Notes to Chapter 1

1. M. Noth, *Geschichte Israels* (2nd edn, Göttingen, 1958), ET: *The History of Israel* (2nd edn, London, 1960), 280-99; P.R. Ackroyd, *Exile and Restoration* (London, 1968), 17-38; E. Janssen, *Juda in der Exilszeit: Ein Beitrag zur Frage der Entstehung des Judentums*, FRLANT 69 (1956). On the question of the numbers deported, see Ackroyd, 21-25.

2. For a recent discussion, see R.P. Carroll, *Jeremiah* (London, 1986), 555-68.

3. Many complex questions are raised concerning the nature and date of the so-called 'Settlement'; cf. N.K. Gottwald, *The Tribes of Yahweh: A Sociology of the Religion of Liberated Israel, 1250-1050 B.C.E.* (New York, 1979), 189-233.

4. Cf. E.W. Nicholson, *Deuteronomy and Tradition* (Oxford, 1967), 1-17.

5. Cf. A. Weiser, *Die Psalmen*, ATD 14/15 (5th edn, Göttingen, 1959), ET: *The Psalms* (London, 1962), 363.

6. J.A. Baker, *The Foolishness of God* (London, 1970), 29.

7. Baker, *Foolishness*, 30. Baker offers a very brief but perceptive reflection on the theological crisis of the Exile. For more comprehensive treatments, see: M. Noth, 'The Jerusalem Catastrophe of 587 B.C., and its Significance for Israel', in *The Laws in the Pentateuch and other studies* (Edinburgh, 1966), 260-80; P.R. Ackroyd, *Exile and Restoration* (London, 1968); R.W. Klein, *Israel in Exile: A Theological Interpretation* (Philadelphia, 1979).

8. As examples of this tendency we may cite: C.F. Whitley, *The Exilic Age* (London, 1957); D. Winton Thomas, 'The Sixth Century B.C.: a Creative Epoch in the History of Israel', *JSS* 6 (1961), 33-46.

9. C.C. Torrey, *Pseudo-Ezekiel and the Original Prophecy* (New Haven, 1930; New York, 1970), 102.

10. J. Smith, *The Book of the Prophet Ezekiel—a New Interpretation* (London, 1931), 95-100.

11. J. Becker, 'Erwägungen zur ezechielischen Frage', in Ruppert, L., Weimar, P. and Zenger, E. (eds.), *Künder des Wortes* (Würzburg, 1982), 137-149.

12. See below.

13. The reference to 'the fifth year of the exile of King Jehoiachin' in 1.2 is generally taken to indicate that Ezekiel began his ministry in 593. Complex

questions are raised by the chronological dates in the book; for a recent discussion of these, including the question of the obscure 'thirtieth year' of 1.1, see E. Kutsch, *Die chronologischen Daten des Ezechielbuches*, Orbis Biblicus et Orientalis 62 (Freiburg & Göttingen, 1985).

14. E.g. W. Eichrodt, *Der Prophet Hesekiel*, ATD 22 (Göttingen, 1959; 3rd edn, 1968), ET: *Ezekiel* (London, 1970), 11; W. Zimmerli, *Ezechiel*, BK 13, 2 vols. (Neukirchen, 1969; 2nd edn, 1979), ET: *Ezekiel 1* (Philadelphia, 1979), 6; cf. W. Zimmerli, 'The Message of the Prophet Ezekiel', *Interpretation* 23 (1969), 132.

15. V. Herntrich, *Ezechielprobleme*, BZAW 61 (Giessen, 1932), 37-130. It should be noted that this question had already been addressed within the rabbinic tradition, for example by Rashi.

16. C.C. Torrey, *Pseudo-Ezekiel and the Original Prophecy* (New Haven, 1930; New York, 1970), 22-44.

17. J. Smith, *The Book of the Prophet Ezekiel—a New Interpretation* (London, 1931), 100.

18. Cf. J. Garscha, *Studien zum Ezechielbuch: Eine redaktionskritische Untersuchung von Ez 1-39*, Europäische Hochschulschriften, XXIII/23 (Bern & Frankfurt, 1974), 294ff.

19. A. Bertholet (with K. Galling), *Hesekiel*, HAT 13 (Tübingen, 1936), 82, 134.

20. W.O.E. Oesterley and T.H. Robinson, working at much the same time as Bertholet, suggested that Ezekiel was active in Jerusalem until 597 and thereafter in Babylonia (*An Introduction to the Books of the Old Testament* [London, 1934], 328-29). Among others who have adopted 'compromise' positions on this question we may note: W.A. Irwin, *The Problem of Ezekiel* (Chicago, 1943), 329; H.W. Robinson, *Two Hebrew Prophets. Studies in Hosea and Ezekiel* (London, 1948), 75-78; J. Steinmann, *Le prophète Ézéchiel et les débuts de l'exil* (Paris, 1953), 9-18.

21. R.H. Pfeiffer, *Introduction to the Old Testament* (New York, 1941), 535-40.

22. W. Zimmerli, *Ezekiel 1* (Philadelphia, 1979), 269. We may compare Ackroyd's comment on ch. 9, which is set (in the context of a vision) in Jerusalem: 'The exiles in Babylonia, who are the prophet's primary audience, are the disobedient to whom it must be said that the judgement upon Jerusalem is the judgement upon themselves' (P.R. Ackroyd, *Exile and Restoration* [London, 1968], 109).

23. J.B. Taylor, *Ezekiel* (London, 1969), 23-24.

24. For a recent defence of the Babylonian location, see M. Greenberg, *Ezekiel, 1-20*, The Anchor Bible 22 (Garden City, New York, 1983), 15-17. A fuller consideration of this and the other major critical questions raised by the book will be found in my commentary on Ezekiel in the New Century Bible series (in preparation).

Notes to Chapter 2

1. P.R. Ackroyd, *Exile and Restoration* (London, 1968), 103.
2. R. Smend, *Der Prophet Ezechiel*, KeH (2nd edn, Leipzig, 1880), xxi.
3. E.g. B. Duhm, *Das Buch Jesaja*, HKAT (Göttingen, 1892); *Das Buch Jeremia*, KHC (Tübingen & Leipzig, 1901).
4. H. Gunkel, 'Die israelitische Literatur', in P. Hinneberg (ed.), *Die Kultur der Gegenwart* (Berlin & Leipzig, 1906), 90.
5. G.B. Gray, *A Critical Introduction to the Old Testament* (London, 1913), 198.
6. S.R. Driver, *An Introduction to the Literature of the Old Testament* (9th edn, Edinburgh, 1913), 279.
7. R. Kraetzschmar, *Das Buch Ezechiel*, HKAT III 3/1 (Göttingen, 1900).
8. J. Herrmann, *Ezechielstudien*, BWAT 2 (Leipzig, 1908).
9. G. Hölscher, *Hesekiel, der Dichter und das Buch*, BZAW 39 (Giessen, 1924), 26-27.
10. G.A. Cooke, *A Critical and Exegetical Commentary on the Book of Ezekiel*, ICC (Edinburgh, 1936), preface, v.
11. The literature was regularly reviewed by C. Kuhl: 'Zur Geschichte der Hesekiel-Forschung', *ThR* NF 5 (1933), 92-118; 'Neuere Hesekielliteratur', *ThR* NF 20 (1952), 1-26; 'Zum Stand der Hesekiel-Forschung', *ThR* NF 24 (1957-58), 1-53. See also: H.H. Rowley, 'The Book of Ezekiel in Modern Study', *BJRL* 36 (1953-54), 146ff. On the more recent debate, see: W. Zimmerli, Preface to 2nd German edn of his commentary, *Ezechiel*, BK 13 (Neukirchen, 1979), available in translation in *Ezekiel 2* (Philadelphia, 1983), xi-xviii; G. Fohrer, 'Neue Literatur zur alttestamentlichen Prophetie (1961-1970)', *ThR* NF 45 (1980), 121-29; B. Lang, *Ezechiel: Der Prophet und das Buch*, Erträge der Forschung 153 (Darmstadt, 1981); J. Lust (ed.), *Ezekiel and his Book: Textual and Literary Criticism and their Interrelation*, Bibliotheca Ephemeridum Theologicarum Lovaniensium LXXIV (Leuven, 1986).
12. This primary concern of Hölscher is, of course, reflected in the title of his book, *Hesekiel, der Dichter und das Buch*.
13. The distinction between poetry and prose as a criterion of authorship characterizes the work of the later part of Duhm's career, e.g. *Das Buch Jesaja*, HKAT (Göttingen, 1892); *Das Buch Jeremia*, KHC (Tübingen & Leipzig, 1901).
14. Cf. E.W. Nicholson, *Preaching to the Exiles* (Oxford, 1970), 3. It must, of course, be stressed that the poetic nature of this material is just one factor in the complex question of its provenance.
15. Cf. Nicholson, *Preaching*, 64.
16. Cf. W. Zimmerli, *Ezekiel 1* (Philadelphia, 1979), 70.

17. G.A. Cooke, *A Critical and Exegetical Commentary on the Book of Ezekiel*, ICC (Edinburgh, 1936), introduction, xxvi; cf. W. Kessler, *Die innere Einheitlichkeit des Buches Ezechiel* (Herrnhut, 1926), where a detailed case for the continuity between poetry and prose is advanced.

18. R.H. Pfeiffer, *An Introduction to the Old Testament* (New York, 1941), 564; A. Bertholet with K. Galling, *Hesekiel* (Tübingen, 1936), xiv; H.G. May, 'The Book of Ezekiel', in *The Interpreter's Bible*, vol. VI (New York & Nashville, 1956), 50-51, 62; E. Vogt, 'Textumdeutungen im Buch Ezechiel', *Sacra Pagina* I (Paris, 1959), 471-94.

19. F. Hitzig, *Der Prophet Ezechiel erklärt*, KeH (Leipzig, 1847); C.H. Cornill, *Das Buch des Propheten Ezechiel* (Leipzig, 1886); G. Jahn, *Das Buch Ezechiel auf Grund der Septuaginta hergestellt, übersetzt und kritisch erklärt* (Leipzig, 1905); J.W. Wevers, *Ezekiel*, New Century Bible (London, 1969).

20. J.W. Wevers, *Ezekiel*, 161. It may be noted in addition that this use of the LXX often involves not only abbreviating the MT, but also at times actually substituting alternative readings from the LXX; e.g. Wevers, *Ezekiel*, 159 (on Ezek. 20.37).

21. E.g. G.A. Cooke, *Ezekiel*, 163; W. Eichrodt, *Der Prophet Hesekiel*, ATD 22 (Göttingen, 1959; 3rd edn, 1968), ET: *Ezekiel* (London, 1970), 199.

22. See especially, G. Fohrer, 'Die Glossen im Buche Ezechiel', *ZAW* 63 (1951), 33-53.

23. E.g. *Ezekiel 1*, 279 (on Ezek. 12.22).

24. J.W. Wevers, *Ezekiel*, 35.

25. K.W. Carley, *Ezekiel among the Prophets* (London, 1975), 54; L. Boadt, 'Textual Problems in Ezekiel and Poetic Analysis of Paired Words', *JBL* 97 (1978), esp. 489-90.

26. G. Hölscher, *Hesekiel, der Dichter und das Buch*, 5-6, 54, 86, 104, 116, 165; H.G. May, 'The Book of Ezekiel', in *The Interpreter's Bible*, vol. VI (New York & Nashville, 1956), 48-49; H. Schulz, *Das Todesrecht im Alten Testament*, BZAW 114 (Berlin, 1969), 163-87; J. Garscha, *Studien zum Ezechielbuch* (Bern & Frankfurt, 1974), 303-305.

27. This is discussed in detail below.

28. Cf. Cooke, *Ezekiel*, 425ff.

29. H. Graf Reventlow, in *Wächter über Israel: Ezechiel und seine Tradition*, BZAW 82 (Berlin, 1962), advances an elaborate thesis presenting Ezekiel as the holder of a cultic 'office'.

30. Cf. M. Burrows, *The Literary Relations of Ezekiel* (Philadelphia, 1925), 19-25; G. Fohrer, *Die Hauptprobleme des Buches Ezechiel*, BZAW 72 (Berlin, 1952), 140-44.

31. S. Herrmann, *Die prophetischen Heilserwartungen im Alten Testament*, BWANT 85 (Stuttgart, 1965), 241ff.

32. R. Liwak, 'Überlieferungsgeschichtliche Probleme des Ezechielbuches.

Eine Studie zu postezechielischen Interpretationen und Kompositionen',
dissertation (Bochum, 1976).

33. Cf. E.W. Nicholson, *Preaching to the Exiles* (Oxford, 1970), 20-37. The
material regarded as deuteronomistic in Jeremiah coincides broadly with the
prose material referred to earlier.

34. See above.

35. W. Zimmerli, *Ezekiel 1*, 46.

36. See Chapter 7 below.

37. We earlier considered the distinction between poetry and prose, which
might be described as a criterion based on consistency of literary form.

38. Wevers, *Ezekiel*, 32.

39. Wevers, *Ezekiel*, 33-34.

40. Cf. M. Noth, *Überlieferungsgeschichte des Pentateuch* (Stuttgart, 1948).
ET: *A History of Pentateuchal Traditions* (Englewood Cliffs, New Jersey,
1972), 30, 230. We may note in passing that by no means all scholars would
favour a source-critical response to such questions; cf. R. Rendtorff, *Das
überlieferungsgeschichtliche Problem des Pentateuch*, BZAW 147 (Berlin &
New York, 1977).

41. W. Zimmerli, *Ezekiel 1*, 69, 349; K. Carley, *Ezekiel among the
Prophets* (London, 1975), 55.

42. See above.

43. Zimmerli warned against the desire 'to press the true flexibility of a
living, spoken, as well as written language into too rigid structural outlines'
(*Ezekiel 2*, xvii).

44. See, e.g., Cooke, *Ezekiel*, 190-91 (on Ezek. 17.22-24).

45. See below, pp. 114f.

46. S. Herrmann, *Die prophetischen Heilserwartungen im Alten Testament*,
BWANT 85 (Stuttgart, 1965), 290.

47. T.M. Raitt, *A Theology of Exile. Judgment/Deliverance in Jeremiah
and Ezekiel* (Philadelphia, 1977), 108-10.

48. We noted earlier that there are literary grounds for regarding 16.44ff.
as an addition. We may now refer to the discussion of W. Eichrodt, in which
he adduces theological as well as literary arguments for regarding both
16.44-58 and 16.59-63 as secondary: *Ezekiel*, 214-20.

49. Cf. O. Kaiser, *Der Prophet Jesaja. Kap 13-39*, ATD 18 (Göttingen,
1973), ET: *Isaiah 13-39* (London, 1974), 173-233; R.N. Whybray, *Isaiah 40-
66* (London, 1975), 20-38.

50. See above, p. 21.

51. Cf. H. Gese, *Der Verfassungsentwurf des Ezechiel (Kap. 40-48)
traditionsgeschichtlich untersucht*, Beiträge zur historischen Theologie 25
(Tübingen, 1957).

52. Cf. K. von Rabenau, 'Das prophetische Zukunftswort im Buch

Hesekiel', in *Studien zur Theologie der alttestamentlichen Überlieferungen*, ed. R. Rendtorff and K. Koch (Neukirchen, 1961), 61-80.

53. The full range of contemporary Ezekiel scholarship is represented in the published proceedings of the 35th Colloquium Biblicum Lovaniense, which met at Leuven in August 1985: J. Lust (ed.), *Ezekiel and his Book : Textual and Literary Criticism and their Interrelation*, Bibliotheca Ephemeridum Theologicarum Lovaniensium LXXIV (Leuven, 1986).

54. J. Garscha, *Studien zum Ezechielbuch. Eine redaktionskritische Untersuchung von Ez 1–39*, Europäische Hochschulschriften, XXIII/23 (Bern & Frankfurt, 1974), 286-88.

55. Ibid., 288-94, 310; cf. 284-86.

56. Ibid., 122-25, 294-303.

57. Ibid., 303-305.

58. Ibid., 305ff.

59. Cf. Zimmerli, *Ezekiel 2*, xiii-xiv.

60. H. Schulz, *Das Todesrecht im Alten Testament*, BZAW 114 (Berlin, 1969) (163-87, 'Die sakralrechtlichen Deklarationsworte bei Deutero-Ezechiel'); H. Simian, *Die theologische Nachgeschichte der Prophetie Ezechiels. Form- und traditionskritische Untersuchung zu Ez. 6; 35; 36*, FZB 14 (Würzburg, 1974); F.L. Hossfeld, *Untersuchungen zu Komposition und Theologie des Ezechielbuches*, FZB 20 (Würzburg, 1977; 2nd edn, 1983); G. Bettenzoli, *Geist der Heiligkeit. Traditionsgeschichtliche Untersuchung des qds-Begriffes im Buch Ezechiel*, Quaderni di Semitistica 8 (Florence, 1979). With the work of these scholars we may compare the attempts of S. Herrmann and R. Liwak to isolate deuteronomistic strata within Ezekiel.

61. E.g. Garscha, *Studien*, 310.

62. Zimmerli criticized Garscha on this count, claiming that his approach 'simply ignores a number of legitimate historical considerations and causes the result reached to appear unconvincing' (*Ezekiel 2*, xiii).

63. Thus, Schulz (*Das Todesrecht*, 163-87) assigns to his 'Deutero-Ezekiel' the passages in which the influence of priestly case law is widely recognized (primarily Ezek. 3.17-21; 14.1-11; 18.1-20; 33.1-20), whereas Garscha explicitly dissociates this material from his 'Deutero-Ezekiel', assigning it instead to his 'Sacral law stratum' (*Studien*, 303-305). Compare Zimmerli's consideration of the notion of a 'Deutero-Ezekiel' in W. Zimmerli, 'Deutero-Ezekiel?', *ZAW* 84 (1972), 501-16; and also Rendtorff's cautionary words about the use of the term 'Deutero-Ezekiel' in R. Rendtorff, *Das Alte Testament: Eine Einführung* (Neukirchen, 1983), ET: *The Old Testament: An Introduction* (London, 1985), 209.

64. J. Muilenburg, 'Ezekiel', in *Peake's Commentary on the Bible*, ed. M. Black and H.H. Rowley (London & Edinburgh, 1962), 569.

65. M. Greenberg, *Ezekiel, 1–20*, The Anchor Bible 22 (Garden City, New York, 1983); 'The Vision of Jerusalem in Ezekiel 8-11: A Holistic

Interpretation', in J.L. Crenshaw and S. Sandmel (eds.), *The Divine Helmsman: Studies on God's Control of Human Events, Presented to Lou H. Silberman* (New York, 1980), 143-64. Cf. also 'Ezekiel', in *Encyclopaedia Judaica*, vol. VI (Jerusalem, 1971).

  66. Greenberg, *Ezekiel 1-20*, 21.

  67. Ibid., 26.

  68. Ibid., 27.

  69. L. Boadt, 'Textual Problems in Ezekiel and Poetic Analysis of Paired Words', *JBL* 97 (1978), 489-99; L. Boadt, *Ezekiel's Oracles against Egypt. A Literary and Philological Study of Ezekiel 29-32*, Biblica et Orientalia 37 (Rome, 1980); M. Nobile, *Una lettura simbolico-strutturalistica di Ezechiele* (Rome, 1982).

  70. R.E. Clements, 'The Chronology of Redaction in Ezekiel 1-24', in J. Lust (ed.), *Ezekiel and his Book: Textual and Literary Criticism and their Interrelation*, Bibliotheca Ephemeridum Theologicarum Lovaniensium LXXIV (Leuven, 1986), 283-94.

Notes to Chapter 3

  1. Noth argued for a Palestinian setting for the Deuteronomistic History: M. Noth, *Überlieferungsgeschichtliche Studien I* (2nd edn, Tübingen, 1957), 96-97, 107ff., ET: *The Deuteronomistic History*, JSOTS 15 (Sheffield, 1981), 141-42. Many have followed him in this view, e.g. E. Janssen, *Juda in der Exilszeit: Ein Beitrag zur Frage der Entstehung des Judentums*, FRLANT 69 (1956), 17-18. However, the case for a Palestinian provenance, though strong, is not conclusive, as is shown by P.R. Ackroyd, *Exile and Restoration* (London, 1968), 65-68.

  2. An earlier form of the exegesis of Ezekiel 18 presented here may be found in my article, 'Individual Responsibility in Ezekiel 18?' in *Studia Biblica 1978*, ed. E.A. Livingstone, JSOTS 11 (Sheffield, 1979), 185-96. The presentation here differs in a number of respects, most significantly in its discussion of the theme of repentance.

  3. Cf. W. Zimmerli, 'Deutero-Ezechiel?', *ZAW* 84 (1972), 501-16. Zimmerli argues that those (such as Schulz) who have attributed this chapter to a post-exilic 'Deutero-Ezekiel' have failed to take adequate note of its dependence upon the immediate historical situation of Ezekiel.

  4. E.g. H. Schulz, *Das Todesrecht im Alten Testament*, BZAW 114 (Berlin, 1969), 163-87. J. Garscha, *Studien zum Ezechielbuch* (Bern & Frankfurt, 1974), 303-305.

  5. See above, p. 25.

  6. See below, p. 55.

  7. G. Fohrer, *Introduction to the Old Testament* (London, 1970), 417.

8. G. von Rad, *Old Testament Theology* (London, 1975), vol. I, 392-94.

9. W. Eichrodt, *Ezekiel* (London, 1970), 231-49.

10. W.H. Brownlee, *Ezekiel 1–19*, Word Biblical Commentary 28 (Waco, Texas, 1986), 50, 284, 292.

11. J. Taylor, *Ezekiel* (London, 1969), 45.

12. A.S. Peake, *The Problem of Suffering in the Old Testament* (London, 1904), 27.

13. B. Lindars, 'Ezekiel and Individual Responsibility', *VT* 15 (1965), 456; see also A. Phillips, *Ancient Israel's Criminal Law* (Oxford, 1970), 32-35.

14. In certain cases (such as the story of Achan in Joshua 7) the contrast between language related to criminal law and that concerning divine retribution can become somewhat blurred, but this does not detract from the significance of the basic distinction.

15. It seems that, in ch. 18 at least, both Ezekiel and his audience assume that Yahweh is powerful and is in control of events; their disagreement concerns the issue of Yahweh's justice. At certain other points in the book it is the power of Yahweh which emerges as the major issue (see Chapter 6 below.

16. The features of the language of priestly law are illustrated in detail in J. Begrich, 'Die priesterliche Tora', *Werden und Wesen des Alten Testaments*, BZAW 66 (Berlin, 1936), 63-88. Analyses of the legal language in Ezekiel may be found in: H.G. Reventlow, *Wächter über Israel. Ezechiel und seine Tradition*, BZAW 82 (Berlin, 1962), 123-30; H. Schulz, *Das Todesrecht im Alten Testament*, BZAW 114 (Berlin, 1969), 163-87.

17. Heb. (Ezek. 18.5): צדיק כי־יהיה צדיק ואיש

18. Heb. (Ezek. 18.21): והרשע כי ישוב מכל־חטאתו (Kethib חֲטָאתוֹ Qere חטאתיו)

19. Heb. (Ezek. 14.4): איש איש מבית ישראל אשר יעלה את־גלוליו אל־לבו

20. W. Zimmerli, 'Die Eigenart der prophetischen Rede des Ezechiel: ein Beitrag zum Problem an Hand von Ez. 14.1-11', *ZAW* 66 (1954), 1-26.

21. Heb. (Lev. 20.9): כי־איש איש אשר יקלל את־אביו ואת־אמו מות יומת ואיש אשר יתן שכבתו בבהמה מות יומת (Lev. 20.15):

22. Heb. (Ezek. 18.9): צדיק הוא חיה יחיה נאם אדני יהוה

23. Heb. (Ezek. 18.13): וחי לא יחיה את כל־התועבות האלה עשה מות יומת (BHS proposes יומת for יומת)

24. This is argued, for example, by H. Schulz, *Das Todesrecht im Alten Testament*, BZAW 114 (Berlin, 1969), 163-87.

25. Heb. (Lev. 18.5): ושמרתם את־חקתי ואת־משפטי אשר יעשה אתם (Lev. 13.17): טהור הוא האדם וחי בהם

26. G. von Rad, '"Gerechtigkeit" und "Leben" in der Kultsprache der Psalmen', *Gesammelte Studien zum Alten Testament*, ThB 8 (1958), 225ff., ET: '"Righteousness" and "Life" in the Cultic Language of the Psalms', *The Problem of the Hexateuch and Other Essays* (Edinburgh & London, 1966),

243-66; W. Zimmerli, '"Leben" und "Tod" im Buche des Propheten Ezechiel', *ThZ* 13 (1957), 494-508. A recent example of interpretation of Ezekiel 18 in the light of entrance liturgies may be found in W.H. Brownlee, *Ezekiel 1-19*, Word Biblical Commentary 28 (Waco, Texas, 1986), 283.

27. The correct reading of the Hebrew of Ezek. 44.5 is disputed. MT reads: שׂמת לבך למבוא הבית BHS proposes: תשׂמת לבך למבוא הבית בכל מוצאי המקדש ולמוצאי המקדש A reading similar to this proposal seems to have been assumed by the RSV translation, quoted in the text.

28. Heb. (Gen. 38.26): צדקה ממני This narrative has commonly been attributed to a Yahwist rather than a Priestly writer (e.g. G. von Rad, *Genesis* [rev. edn, London, 1972], 357). The validity of a documentary analysis of the Pentateuch is certainly not to be taken for granted (see below, Chapter 4). Nevertheless, this example may at least serve as an indication of the broad range of legal language to which the positive declarations of Ezekiel 18 have affinities.

29. See above. This parallel between the lists of ch. 18 and of the Psalter may strengthen the argument of those who would trace the origin of the positive declarations of ch. 18 (e.g. 'He is righteous') to a liturgy of entrance.

30. A further related feature is the use of the phrase 'to suffer for the iniquity of' (נשׂא בעון) in 18.19-20 (cf. Lev. 17.16).

31. See above.

32. Zimmerli showed how in the book of Ezekiel the existing individual reference of laws is often taken and reapplied. Thus, for example, in 22.2-4 language which would normally be used in the trial of an individual is applied to the fate of the city of Jerusalem. Cf. W. Zimmerli, 'Die Eigenart der prophetischen Rede des Ezechiel. Ein Beitrag zum Problem an hand von Ez. 14.1-11', *ZAW* 66 (1954), 1-26.

33. Cf. Ezek. 8.12; 9.9; 11.15; 12.27; 33.10; 37.11.

34. In 16.44, a current proverb is cited *against* the people: 'Behold, everyone who uses proverbs will use this proverb about you, "Like mother, like daughter"'. On the place of proverbs in the Old Testament, see further: O. Eissfeldt, *Der Maschal im Alten Testament*, BZAW 24 (Giessen, 1913); H.W. Wolff, 'Das Zitat im Prophetenspruch', *BhEvTh* 4 (Munich, 1937); C.R. Fontaine, *Traditional Sayings in the Old Testament: A Contextual Study* (Sheffield, 1982).

35. It should be noted that Jer. 31.29-30 and Ezekiel 18 make very different points: the author of Jer. 31.29-30 apparently agrees that the 'sour grapes' proverb paints an accurate picture, but promises that life will be fairer in the coming age of blessing. Ezekiel 18, on the other hand, asserts firmly that here and now the proverb is inaccurate and must not be used. Jer. 31.29-30 may be part of deuteronomistic redaction of the book of Jeremiah, as is suggested by E.W. Nicholson (*Preaching to the Exiles* [Oxford, 1970],

85). Nicholson in fact argues that the prose tradition of the book of Jeremiah (to which the so-called Book of Consolation in Jeremiah 30–31 seems closely related) originated, in large measure, among the exiles in Babylonia (*Preaching to the Exiles*, 131). This prompts the interesting speculation that there could conceivably be some connection between the use of the 'sour grapes' proverb evidenced in Jeremiah 31 and the position to which Ezekiel 18 is a polemical response.

36. D.F. Morgan, *Wisdom in the Old Testament Traditions* (Atlanta & Oxford, 1981), 109-10.

37. K.D. Sakenfeld, 'Ezekiel 18.25-32', *Interpretation* 32 (1978), 297.

38. Among many valuable recent contributions to the elucidation of sophisticated argumentation in the Old Testament, we may note: A. Gibson, *Biblical Semantic Logic* (Oxford, 1981); E.M. Good, *Irony in the Old Testament* (2nd edn, Sheffield, 1981); A. Graffy, *A Prophet Confronts his People*, Analecta Biblica 104 (Rome, 1984).

39. For discussion of the location of Ezekiel's ministry, see pp. 18f. above.

40. J. Battersby Harford, *Studies in the Book of Ezekiel* (Cambridge, 1935), 48.

41. W. Eichrodt, *Ezekiel* (London, 1970), 236. Eichrodt offers this as just one of the senses which the word 'fathers' in the proverb may convey.

42. D. Daube, *Studies in Biblical Law* (Cambridge, 1947), 184.

43. W. Zimmerli, *Old Testament Theology in Outline* (Edinburgh, 1978), 213. In Ezek. 20.8, Israel is represented as rebellious even in Egypt, before the Exodus.

44. See below, Chapter 3, note 50.

45. K.D. Sakenfeld, 'Ezekiel 18.25-32', *Interpretation* 32 (1978), 297-98.

46. The theme of the radical theocentricity of the book of Ezekiel is explored in detail in Chapter 6 below.

47. The word נפש should not be taken to refer to the 'soul' in contrast to the 'body'; such a dichotomy does not characterize Old Testament anthropology (cf. H.W. Wolff, *The Anthropology of the Old Testament* [London, 1974], 10-25). נפש may be taken to mean simply 'person': 'the person that sins shall die'.

48. See below, pp. 83f.

49. There has been much discussion of the meaning of the words 'life' and 'death' in Ezekiel 18 (see, for example, W.H. Brownlee, *Ezekiel 1–19*, Word Biblical Commentary 28 [Waco, Texas, 1986], 292). However, a correct understanding of these words depends upon a recognition of the adaptation of legal formulae within 18.1-20. The references to life and death within these verses all occur within statements of legal principle or specific legal judgments; they refer quite literally to life and death. As should be clear by now, however, this legal discussion serves as an analogy for Ezekiel's discussion of responsibility for the disaster of exile. See below, Chapter 3,

note 62, for discussion of the references to 'life' and 'death' in 18.21-32.

50. Is the insistence that the present disaster is not the result of the sins of previous generations contradicted by Ezekiel 20? 20.4 ('Will you judge them, son of man, will you judge them? Then let them know the abominations of their fathers') introduces a long survey of the sins of Israel from the beginning of her history, and might be understood to imply that responsibility for the sins of the fathers rests on the present generation. However, it becomes clear in 20.30 that the purpose of the extended historical review has rather been simply illustrative and that what matters is the response of the present generation, 'Will you defile yourselves after the manner of your fathers?' It is certainly implied that the present generation follows all too closely the ways of its ancestors (cf. Ezek. 16.44, 'Everyone who uses proverbs will use this proverb about you, "Like mother, like daughter"'), but the moral independence of generations argued for so strongly in ch. 18 is not contradicted here in ch. 20.

51. Most notably Zimmerli's article, 'Die Eigenart der prophetischen Rede des Ezechiel. Ein Beitrag zum Problem an Hand von Ez. 14.1-11', *ZAW* 66 (1954), 1-26.

52. See above, p. 40.

53. W. Zimmerli, 'The Message of the Prophet Ezekiel', *Interpretation* 23 (1969), 156-57. Zimmerli first describes Ezek. 18.4-20 in a way which appears to acknowledge its corporate concern: 'the prophet passionately proclaims that each generation is responsible for its own action and receives life or death accordingly', but then, speaking of this same section of the chapter, he goes on to interpret the positive declarations of Ezek. 18.9, 17 as evidence of a concern for individual conversion.

54. W. Zimmerli, *Old Testament Theology in Outline* (Edinburgh, 1978), 213.

55. Heb. (Ezek. 18.19): מרע לא־נשא חבן בעון האב

56. See above, p. 42.

57. Since Deut. 24.16 seems likely to be an older law quoted by the Deuteronomistic legislators (cf. A.D.H. Mayes, *Deuteronomy* [London, 1979], 326) and is, moreover, quoted by the Deuteronomistic Historians (2 Kgs 14.6), it seems unlikely that Ezek. 18.20 has influenced Deut. 24.16. On the other hand, that Ezek. 18.20 has been influenced by Deut. 24.16 must be recognized as a real possibility.

58. The possibility of a father suffering for the sins of a son does not appear explicitly in any of Ezekiel's three test-cases, though we may note that the righteous man of 18.5-9 (of whom it is said 'He shall surely live') is the father of the wicked man of vv. 10-13.

59. A.D.H. Mayes, *Deuteronomy*, 323.

60. See p. 43 above. See also: A. Phillips, *Ancient Israel's Criminal Law* (Oxford, 1970), 34; A. Phillips, 'Double for all her Sins', *ZAW* 94 (1982), 131.

61. K.D. Sakenfeld, 'Ezekiel 18.25-32', *Interpretation* 32 (1978), 297.

62. We argued earlier that the meaning of 'life' and 'death' in Ezek. 18.1-20 depended upon the nature of the reapplication of legal language within that section of the chapter, dealing with the question of responsibility for the disaster of exile (see above, Chapter 3, note 49). What do the words 'life' and 'death' signify here in this section, 18.21-32, with its prospective talk of repentance? There are no good grounds for believing that these words should be understood eschatologically (as they were, for example, by G. Hölscher, *Hesekiel: der Dichter und das Buch*, BZAW 39 [Giessen, 1924], 102-105). Nor (as we shall see) is there any realistic sense in which the prophet could here be offering to the penitent exemption from the current disaster. Rather, 'life' here seems to refer to fulness of relationship with God, and 'death' to estrangement from God (see W. Zimmerli, '"Leben" und "Tod" im Buche des Propheten Ezechiel', *ThZ* 13 [1957], 494-508).

63. The coherence of Ezek. 18.1-32, including the interweaving of themes which we have highlighted, strongly suggests that the chapter is an integral unit. Nevertheless, as we shall see below (Chapter 3, note 70), some scholars regard the shift to talk of repentance at 18.21 as evidence of the composite nature of the chapter.

64. Verses 25 and 29 feature an attractive play on the word 'way' (דרך) or 'ways' (דרכים). When Israel complains about Yahweh's 'way', the reference is to Yahweh's manner of conducting justice; when Ezekiel challenges Israel in the words 'Is it not your ways that are not just?', the reference is both to the actual behaviour of Israel and also to her assessment of the situation and of Yahweh's justice.

65. For the sake of convenience, we noted examples of legal language from Ezek. 18.21-32 in our earlier review of such usage.

66. In Ezek. 14.12ff. we find a comparable case of freedom in adapting legal style (see below, Chapter 4, note 37).

67. M. Greenberg, *Ezekiel 1–20* Anchor Bible 22 (Garden City, New York, 1983), 340; cf. 334: 'In the second section, the principle of God's justice, namely that the past does not determine the evaluation of the present, is extended into the life of the individual'.

68. The fact that Ezekiel uses verbs in the plural when addressing his audience (e.g. Ezek. 18.31: עשו; תמתו) should not be allowed to obscure this corporate emphasis.

69. K.D. Sakenfeld, 'Ezekiel 18.25-32', *Interpretation*, 32 (1978), 296, expresses this well: 'The call to repentance is addressed to the community *as a whole*, and it is the restoration of the whole people to life before God for which Ezekiel presses'.

70. E.g. A. Graffy, *A Prophet Confronts his People*, Analecta Biblica 104 (Rome, 1984), 58-59: 'It is in 33.11-20 that the material concerning the possibility of change in the life of an individual fits better as a reply to the

quotation in v.10 ... In Ezek. 18.21-32, on the other hand, the material is a later addition'. See below, note 87.

71. W. Zimmerli, *Ezekiel 1* (Philadelphia, 1979), 377-78 (cf. *Ezekiel 2* [Philadelphia, 1983], 189-90). Zimmerli advanced a number of arguments in favour of dating ch. 18 after 587, none of which carry conviction. Thus, for example, whilst it is true that the saying in Lam. 5.7, 'Our fathers sinned and are no more; and we bear their iniquities', is similar to the 'sour grapes' proverb, the (likely) Palestinian provenance of the book of Lamentations does not mean that our proverb must have been spoken in Palestine, after the fall of Jerusalem. Or again, the fact that Jer. 31.29 (which also quotes the 'sour grapes' proverb; see above, note 35) is probably later than 587 does not necessarily mean that Ezekiel 18 must be so late.

72. W. Zimmerli, *Ezekiel 1*, 369, 377.

73. W. Zimmerli, *Ezekiel 1*, 377-78; cf. 281-82. For discussion of the complex question of the location of Ezekiel's ministry, see above.

74. See above, p. 43.

75. W. Zimmerli, *Ezekiel 1*, 72.

76. W. Zimmerli, *Ezekiel 1*, 378, note 17.

77. W. Zimmerli, *Ezekiel 1*, 72. Zimmerli's dating of Ezekiel 18 is closely related to his understanding of the place of 3.16b-21 and 33.1-20. The danger of circularity of argument often attends a cumulative case of the kind which Zimmerli advanced for regarding these three passages as inaugurating a new phase of the prophet's ministry after 587 (see also note 87 below). When particular elements of the argument are challenged, the whole begins to look less secure.

78. With rare exceptions (11.14-21; 16.59-63; 17.22-24; 20.40-44), all of the hopeful material in Ezekiel is found after the announcement of the fall of Jerusalem at 33.21-22. As with so many features of the book, it is difficult to know to what extent this schema derives from the prophet and how much it owes to editors.

79. Cf. *Ezekiel 1*, 386-87; also *Ezekiel 2*, 189-90.

80. See below, especially Chapter 8.

81. The theme of the imminence of the judgment upon Jerusalem is particularly prominent in Ezekiel 9; see detailed exegesis in Chapter 4 below.

82. Ezek. 33.1-20, rather than introducing a new phase of the prophet's ministry suited to the situation after 587 (as Zimmerli argued: *Ezekiel 2*, 189-90), in fact recapitulates themes of chs. 1-24 as a prelude to the announcement of the final judgment which follows in 33.21-22. See further below, note 87.

83. In addition to the references in ch. 18, explicit mention of repentance, using the verb שוב, is found at 3.19; 13.22; 14.6; 33.9, 11, 12, 14, 19. (On 14.6, see further below, Chapter 4).

84. E.W. Heaton, *The Old Testament Prophets* (rev. edn. London, 1977), 117.

85. On the range of meaning of the words 'life' and 'death' in ch. 18, see above, notes 49 and 62. At points this affords a rich subtlety: the words 'Why will you die, O house of Israel?' (18.31) poignantly acknowledge the fact that Israel is dying, suffering the fully deserved punishment of defeat and exile; and yet this question also anticipates that future which Yahweh wishes for his people.

86. W. Zimmerli, *Ezekiel 2*, 189-90; cf. *Ezekiel 1*, 144.

87. Further comment on the place of Ezek. 3.16-21 and 33.1-20 is called for here. As we mentioned above (note 82), there is reason to believe that, rather than inaugurating a new period of the prophet's ministry, 33.1-20 recapitulates themes of 1-24, bringing the pre-587 phase to a climax before the final blow falls. It is important that this material precedes rather than follows the announcement of 33.21-22.

Ezek. 33.1-20 has close links with material earlier in the book. 33.1-9 reintroduces the watchman motif which first occurs in 3.16-21. It may be that 3.16b-21 is secondary in its present position and dependent on both 33 and 18, as Zimmerli plausibly argued (*Ezekiel 1*, 143). Nevertheless, it is important to take account of the fact that the two watchman passages now form 'bookends' around the pre-587 ministry of Ezekiel. It seems reasonable to suggest, moreover, that if redactors have indeed interpolated the earlier of the two watchman passages, this itself is an indication that they understood the watchman role to relate to the period prior to the fall.

33.10-20 is based on elements drawn from ch. 18. Most scholars have taken the words of the people in 33.10 as an admission of responsibility (e.g. Zimmerli, *Ezekiel 2*, 187; Eichrodt, *Ezekiel*, 453; Greenberg, *Ezekiel 1-20*, 341). However, vv. 17 and 20 indicate that the prophet's audience has still not accepted responsibility. Perhaps therefore פשעינו וחטאתינו in v. 10 should be taken to refer not to (acknowledged) sins but rather to (undeserved) punishments (cf. Dan. 8.12, 13; 9.24; Zech. 14.19); in which case, the popular saying of 33.10 would mean precisely the same as the 'sour grapes' proverb of 18.2. If this is correct, 33.10-20, though less carefully argued, is in fact very similar to ch. 18. The immediate function of the repentance motif (vv. 11-16, 18-19) is again to highlight responsibility for the impending final judgment, as is indicated by the fact that the section culminates with the latter theme in vv. 17 and 20.

88. R.R. Wilson, 'An Interpretation of Ezekiel's Dumbness', *VT* 22 (1972), 94-96.

89. The form of these sentences seems to owe something to the test-case style of legal language, but the imagery used is that of the watchman who warns a city of impending military threat (cf. 2 Sam. 18.24-27; 2 Kgs 9.17ff.). In these verses (33.1-6), the watchman analogy is introduced in general

terms, only to be applied specifically to Ezekiel in vv. 7-9.

90. R.R. Wilson, 'Ezekiel's Dumbness', 96.

91. Wilson reviews the various explanations which have been proposed (ibid., 91-92).

92. Ibid., 98-100.

93. Ibid., 101.

94. Ezek. 2.5, 6, 7; 3.9, 26, 27.

95. In spite of the placing of 33.33 after the reference to the announcement of the fall of the city in 33.21-22, it clearly still anticipates that event.

Notes to Chapter 4

1. An earlier form of the exegeses of Ezekiel 9 and 14.12-23 presented here may be found in my paper read to the Leuven Ezekiel Colloquium in August 1985: 'Ezekiel and Individual Responsibility', in *Ezekiel and his Book: Textual and Literary Criticism and their Interrelation*, ed. J. Lust (Leuven, 1986), 317-21.

2. With this we may compare Jer. 5.1, 'Run to and fro through the streets of Jerusalem, look and take note! Search her squares to see if you can find a man, one who does justice and seeks truth; that I may pardon her'. This last phrase (if ואסלח לה is retained; cf. BH3 in loc.) may envisage a situation in which the merits of righteous individuals might secure the pardon of the whole city. It is conceivable (though unlikely) that such a possibility is entertained at Ezek. 22.30, 'And I sought for a man among them who should build up the wall and stand in the breach before me for the land, that I should not destroy it; but I found none'. We may note, however, that in ch. 9 there is absolutely no suggestion that the merits of any righteous would benefit others. Indeed, as we shall see, vv. 5-6 in particular rule out such a possibility.

3. J. Garscha, *Studien zum Ezechielbuch* (Bern & Frankfurt, 1974), 256-58, 296-97.

4. G. Hölscher, *Hesekiel: Der Dichter und das Buch*, BZAW 39 (Giessen, 1924), 69-86.

5. E.g. W. Eichrodt, *Ezekiel* (London, 1970), 112-19; W. Zimmerli, *Ezekiel I* (Philadelphia, 1979), 233-34.

6. W. Zimmerli, 'Das Wort des göttlichen Selbsterweises (Erweiswort), eine prophetische Gattung', in *Mélanges A. Robert* (Paris, 1957), 154-64; ET: 'The Word of Divine Self-Manifestation (Proof-Saying): A Prophetic Genre', in W. Zimmerli, *I am Yahweh*, ed. W. Brueggemann (Atlanta, 1982), 99-110.

7. See, for example, J.B. Taylor, *Ezekiel* (London, 1969), 44-46.

8. We may note incidentally that in Jeremiah 5 it is made clear that the search for righteous described there proved fruitless (see especially vv. 4-5).

9. It is, for example, inappropriate to ask questions about the whereabouts of Jeremiah during the search. Zimmerli suggested that 9.4 at least gives room for a knowledge on Ezekiel's part of a preaching similar to his own among those who were not exiled in 597 (*Ezekiel 1* [Philadelphia, 1979], 46). It is, however, unreasonable to press material such as ch. 9 far in discussing such questions.

10. It is impossible to say with certainty upon what basis little children are held to be included in the general punishment in ch. 9. There would seem to be two main possibilities: either they are held to share in the collective responsibility of the nation; or they are afflicted as part of the property of the wicked, on the basis of what Daube has called 'Ruler Punishment' (D. Daube, *Studies in Biblical Law* [Cambridge, 1947], 161ff).

11. Note also that in ch. 10 burning coals are scattered indiscriminately over the city; such a punishment is inevitably collective.

12. Y. Kaufmann, *The Religion of Israel* (London, 1961), 439.

13. See below, Chapter 5.

14. The dialogue of Gen. 18.20-33 and one version of the Flood narrative in Genesis 6—9 have commonly been attributed to the early monarchic period (e.g. G. von Rad, *Das erste Buch Mose, Genesis*, ATD 2-4 (Göttingen, 1949—9th edn, 1972), ET: *Genesis* (London & Philadelphia, 1961; rev. edn, 1972), 116-25, 210-15). However, this depends upon the isolation of the so-called Yahwistic work as a distinct and early source; this assumption has come under renewed criticism in recent years, in (among others) the following works: J. Van Seters, *Abraham in History and Tradition* (New Haven & London, 1975); H.H. Schmid, *Der sogenannte Jahwist: Beobachtungen und Fragen zur Pentateuchforschung* (Zürich, 1976); R. Rendtorff, *Das überlieferungsgeschichtliche Problem des Pentateuch*, BZAW 147 (Berlin, 1977); R.N. Whybray, *The Making of the Pentateuch: A Methodological Study*, JSOTS 53 (Sheffield, 1987).

15. For a discussion of the broader Old Testament picture with regard to collective and individual responsibility, see Chapter 5 below.

16. P.R. Ackroyd, *Exile and Restoration* (London, 1968), 109.

17. E.g. J. Garscha, *Studien zum Ezechielbuch* (Bern & Frankfurt, 1974), 266-67.

18. See above, p. 25.

19. W. Zimmerli, 'Die Eigenart der prophetischen Rede des Ezechiel. Ein Beitrag zum Problem an Hand von Ez. 14.1-11', *ZAW* 66 (1954), 1-26.

20. Cf. W. Zimmerli, 'Deutero-Ezechiel?', *ZAW* 84 (1972), 501-16.

21. G. Fohrer, 'Die Glossen im Buche Ezechiel', *ZAW* 63 (1951), 33-53.

22. See above, p. 24.

23. For a fuller defence of the unity of the passage, see Zimmerli, *Ezekiel 1*, 305-306.

24. See Chapter 3 above.
25. Heb. (Ezek. 14.4): איש איש מבית ישראל אשר
26. W. Zimmerli, *Ezekiel 1*, 302-305.
27. Heb. (Ezek. 14.8): והכרתיו מתוך עמי
28. Cf. W. Zimmerli, *Ezekiel 1*, 303, 305. The very similar phrase found in Ezek. 14.9, והשמדתיו מתוך עמי ישראל ('I will destroy him from the midst of my people Israel') should be understood in the same way.
29. Heb. (Ezek. 14.10): ונשאו עונם
30. W. Zimmerli, *Ezekiel 1*, 303-305. Cf. A. Phillips, *Ancient Israel's Criminal Law* (Oxford, 1970), 28-32.
31. Heb. (Ezek. 14.5): נזרו מעלי בגלוליהם כלם
32. W. Zimmerli, 'Die Eigenart der prophetischen Rede des Ezechiel', *ZAW* 66 (1954), 1-26. In our discussion of Ezekiel 18 this insight helped us demonstrate the collective nature of the concerns of that chapter. Indeed, we followed through the implications of this feature of the method of Ezekiel in a more consistent manner than Zimmerli apparently wished to. However, in his consideration of 14.1-11 we see Zimmerli himself employing this insight in a very thoroughgoing way.
33. W. Zimmerli, *Ezekiel 1*, 306, 307.
34. It seems very probable that 14.1-11 relates to the period before the final collapse of Jerusalem in 587. Judgment is clearly anticipated throughout the passage; moreover, as we have noted before, when a new future comes to be spoken of in Ezekiel, this is in spite of rather than because of Israel's behaviour, and so the call to repentance in 14.6 cannot be regarded as evidence of a post-587 perspective. See above for discussion of whether ch. 18 relates to the period before or after 587.
35. R.R. Wilson, 'An Interpretation of Ezekiel's Dumbness', *VT* 22 (1972), 103. See above for further discussion of Wilson's contribution. It should be noted that, for Wilson, the dumbness theme and also (by implication at least) that of the refusal of 'inquiry' are secondary motifs, with the apologetic purpose of explaining why final disaster came to the nation in spite of the prophet's activity.
36. As H.W. Wolff has demonstrated, a call to repentance indicates at least some openness to the possibility of a future ('Das Thema "Umkehr" in der alttestamentlichen Prophetie', *ZThK* 48 [1951], 129-48).
37. The presence of כי after the subject (ארץ) in 14.13 is a clear indication of this format (cf. Ezek. 14.9; 18.5; Lev. 19.20). We may note an important difference between the use of such language here and in Ezek. 18.1-20. Within 18.1-20, cases are presented in the actual form of legal cases and the theological implications for Ezekiel's audience are drawn by analogy. Here in 14.12-20, however, the case format is followed less closely, for the cases cited actually refer directly to Yahweh's activity in history. This is not unlike the phenomenon we noted in Ezek. 18.21-32, where we found a less careful

distinction between legal and theological discourse than in the first half of that chapter.

38. We may compare similar lists of forms of punishment in Ezek. 5.1-4, 16-17; 6.11-12; 12.16. A close parallel is found also in the four-fold lists of Jer. 15.2, 3; in fact, J.W. Miller has argued that Ezekiel 14 is dependent upon these verses of Jeremiah (J.W. Miller, *Das Verhältnis Jeremias und Hesekiels sprachlich und theologisch untersucht* [Assen, 1955], 93).

39. All three figures were, it seems, of international rather than merely Israelite renown (cf. W. Eichrodt, *Ezekiel* [London, 1970], 188-89; J. Day has more recently defended the identification of the Daniel of Ezek. 14.12-20 with the figure alluded to in the Ugaritic Aqhat epic: J. Day, 'The Daniel of Ugarit and Ezekiel and the Hero of the Book of Daniel', *VT* 30 [1980], 174-84). This international perspective is appropriate since Ezek. 14.12-20 is presented (formally at least) as illustrating a general principle.

It should be noted that, despite the use of the names of heroic figures, the concern in Ezekiel 14 is not with the question of whether the deeds of previous generations affect the present generation (as we have suggested is the case in ch. 18). Rather, these heroic figures simply represent hypothetical righteous individuals within the present generation.

40. We may perhaps compare Amos 1–2, where a series of oracles of judgment against the various foreign nations builds up to the really important oracle of the sequence, that against Israel (Amos 2.6ff.) (cf. J. Barton, *Amos's Oracles Against the Nations* [Cambridge, 1980]).

41. E.g. J. Garscha, *Studien zum Ezechielbuch* (Bern & Frankfurt, 1974), 267-69.

42. See above, pp. 24f.

43. Cf. W. Zimmerli, *Ezekiel 1* (Philadelphia, 1979), 312.

44. D.M.G. Stalker, *Ezekiel* (London, 1968), 34.

45. J.B. Taylor, *Ezekiel* (London, 1969), 45.

46. See above, pp. 62ff.

47. We may compare also Ezek. 18.10-13, which presents the legal case of the wicked son of a righteous man and declares that 'he shall surely die'. As we saw earlier, however, the concern in ch. 18 is with the question of the relationship between generations of Israel rather than with the moral independence of individuals.

48. The motif of Noah's family being spared with him (even though it is Noah who is the righteous man) is a consistent feature of the Genesis Flood narrative as a whole. This is true both of those parts which have often been regarded as pre-exilic Yahwist material (Gen. 7.1, 7; cf. 6.8) and of those which have often been regarded as exilic Priestly material (Gen. 6.18; cf. 6.9). (A 'documentary hypothesis' is, of course, not to be taken for granted [cf. Chapter 4, note 14]).

Eichrodt (*Ezekiel*, 188-89) emphasizes Noah's cursing of his son Canaan in

Gen. 9.24-25 and argues that even the Noah of Genesis is regarded as a figure who could not deliver his son. However, it is surely more likely that Ezekiel is contradicting the assumption that a man as righteous as Noah would naturally be able to deliver his own sons and daughters. Indeed, it is probable that all three heroic figures are presented as paragons whom one would expect to be able to deliver their children. For further discussion, see J. Day, 'The Daniel of Ugarit and Ezekiel and the Hero of the Book of Daniel', *VT* 30 (1980), 174-84 and also S. Spiegel, 'Noah, Daniel and Job, Touching on Canaanite Relics in the Legends of the Jews', in *Louis Ginzberg Jubilee Volume* (New York, 1945), 305-55.

49. See Chapter 5 for a consideration of collective and individual responsibility in the wider Old Testament.

50. This is a consistent feature of the Passover narrative as a whole, both those sections which have often been regarded as Yahwist (e.g. Exod. 11.7) and those which have often been regarded as Priestly (e.g. Exod. 12.13).

51. D. Daube, *Studies in Biblical Law* (Cambridge, 1947), 157-58.

52. See BDB, 65; also G-K, 484.

53. Verses 12-20 can surely never have stood alone as a general doctrinal section unrelated to the specific case of Jerusalem, as was believed by A. Bertholet (*Das Buch Hesekiel erklärt*, KHC 12 [Freiburg, 1897], 74). Verse 21 is required to give vv. 12-20 relevance to Ezekiel's audience.

54. The recognition of the use of a test-case format has played an important role in our consideration of both ch. 18 and Ezek. 14.12ff. However, it is important to see that this role is significantly different in the two instances. Our exegesis of ch. 18 depended upon the insight that the appearance of particular cases was a feature of the prophet's teaching technique and not evidence of an individualistic concern. In 14.12ff., on the other hand, we have acknowledged an element of individualism, but we have seen that it is only because of the test-case format that the rigorous application of the principle of individual responsibility appears general and theoretical.

55. We may compare Jer. 15.1, which may well have had some influence on Ezek. 14.12ff. (cf. Miller, *Verhältnis*, 93), 'Though Moses and Samuel stood before me, yet my heart would not turn toward this people'. This verse certainly seems to be a response to the particular wickedness of Jeremiah's contemporaries, rather than a theoretical denial of the efficacy of the prayers of great and holy men.

56. E.g. J.W. Wevers, *Ezekiel* (London, 1969), 114: 'Obviously, some member of the Ezekiel school after 586 B.C. realizing the actual state of affairs wanted to justify the existence of survivors within the framework of Ezekiel's argument'.

57. It is proper that we should attempt to make sense of vv. 22-23 in relation to the preceding verses, before entertaining the hypothesis that they

constitute an independent addition (see discussion of methodology above).

58. The word הנה ('behold!'), which occurs twice in v. 22, seems to express some natural surprise at the appearance of these survivors.

59. With this we may compare Ezek. 12.16, 'But I will let a few of them escape . . . that they may confess all their abominations among the nations where they go'. Also worthy of comparison is the more common motif of the self-loathing of survivors (Ezek. 6.8-9; 7.16; 16.54, 63; 20.43; 36.31-32).

60. On which see Chapter 6 below.

61. There would seem to be no good grounds for denying these words to Ezekiel. They express the predominant theme of chs. 1-24, judgment upon the nation, employing the now familiar motif of the sword (e.g. Ezek. 5.12, 17; 6.3, 11-12; 14.17-18, 21).

62. W.A. Irwin, *The Problem of Ezekiel* (Chicago, 1943), 331-32. It seems that even in ancient times some found difficulty with the words of Ezek. 21.8, 9 (Eng. 3, 4). Where the MT has צדיק ורשע LXX reads ἄδικον καὶ ἄνομον. Zimmerli described this as a 'classical example of a correction for dogmatic reasons' (*Ezekiel 1*, 421).

Notes to Chapter 5

1. F. Baumgärtel, *Die Eigenart der alttestamentlichen Frömmigkeit* (Schwerin, 1932).

2. W. Eichrodt, *Theologie des Alten Testaments* (Göttingen & Stuttgart, 1933ff.), ET: *Theology of the Old Testament* (London, 1961, 1967), vol. II, 231ff.

3. See, for example, J. Rhymer and A. Bullen, *Companion to the Good News Old Testament* (London, 1976), 186.

4. See, for example, O. Eissfeldt, *Einleitung in das Alte Testament* (Tübingen, 1934), ET: *The Old Testament: An Introduction* (Oxford, 1965), 467.

5. See, for example, A.S. Peake, *The Problem of Suffering in the Old Testament* (London, 1904), 83-103, 118-36.

6. The five issues of method which are discussed in the text are those which bear most directly upon the viability of the developmental hypothesis. However, reference must also be made here to the influential theory of 'corporate personality'. Some scholars, recognizing that much Old Testament material seems to exhibit a rather more collective understanding of responsibility than that to which we are generally accustomed, have sought to provide a psychological explanation for such phenomena. Thus, for example, H. Wheeler Robinson explained cases such as that of Achan in Joshua 7, where Achan's family and possessions are destroyed with him, in terms of his notion of 'Corporate Personality' (see especially 'The Hebrew

Conception of Corporate Personality', in *Werden und Wesen des Alten Testaments* BZAW 66 [Berlin, 1936]. The essay has been reissued in H. Wheeler Robinson, *Corporate Personality in Ancient Israel* [Philadelphia, 1980; Edinburgh, 1981], 25-44). Drawing on the anthropological work of Levy-Bruhl and Durkheim, Robinson claimed that much of the Old Testament is to be understood in the light of his belief that the individual was not clearly distinguished from the group to which he belonged. In a rather similar way, J. Pedersen spoke of 'Psychic Community' (*Israel: its Life and Culture, I-II* [London & Copenhagen, 1926], 292) and A.R. Johnson of the group as a 'Psychical Whole' (*The One and the Many in the Israelite Conception of God* [Cardiff, 1942; 2nd edn, 1961], 8).

The influence of such notions on biblical studies has been considerable. Robinson himself applied his concept of 'Corporate Personality' to a wide range of problems in Old Testament studies (see, for example, H. Wheeler Robinson, *The Cross of the Servant* [London, 1926]). However, recent decades have seen something of a reaction. J.R. Porter warned that such notions had perhaps been applied too widely and with insufficient care ('The Legal Aspects of the Concept of "Corporate Personality" in the Old Testament', *VT* 15 [1965], 361-80), whilst J.W. Rogerson has been particularly critical of Robinson's implication that the ancient Israelite lacked the awareness of being an individual which is part of the experience of the modern human being ('The Hebrew Conception of Corporate Personality: a Re-examination', *JTS* 211 [1970], 1-16). Whilst Robinson's work remains of importance (not least as a pioneering example of the use of anthropological insights in the study of the Bible), it lies beyond the scope of the available evidence to make confident assertions about the distinctive psychologies of ancient peoples. The discussion of responsibility in the Old Testament is better conducted in a way which does not depend upon sweeping psychological theories.

7. J.R. Porter, 'The Legal Aspects of the Concept of 'Corporate Personality' in the Old Testament', *VT* 15 (1965), 363.

8. K. Koch, 'Gibt es ein Vergeltungsdogma im Alten Testament?', *ZThK* 52 (1955), 1-42; ET: 'Is there a Doctrine of Retribution in the Old Testament?', in J.L. Crenshaw (ed.), *Theodicy in the Old Testament* (Philadelphia & London, 1983), 57-87.

9. D. Daube, *Studies in Biblical Law* (Cambridge, 1947), 161-63. Daube used the term 'Ruler Punishment' to describe such an understanding.

10. A distinction stated particularly clearly by B. Lindars, in 'Ezekiel and Individual Responsibility', *VT* 15 (1965), 456. See our discussion above.

11. See below.

12. Clearly any full-scale exploration of collective and individual responsibility in the Old Testament would require a thorough examination of the function of language about responsibility in the different parts of the

literature, and would need to draw upon a wealth of sociological and anthropological expertise. Certain kinds of reference might appropriately be handled separately, so as to avoid distortion of the broader picture; thus, for example, references to family solidarity might constitute one such special case.

13. Wheeler Robinson cited this as an example of 'corporate personality' (*Corporate Personality in Ancient Israel* [Philadelphia, 1980; Edinburgh, 1981], 26), but it might alternatively be regarded as an instance of Daube's 'Ruler Punishment', Achan being deprived of his property (including his family) as well as his life (Daube, *Studies in Biblical Law*, 161ff.).

14. In this complexity, the story of Achan has important affinities with the notion of excommunication, which (as we saw earlier, Chapter 4) is characterized by a striking ambivalence, involving as it does not only a high consciousness of the importance of the community and of the necessity to preserve it, but also a strong awareness of the need to isolate the sinful individual who poses a threat to the community.

15. A valuable discussion of this passage may be found in C.S. Rodd, 'Shall not the Judge of all the earth do what is just? (Gen.18.25)', *ET* 83 (1972), 137-39.

16. Daube, *Studies in Biblical Law*, 155.

17. Note that the concerns of Joshua 7 and of Genesis 18 differ markedly. Joshua 7 is so aware of the threat posed to the righteous community by the unrighteous individual that Achan is isolated and destroyed, and his family with him. In contrast to this, Genesis 18 is so conscious of the injustice of a righteous minority being punished that it is envisaged that the unrighteous majority might be spared.

18. Among other passages manifesting (at least in the final form of the text) a stark juxtaposition of more collective and more individualistic elements may be mentioned Numbers 16 and Deuteronomy 29 (esp. vv. 15ff. [Eng. 16ff.]).

19. See above, Chapter 4, note 14.

20. J.R. Porter, 'The Legal Aspects of the Concept of 'Corporate Personality' in the Old Testament', *VT* 15 (1965), 365.

21. A.D.H. Mayes, *Deuteronomy* (London, 1979), 326.

22. See above, pp. 48f.

23. Genesis 18 has most commonly been attributed to a Yahwist writer, or writers, working in the early monarchy (see, for example, M. Noth, *Überlieferungsgeschichte des Pentateuch* [Stuttgart, 1948], ET: *A History of Pentateuchal Traditions* [Englewood Cliffs, New Jersey, 1972] 263). However, though this view is still widely held, many recent critics have raised serious questions about such an early dating (see above, Chapter 4, note 14).

On the probable continuity of the Flood story of Genesis 6-9 with pre-Israelite traditions, see G. von Rad, *Das erste Buch Mose, Genesis* ATD 2-4

(Göttingen, 1949ff.; 9th edn, 1972); ET: *Genesis* (London & Philadelphia, 1961; rev. edn, 1972), 123-24.

24. A judicious treatment of these questions may be found in J. Hempel, *Das Ethos des Alten Testaments*, BZAW 67 (Berlin, 1938; 2nd edn, 1964), 32ff.

25. Daube, *Studies in Biblical Law*, 160-61.

26. Cf. H.W. Wolff, *Dodekapropheton 2, Joel und Amos* (Neukirchen-Vluyn, 1969; 2nd edn, 1975), ET: *Joel and Amos* (Philadelphia, 1977), 103-106.

27. J.M. Robinson and H. Koester, *Trajectories through Early Christianity* (Philadelphia, 1971). The model has already been applied to Old Testament studies by W. Brueggemann, in 'Trajectories in Old Testament Literature and the Sociology of Ancient Israel', *JBL* 98 (1979), 161-85.

28. To use more technical language, a full 'synchronic' understanding of each period would be necessary before a 'diachronic' picture could be drawn with any confidence—and our sources are surely too selective ever to permit this.

Notes to Chapter 6

1. See chart on p. 91. All the occurrences of the basic formula are listed, together with a number of those of variant forms. In a few cases it is difficult to be certain precisely where to place a particular verse, whether because the subject of the verb ידע is ambiguous (e.g. Ezek. 12.16; see below, note 5) or because of other difficulties relating to the interpretation of the verse (e.g. Ezek. 29.16; see below, note 7). It will be noted that 28.26 and 39.28 are especially complex verses and that they therefore appear in more than one category on the chart.

2. Category 'A' on chart.

3. Category 'G' on chart.

4. Category 'E' on chart.

5. Category 'C' on chart. It is conceivable that 12.16 speaks of the nations coming to know that 'I am Yahweh' when the exiled Israelites confess their abominations (category 'C'), but it is more likely that (as in the preceding verse) the reference is to Israel coming to know that 'I am Yahweh' when she is punished (category 'G'). In Ezek. 21.4 (Eng. 20.48) we read, in a variation of the formula, that 'All flesh shall see that I the LORD have kindled (fire in the South)'. Similarly, in Ezek. 21.10 (Eng. 21.5) it is said that 'All flesh shall know that I the LORD have drawn my sword (against Israel)'. These uses of the phrase 'all flesh' are to be understood as general rhetorical references rather than as relating specifically to the nations. These verses cannot, then, be said to belong to category 'C'.

6. Category 'H' on chart.

7. Thus it will be seen that categories 'B' and 'F' on our chart are both empty. The restoration of Egypt which is envisaged in Ezek. 29.13-16 in fact amounts to a humiliation, and so 29.16 is placed not in category 'B' but in category 'A'.

8. Category 'D' on chart.

9. It will be seen that categories 'A', 'G' and 'H' account for the vast majority of the examples of our formula. We shall return to consider these categories more closely later.

10. G. Hölscher, *Hesekiel, der Dichter und das Buch*, 26-27.

11. S. Herrmann, *Die prophetischen Heilserwartungen*, 241ff.

12. See our discussion concerning the use of the distinction between poetry and prose and of theological content as criteria in making decisions about authorship (Chapter 2).

13. For the grounds for regarding 16.62 as secondary, see also Chapter 2, note 48. 28.26 forms part of a short section (28.25-26) found between the oracles against Tyre and Sidon and those against Egypt. A number of features suggest that this section may well be redactional: it begins with a fresh introductory formula; it uses language uncharacteristic of the book (notably כרם, which is found only here); and it attempts to summarize the purpose of the foreign nation oracles in a systematic way (cf. W. Zimmerli, *Ezekiel 2*, 100-101). It is in connexion with references to the deliverance of Israel that the possibility of redactional provenance most often arises (as in the two examples just cited). It is, however, as we have seen, by no means easy to discriminate with confidence between primary and secondary material in the book of Ezekiel (Chapter 2). For discussion of the authorship of each of the occurrences of the 'I am Yahweh' formula see my commentary on Ezekiel in the New Century Bible series (in preparation).

14. See above, Chapter 2.

15. G. Fohrer, *Introduction*, 409.

16. A number of Zimmerli's writings concern the formula, notably 'Ich bin Jahwe' (1953); *Erkenntnis Gottes* (1954); and 'Das Wort des göttlichen Selbsterweises' (1957); for full details see bibliography (Zimmerli items 2, 4 and 5). These are available in ET in W. Zimmerli, *I am Yahweh*, ed. W. Brueggemann (Atlanta, 1982). It may be suggested, moreover, that Zimmerli's concern with this formula in Ezekiel profoundly influenced his exposition of the theology of the Old Testament as a whole, as presented in his *Grundriss der alttestamentlichen Theologie* (Stuttgart, 1972; 2nd edn, 1975); ET: *Old Testament Theology in Outline* (Edinburgh, 1978).

17. Exod. 6.2ff. has often been regarded as Priestly material, e.g. M. Noth, *A History of Pentateuchal Traditions*, 18.

18. Exod. 20.1ff. has often been regarded as Elohist material, e.g. M. Noth, *A History of Pentateuchal Traditions*, 36. However, this and many other

aspects of the so-called 'documentary hypothesis' have been much debated recently (cf. Chapter 4, note 14).

19. Lev. 17-26 has commonly been understood to constitute a distinct work, the so-called Holiness Code. In these chapters, the words 'I am Yahweh' are appended to a number of legal stipulations; this is one of the grounds on which Reventlow has argued for a close affinity between Ezekiel and the Holiness Code (see H. Graf Reventlow, *Wächter über Israel* [Berlin, 1962], 50ff.).

20. Blank regarded the use of the phrase 'I am Yahweh' in Ezekiel as later than and dependent upon Deutero-Isaiah; he argued that its primary purpose was to assert a doctrine of monotheism. The possibility that the use of the phrase in Ezekiel may in part reflect an increasing emphasis on the theme of monotheism in the exilic period is not to be ruled out. However, there are no good grounds for believing Ezekiel to be dependent on Deutero-Isaiah here (see Sheldon H. Blank, 'Studies in Deutero-Isaiah', *HUCA* 15 [1940], 14ff.).

21. Cf. also 1 Kgs 17.24 and 2 Kgs 5.8, 15 and 19.19.

22. W. Zimmerli, 'Das Wort des göttlichen Selbsterweises', 154ff.

23. G. von Rad, *Der heilige Krieg im alten Israel*, ATANT 20 (1951), 7ff.

24. K.W. Carley, *Ezekiel among the Prophets* (London, 1975), 38-39.

25. G. Fohrer, *Introduction*, 104.

26. G. Fohrer, 'Remarks on Modern Interpretation of the Prophets', *JBL* 80 (1961), 310.

27. Fohrer cites Exod. 7.17; 8.6, 18 (Eng. 8.10, 22); 9.29; 11.7. Which background is the more likely? On the whole, the Exodus references tend perhaps to be closer in form to the wording in Ezekiel. It may be of value to reflect on the categories into which the examples cited from Kings and Exodus would fall on our chart. Of Zimmerli's examples, 1 Kgs 20.13, 28 would belong in category 'E' and 2 Kgs 19.19 in category 'D', both categories in which there are few cases in Ezekiel. The remaining examples cited by Zimmerli (1 Kgs 17.24 and 2 Kgs 5.8, 15) would belong in category 'B', of which there are no cases in Ezekiel. Of Fohrer's examples, whilst Exod. 8.6 (Eng. 8.10) and 9.29 would belong in category 'B' on our chart, a use not found in Ezekiel, 7.17 would belong in category 'A', one of the major Ezekiel uses, whilst 8.18 (Eng. 8.22) and 11.7 would belong in category 'D', which (though itself a minor category) is closely related to category 'A'. It might be argued that such a breakdown points in favour of a background in Exodus, but it must be acknowledged that the sample is small and the evidence inconclusive.

28. Categories 'A', 'G' and 'H' on our chart.

29. Category 'A'.

30. Category 'H'.

31. Such an extension would account not only for the cases in the major

category 'H', in which it is said that Israel will come to know that 'I am Yahweh' when Yahweh delivers her, but also for the cases in the minor category 'D', in which it is said that the nations will come to know that 'I am Yahweh' when Yahweh delivers Israel.

32. Category 'G'.

33. This must, of course, remain a hypothesis. Moreover, if such an inversion of an established form has taken place, we are clearly not in a position to know whether this was an innovation by Ezekiel or a part of the tradition which he inherited.

34. We have seen that it is likely that our formula had its origin in oracles against the nations (a theme to which that of the deliverance of Israel is closely related) and that its use in relation to Yahweh's punishment of Israel may represent an advanced stage in the development of the formula. Paradoxically, however, within the book of Ezekiel itself it is (as we have noted) in connexion with references to the deliverance of Israel that the possibility of redactional provenance most often arises (e.g. Ezek. 16.62; 28.26). It seems probable that all three major categories ('A', 'G' and 'H') were well represented in the usage of Ezekiel himself, but that one of these in particular, namely category 'H', was much elaborated in the redactional tradition.

35. It was this concern with evidence or proof which caused Zimmerli to dub the formula which we are considering 'das Erweiswort' or 'the proof-saying' (W. Zimmerli, 'Das Wort des göttlichen Selbstserweises', in *Mélanges A. Robert* [Paris, 1957], 154).

36. The formula normally begins with a waw-consecutive construction (either וידעתם or וידעו. Only occasionally is an explicit purpose clause found, as in Ezek. 20.26: למען ידעו אשר אני יהוה).

37. This statement may be qualified to a limited extent. Reference to the 'I am Yahweh' formula always follows mention of some decisive action of Yahweh which gives an insight into his nature. Moreover, variations on the basic formula occasionally expand it to give more information of this kind, as in Ezek. 5.13: '... and they shall know that I, the LORD, have spoken in my jealousy, when I spend my fury upon them'. Nevertheless, the overriding impression is of a terse and cryptic saying.

38. Occasionally, specific groups or individuals, to whom reference is made in the third person, are condemned, and then this is followed by a rather indeterminate address in the second person, as in Ezek. 13.9 and 14.8: 'and you shall know ... ' (Cf. B.S. Childs, *Introduction to the Old Testament as Scripture* [London, 1979], 361-62.)

39. H. Graf Reventlow, 'Die Völker als Jahwes Zeugen bei Ezechiel', *ZAW* 71 (1959), 33-43.

40. E.g. P.R. Ackroyd, *Exile and Restoration*, 115. We may note in passing that it should not be assumed without question that universalism is a

prominent feature of Deutero-Isaiah (cf. R.N. Whybray, *Isaiah 40-66*, New Century Bible Commentary [Grand Rapids & London, 1975], 31-32).

41. The material which concerns us here falls in to categories 'A' and 'D' on our chart.

42. Category 'B'; see note 7 above. We may observe that 16.53ff. (which may well be part of redactional elaboration; see above p. 26 and also Chapter 2, note 48) envisages the restoration of Sodom and Samaria. However, this is an incidental motif in the tirade against the wicked foundling Israel, related to the theme that her sins are worse than theirs. The 'I am Yahweh' formula is, in any case, not used here.

43. Category 'C'; see note 5 above. We may observe that Ezek. 5.15 (which does not employ the formula) says that Israel will be 'a reproach and a taunt, a warning and a horror' to the nations round about. However, the focus here is on Israel's sin and punishment; there is no suggestion that the nations will learn from Israel's fate. Carley offers the following generalizing summary of the usage of the 'I am Yahweh' formula: 'It is Israel who will be given into the hands of Yahweh's avengers and Israel's neighbours will acknowledge Yahweh in his historical activity' (*Ezekiel among the Prophets*, 39-40). In the light of our detailed survey of the application of the formula this may be seen to be somewhat misleading.

44. Category 'A'.

45. Category 'D'.

46. It is clear from the contexts of the verses in category 'D' that it is envisaged that Israel's deliverance will be at the expense of the nations.

47. This range of closely associated phrases would seem to constitute another feature of the style of the prophet Ezekiel which has become a mark also of the redactional strata of the book. A couple of examples of references which may be secondary must suffice here. We have already seen that the passage in which 28.25 occurs (28.25-26) is likely to be redactional (see above, Chapter 6, note 13). There are grounds for believing that the passage in which 39.27 occurs (39.23-29) may also be an addition. Thus, for example, it shows no awareness of the Gog material which precedes it, and it contains a number of features uncharacteristic of the book, e.g. 'hiding the face', found in 39.23, 24, 29 (cf. W. Zimmerli, *Ezekiel 2*, 319-21).

48. Reventlow, 'Die Völker', 35-36.

49. Cf. G.M. Tucker, 'Witnesses and Dates in Israelite Contracts', *CBQ* 28 (1966), 42ff.

50. The case which might be thought most likely to favour Reventlow's view is 5.6-8, where the declaration that Yahweh will judge Jerusalem 'in the sight of the nations' (5.8) appears straight after the statement that Jerusalem is more wicked than the nations round about (5.6-7). However, the focus here is entirely upon Yahweh's judgment of Jerusalem. The motif in vv. 6-7 is to be understood as hyperbole, indicating the magnitude of Israel's sin, and certainly not as evidence of the conversion of the nations.

51. It should be noted that we are not arguing for close verbal similarity to or dependence upon such texts. Rather, they are cited simply as examples of rhetorical appeals to witnesses.

52. Cf. K. Nielsen, *Yahweh as Prosecutor and Judge: an Investigation of the Prophetic Lawsuit (Rîb Pattern)*, JSOTS 9 (Sheffield, 1978), 13.

53. A number of scholars have favoured the view that there is not to be found in Ezekiel a positive concern for the nations, notably: G.A. Cooke, *The Book of Ezekiel* (Edinburgh, 1936), xxxi; H. Wheeler Robinson, *Two Hebrew Prophets* (London, 1948), 124; Y. Kaufmann, *The Religion of Israel* (London, 1961), 446.

54. The motif of self-loathing is a recurrent one in Ezekiel, e.g. 6.9; 16.54, 63; 20.43; 36.31, 32. Some of the cases appear to be redactional (e.g. 16.54, 63; see Chapter 2, note 48).

55. See above. We suggested that the call to repentance also testifies to the yearning of Yahweh for the obedience of his people; we learn in 36.26-27 (cf. 11.19-20) that this desire is to be satisfied through a remarkable divine initiative whereby Yahweh will grant as gift that which he previously demanded.

56. In passing, however, it is of interest to note the interpretation of Isa. 40.2 offered by A. Phillips. Commenting on the problematic words 'she has received from the LORD's hand double for all her sins', Phillips argues that this is to be understood as part of a promise addressed to a second, innocent, exilic generation. The deportation was a fully deserved punishment, but now that the sinful generation has passed on, the restoration of Israel becomes appropriate (cf. A. Phillips, 'Double for all her Sins', *ZAW* 94/1 [1982], 130-32).

57. Cf. W. Eichrodt, *Ezekiel*, 205-206; also W. Zimmerli, *Ezekiel 1*, 339-40. It may be conceded that vv. 9-14 yield more evidence of particular affection, but even in these verses there appear to be significant elements of ceremonial formality.

58. It is likely that the latter part of Ezekiel 16, which speaks of restoration (16.53ff.), is a redactional elaboration (see above p. 26, and also Chapter 2, note 48).

59. As with other formulae we have considered, the various phrases referring to the divine 'name' seem to characterize both the style of the prophet Ezekiel himself and also the redactional tradition which followed him. Among references which may well be redactional are 20.44; 39.25; 43.7, 8.

60. The 'name' is spoken of as 'defiled' (ממא) at 43.7, 8.

61. It is generally conceded that the etymology of the word remains obscure. Cf. BDB, 1027; H. Bietenhard, ὄνομα, *Theologisches Wörterbuch zum Neuen Testament* (ed. G. Friedrich); ET: *Theological Dictionary of the New Testament* (ed. G.W. Bromiley), vol. V, 252. Barr has, in any case,

taught us to be wary of giving undue weight to supposed etymologies; cf. J. Barr, *The Semantics of Biblical Language* (Oxford, 1961), 107-60.

62. Cf. J. Pedersen, *Israel I-II* (London & Copenhagen, 1926), 247-48.

63. Seven of the fourteen cases of the word in the book of Ezekiel occur in these two passages.

64. The motif of Yahweh sparing his people lest the nations think him weak is found elsewehere in the Old Testament, e.g. Num. 14.13-19; Deut. 32.26-27; Ps. 79.8-10; Joel 2.17. With these examples we may contrast other cases, where the nations are portrayed as perceiving the justice of Yahweh's punishment of his people, e.g. Deut. 29.23-27 (Eng. 29.24-28); 1 Kgs 9.7-9; Jer. 50.7.

65. Our intention is simply to suggest that the aspect of Yahweh's reputation which is most prominent here is his power. The argument does not rest upon the widespread notion that names in the Old Testament necessarily had an intrinsic power. For a careful discussion of the latter, see J. Barr, 'The Symbolism of Names in the Old Testament', *BJRL* 52/1 (1969), 11-29.

66. H.W. Robinson, *Two Hebrew Prophets* (London, 1948), 96.

67. K.W. Carley, *Ezekiel among the Prophets* (London, 1975), 59.

68. This understanding of Ezekiel's presentation would seem to be supported by a further factor. On a number of occasions in the Old Testament, the 'name' of Yahweh appears to be used as a periphrasis for Yahweh himself. For example, in Ps. 54.6, we read 'I will give thanks to thy name, O LORD, for it is good'. We may discern an element of periphrasis in Ezekiel too, for when we read that Yahweh acts to deliver Israel 'for the sake of his name', this seems to amount to a statement that he acts 'for his own sake'.

69. This phrase occurs nine times: 20.39; 36.20, 21, 22; 39.7 (twice); 39.25; 43.7, 8.

70. The Niphal form occurs six times: 20.41; 28.22, 25; 36.23b; 38.16; 39.27.

71. As with other features of the language of the book of Ezekiel, the verb קדש is a feature both of material which is likely to be primary (e.g. 36.23) and also of material which may well be secondary (e.g. 20.41). It would thus appear to furnish yet another example of continuity between the style of the prophet and the redactional tradition which followed him.

72. O. Procksch, ἅγιος, *Theologisches Wörterbuch zum Neuen Testament* (ed. G. Kittel); ET: *Theological Dictionary of the New Testament* (ed. G.W. Bromiley), vol. I, 90.

73. The etymology most widely (though by no means confidently) proposed for the root ἅγιος relates to the notion of 'separateness' or 'apartness' (cf. BDB, 871; Procksch, 89). Usage in Ezekiel would seem to cohere with such a sense, since the notion of Yahweh's 'otherness' (which is

nevertheless made manifest) is prominent. However, Barr has rightly made us wary of arguments based on postulated etymologies (*Semantics*, 107-60).

74. H. Graf Reventlow, *Wächter über Israel: Ezechiel und seine Tradition*, BZAW 82 (Berlin, 1962).

75. G. Bettenzoli, *Geist der Heiligkeit. Traditionsgeschichtliche Untersuchung des QDS-Begriffes im Buch Ezechiel* (Florence, 1979). Bettenzoli regards Ezekiel's usage as being shaped by the prophetic tradition, notably Isaiah, together with sacral-legal traditions.

76. J. Muilenburg, 'Holiness', *The Interpreter's Dictionary of the Bible* (New York & Nashville, 1962), vol. II, 622.

77. It is the *nations* who come to know that 'I am Yahweh' at 28.23; 36.23; 38.23 (and 38.16), whilst at 20.42; 28.26; 39.28 *Israel* comes to know that 'I am Yahweh'.

78. In connexion with the theme of Yahweh's power, we may note the use in 38.23 of the Hithpael of the verb גדל alongside the Hithpael of קדש.

79. It will have become clear that the radical theocentricity of Ezekiel is evidenced in a wide range of features of the book. For a fuller demonstration of this (including treatment of the recurrent motif of the Glory of Yahweh), see my commentary on Ezekiel in the New Century Bible series (in preparation).

Notes to Chapter 7

1. H.W. Wolff, *Anthropologie des Alten Testaments* (Munich, 1973), ET: *Anthropology of the Old Testament* (London, 1974), 40.

2. The word is used of God only 26 times, e.g. Job 10.13. Even rarer uses may be noted: of the sea (Ezek. 28.8), of heaven (Deut. 4.11) and of a tree (2 Sam. 18.14).

3. In what follows, statements about לב are to be taken to refer also to the longer form of the word, unless otherwise indicated.

4. Ezek. 21.12, 20 (Eng. 7, 15); cf. 32.9.

5. Cf. also Ezek. 3.10; 13.2, 17; 40.4.

6. It is interesting to note that the verbal roots found here are used of the hardening of Pharaoh's heart by Yahweh at Exod. 4.21 (חזק) and Exod. 7.3 (קשה) respectively. The divine act which is promised in Ezek. 11.19 and 36.26 may be said to amount to the antithesis of the hardening of the heart.

7. Replaced, that is, with a 'heart of flesh'. Wolff notes that the remarkably positive sense which בשר ('flesh') has here (that which is sensitive, responsive) is absolutely unparalleled (*Anthropology*, 29).

8. Both 11.19 and 36.26 speak of the replacement of the 'heart of stone'

with a 'heart of flesh'. It should be noted, however, that the MT at 11.19
speaks not of a 'new heart' (לב חדש) but of 'one heart' (לב אחד). LXX reads
καρδίαν ἑτέραν; Zimmerli (*Ezekiel 1*, 230) and Wolff (*Anthropology*, 54)
emend the Hebrew to לב אחר (cf. also 1 Sam. 10.9). On the basis of the
Syriac and a few Hebrew MSS, Herrmann (*Heilserwartungen*, 245) and
Reventlow (*Wächter*, 53) emend 11.19 to לב חדש (as 36.26; 18.31). However,
the MT of 11.19 is not so difficult as to demand emendation; reference is
made to לב אחר in a very similar context in MT of Jer. 32.39. The MT of
Ezek. 11.19 may imply an 'undivided heart' or could possibly reflect hopes of
renewed national unity (cf. Ezek. 37.22).

9. D. Lys, *Ruach. Le souffle dans l'Ancien Testament*, EHPhR 56 (1962),
336.

10. It may be noted that reference to the spirit of Yahweh is conspicuously
rare in classical prophecy (particularly Jeremiah) outside Ezekiel. W.
Zimmerli (*Ezekiel 1*, 42) and K.W. Carley (*Ezekiel among the Prophets*, 23ff.)
have emphasized this apparent link between Ezekiel and pre-classical
prophecy.

11. In this use of the word we are clearly still quite close to the sense of רוח
as 'wind', as a powerful force at Yahweh's disposal.

12. It should be noted that this explicit reference to the spirit of Yahweh in
36.27 is not to be found in 11.19-20.

13. We may note also Ezek. 39.29: '. . . when I pour out my spirit upon the
house of Israel'.

14. This use of רוח is close to the sense of לב as the rational or intellectual
faculty (see above).

15. This use of רוח is close to the sense of לב as the seat of the emotions
(see above).

16. Fohrer would omit the reference to רוח חדשה in 36.26 as a redundant
gloss based on רוחי in 36.27 (G. Fohrer, *Ezechiel* [Tübingen, 1955], 203).
However, there seems to be no compelling reason to emend the MT, with its
parallelism between 'new heart' and 'new spirit' and its subtle play on
'anthropological' and 'theological' senses of רוח.

17. See above.

18. See above, Chapter 7, note 8.

19. H.W. Wolff, *Anthropology*, 38.

20. Cf. W. Eichrodt, *Ezekiel*, 499.

21. These verses feature the double-sided formula; the single-sided
formula occurs at Ezek. 34.24 ('I, the LORD, will be their God').

22. See below.

23. G. von Rad, *Old Testament Theology*, vol. II, 235.

24. Heb. (Ezek. 11.16): ואהי להם למקדש מעט בארצות אשר־באו שם

25. W. Zimmerli, *Ezekiel 1*, 262.

26. W. Eichrodt, *Ezekiel*, 501.

27. W. Eichrodt, *Ezekiel*, 500.

28. The MT of Ezek. 11.15 refers to אנשי גאלתך ('men of your kindred'), but some scholars prefer to follow the LXX and Syriac (hence RSV: 'your fellow exiles'; cf. BHS). However, whether explicit reference is made to the exiles or not, it is clear that they are intended because of the contrast with the inhabitants of Jerusalem.

29. See above. The word רוח is, of course, used in a 'theological' as well as an 'anthropological' sense in 36.26-27.

30. In passing, we may perhaps compare the New Testament concept of the Church as the 'Body of Christ'.

31. See above, Chapter 7, note 8.

32. W. Eichrodt, *Ezekiel*, 501.

33. Cf. W. Zimmerli, *Der Mensch und seine Hoffnung im Alten Testament* (Göttingen, 1968), ET: *Man and his Hope in the Old Testament*, SBTh II/20 (London, 1971), 119.

34. There are three other hopeful passages within the part of the book (chs 1-24) generally concerned with judgment upon Israel. These are 16.59-63; 17.22-24; 20.40-44.

35. Such a view can only be advanced with caution, however, since Ezek. 33.23ff. might possibly be taken to suggest that the Jerusalem community was slow to relinquish its pretensions even after 587.

36. Within 11.14-21, it seems likely that v. 17 is a later addition. Unlike vv. 16 and 19-21, v. 17 is couched in the second person; moreover, it begins with a redundant repetition of the introduction to v. 16, 'Therefore say, "Thus says the Lord GOD"'. Verse 18, which assumes v. 17 but is couched in the third person, may be regarded as a further addition. This would leave vv. 14-16 and 19-21 as the basic text. This view (favoured by Zimmerli, *Ezekiel 1*, 230) is to be preferred to that of Eichrodt, who regarded 11.19-20 as a gloss from 36.26-27 (W. Eichrodt, *Ezekiel*, 111).

37. The other three hopeful passages within Ezekiel 1-24 (16.59-63; 17.22-24; 20.40-44) lack such evidence of early date and for this reason, among others, they are widely regarded as redactional additions.

38. Ezek. 35, containing a denunciation of Edom, represents an exception to the general rule that from 33.21-22 the emphasis of the book is directly upon the restoration of Israel.

39. We may compare a number of verses within 34-37 which have particular affinities to the promise of a 'new heart' and a 'new spirit'. 37.23 speaks of Yahweh saving his people from their backslidings and cleansing them. We have already noted the similarity between 36.26-27 and the reference to the placing of Yahweh's spirit within Israel at 37.14. We may also compare 34.16, where Yahweh is spoken of as a shepherd bringing back the strayed, binding up the crippled and strengthening the weak sheep.

40. The motif of sprinkling here is to be understood as a metaphorical

image drawn from the cult. Priestly terminology is employed (e.g. טמאה, 'uncleanness'). A similar use of such imagery is found in Ps. 51.9 (Eng. 51.7). As the denial of cleansing was part of the judgment (cf. Ezek. 24.13-14), so now cleansing forms part of the restoration. This is one of a number of respects in which features of the earlier judgement are reversed (cf. 36.1ff., where the mountains of Israel, condemned in 6.1ff., are now the recipients of a word of assurance; or again, 36.37-38, where 'inquiry' of Yahweh, denied in 14.1ff., is now again permitted).

41. S. Herrmann, *Die prophetischen Heilserwartungen im Alten Testament*, BWANT 85, NF 5 (Stuttgart, 1965), 241ff. Kaiser has followed Herrmann, e.g. O. Kaiser, *Einleitung in das Alte Testament* (Gütersloh, 1969); ET: *Introduction to the Old Testament* (Oxford, 1975), 257. Of course, the complexity of Herrmann's position should not be underestimated; he discerns in his secondary material deuteronomistic influence (see below). Nevertheless, the point remains that he is inclined to regard hope of restoration as, in itself, a sign of redactional provenance.

42. See Chapter 2 above.

43. Cf. W. Zimmerli, *Man and his Hope in the Old Testament*, SBTh II/20 (London, 1971), 117-18.

44. An important indication that the motif of Yahweh acting for the sake of his 'name' derives from Ezekiel himself is its occurrence even in Ezek. 20 (vv. 9, 14, 22), a chapter concerned not with announcing future restoration but rather with reviewing Israel's sin from the beginning of her history. (To suggest that the motif was a feature of the prophet is not, of course, to deny that it was taken up also in the redactional tradition; see above, Chapter 6, note 59.)

45. T.M. Raitt, *A Theology of Exile: Judgment/Deliverance in Jeremiah and Ezekiel* (Philadelphia, 1977), 126.

46. Ibid., 126.

47. We saw this to be the case with the 'I am Yahweh' formula which we considered in Chapter 6. Thus the occurrence of this formula here (36.11, 23, 38) cannot be taken as conclusive evidence that this material is primary.

48. These two sections (36.33-36, 37-38), each with its own separate introductory formula, are widely regarded as secondary. Eichrodt noted that 'they represent special longings on the part of the later generation, such as the erection of fortified cities and the increase of the diminished population . . ., things which the returned exiles were particularly disappointed to see withheld, and which were therefore brought into the picture of the future' (W. Eichrodt, *Ezekiel*, 503-54). Zimmerli saw the phrase עוד זאת (36.37) as evidence of a secondary addition (cf. 20.27), and also detected marked affinities with Second Isaiah in both sections (W. Zimmerli, *Ezekiel 2*, 246).

49. In the oldest Greek manuscript, Codex 967, the whole passage 36.23b-

38 is missing, but there are no compelling grounds to believe that this entire section was missing from an original Hebrew text. The account of the vindication of Yahweh's 'name' is far from complete at 36.23a and, moreover, the 'inclusio' formed by 36.22 and 36.32 is to be noted (cf. Zimmerli, *Ezekiel 2*, 242, 245).

50. We must, moreover, heed the warning of Fohrer concerning the need for caution in suggesting literary affinities, since many features may have been general currency. This is particularly important in view of the partial and selective nature of our sources. See G. Fohrer, *Die Hauptprobleme des Buches Ezechiel*, BZAW 72 (Berlin, 1952), 135ff.

51. For a fuller consideration of the points of similarity between Jeremiah 24 and our Ezekiel texts, see J.W. Miller, *Das Verhältnis Jeremias und Hesekiels sprachlich und theologisch untersucht* (Assen, 1955), 96-97.

52. See above, Chapter 7, note 8.

53. On the theme of 'the New' in exilic prophecy, see H.W. Wolff, 'Prophecy from the Eighth through the Fifth Century', *Interpretation* 32 (1978), 17-30.

54. See further: Miller, *Verhältnis*, 65-66, 98-99, 118-19.

55. G. von Rad, *Old Testament Theology*, vol. II, 235.

56. Within Ezekiel 34–37, we may note affinities between the condemnation of the bad shepherds in ch. 34 and Jeremiah 23.1ff., and between the dry bones of Ezekiel 37 and Jer. 8.1-3. Noteworthy also is the parallel between the hope of a Davidic restoration in Ezek. 34.24; 37.22, 24-25 and Jer. 23.5-6; 33.14ff.

57. M. Burrows, *The Literary Relations of Ezekiel* (Philadelphia, 1925), 15; J.W. Miller, *Verhältnis*, 21ff.; W. Zimmerli, *Ezekiel 1*, 44-46.

58. E.g. K.W. Carley, *Ezekiel among the Prophets*, 56-57.

59. Cf. E.W. Nicholson, *Preaching to the Exiles* (Oxford, 1970), 81-84.

60. E.g. M. Burrows, *Literary Relations*, 19-25; G. Fohrer, *Die Hauptprobleme des Buches Ezechiel*, BZAW 72 (Berlin, 1952), 140-44; E. Balla, *Die Botschaft der Propheten* (Tübingen, 1958), 284-85. In contrast, Zimmerli was markedly reluctant to give much weight to the influence of Deuteronomy upon the book of Ezekiel; cf. *Ezekiel 1*, 46. On deuteronomistic features within the book of Ezekiel, see also above, p. 26.

61. See above, p. 111.

62. H. Graf Reventlow has argued otherwise, regarding the concept of 'covenant' as a major focus of the book (see especially his *Wächter über Israel: Ezechiel und seine Tradition*, BZAW 82 [Berlin, 1962]). He emphasizes the affinities between the book of Ezekiel and the Holiness Code of Leviticus 17–26 (for example, the blessings associated with the 'covenant of peace' in Ezek. 34.25ff. and those promised in Lev. 26.4ff.) The existence of such points of contact may be acknowledged, but Reventlow goes beyond the evidence when he defines the Holiness Code as a ritual for a cultic ceremony

(a thesis advanced in more detail in his *Das Heiligkeitsgesetz formgeschichtlich untersucht*, WMANT 6 [Neukirchen, 1961]) and proceeds to speak of Ezekiel as the holder of a cultic office in a 'covenant' festival tradition.

63. There is a possibility that these references to a 'covenant of peace' and an 'everlasting covenant' (Ezek. 34.25; 37.26) are redactional (von Rad regarded them as coming from Ezekiel himself [Old Testament Theology, vol. II, 235], whilst Zimmerli attributed them to his posited 'School' [*Outline*, 212]). The reference to an 'everlasting covenant' in 16.60 is very probably secondary (see above). Nevertheless, our purpose here is simply to illustrate the association between our formula and the word בְּרִית ('covenant').

64. The formula (and variations upon it) is evidenced in a wide range of strata in this period: the Priestly strand of the Pentateuch, if such is to be isolated (e.g. Gen. 17.8; Exod. 6.7); the so-called Holiness Code (e.g. Lev. 26.12, 45); Zech. 8.8. However, the bulk of the references are to be found in Deuteronomy, the Deuteronomistic History and (above all) Jeremiah (e.g. Deut. 26.17-18; 29.12 [Eng. 13]; 2 Sam. 7.24; Jer. 7.23; 11.4; 24.7; 30.22; 31.1, 33; 32.38).

65. E.W. Nicholson, *God and his People: Covenant and Theology in the Old Testament* (Oxford, 1986), vi. Whilst Nicholson finds what he calls pre-Deuteronomic 'covenant' references in Hos. 6.7 and 8.1 and in Exod. 24.3-8, Perlitt argues that the theological notion of 'covenant' was completely unknown to the eighth-century prophets. Cf. L. Perlitt, *Bundestheologie im Alten Testament*, WMANT 36 (Neukirchen-Vluyn, 1969).

66. The fact that the longer form לבב is generally used in Deuteronomy, whereas in Ezekiel (and Jeremiah) the shorter form לב is much the more common, should not be allowed to obscure the similarity in usage.

67. Cf. Deut. 4.29; 10.12; 11.13; 13.4 (Eng. 3); 26.16.

68. E.g. Josh. 24.23; 1 Kgs 8.48; 2 Kgs 23.25. On the 'heart' as the place of moral response, see above.

69. Cf. A.D.H. Mayes, *Deuteronomy* (London, 1979), 367-68; E.W. Nicholson, *Deuteronomy and Tradition* (Oxford, 1967), 35-36.

70. R.E. Clements postulates a wide-ranging process of elaboration of the exilic prophetic texts in the direction of a harmonized expression of hope, but suggests that it would be wrong to lay too much emphasis on the deuteronomistic character of this process (R.E. Clements, 'The Chronology of Redaction in Ezekiel 1-24', in J. Lust [ed.], *Ezekiel and his Book: Textual and Literary Criticism and their Interrelation* [Leuven, 1986], 283-94). See also Clements's earlier essay, 'Patterns in the Prophetic Canon', in G.W. Coats and B.O. Long (eds.), *Canon and Authority* (Philadelphia, 1977), 42-55.

71. It is interesting to note that if Van Seters were correct in his proposal to redate the work of the Yahwist to the sixth century, the expression of unconditional promises in the exilic age would be even more widely attested.

He writes of the Yahwist: 'It is to the despairing community of the exile that the unbreakable promises of the patriarchs are addressed' (J. Van Seters, *Abraham in History and Tradition* [New Haven & London, 1975], 311).

72. S. Herrmann adopts this position in a number of his works: *Die prophetischen Heilserwartungen im Alten Testament*, BWANT 85 (Stuttgart, 1965), 241ff.; 'Die konstruktive Restauration. Das Deuteronomium als Mitte biblischer Theologie', in *Probleme biblischer Theologie. Festschrift G. von Rad* (Munich, 1971), 155-70; see also *Geschichte Israels in alttestamentlicher Zeit* (Munich, 1973); ET: *A History of Israel in Old Testament Times* (London, 1975), 292, 297.

73. See above, pp. 114f.

74. See above.

75. The affinities between Ezekiel and pre-classical prophecy are explored in detail by K.W. Carley, *Ezekiel among the Prophets*, 13-47.

76. In Chapter 6 we showed that a radical theocentricity was a characteristic feature both of the prophet Ezekiel and of the redactional tradition which followed him. Earlier in the present chapter we argued that Ezek. 36.16ff. has a strong claim to be regarded as coming from Ezekiel himself.

77. See above, Chapter 2.

78. Cf. E.W. Nicholson, *Preaching to the Exiles*, 116-35.

79. The sequence proposed here must remain conjectural. It will be explored more fully in my commentary on Ezekiel in the New Century Bible series (in preparation).

Notes to Chapter 8

1. Cf. Nicholson's reflections on the 'new covenant' prophecy of Jer. 31.31-34: E.W. Nicholson, *God and his People: Covenant and Theology in the Old Testament* (Oxford, 1986), 216.

2. Cf. Carroll's stimulating discussion in relation to Jer. 31.31-34: R.P. Carroll, *From Chaos to Covenant: Uses of Prophecy in the Book of Jeremiah* (London, 1981), 215-25.

BIBLIOGRAPHY

Ackroyd, P.R., *Exile and Restoration* (London, 1968).

Andrew, M.E., *Responsibility and Restoration* (Otago, New Zealand, 1985).

Baker, J.A., *The Foolishness of God* (London, 1970).

Balla, E., *Die Botschaft der Propheten* (Tübingen, 1958).

Baltzer, D., *Ezechiel und Deuterojesaja*, BZAW 121 (Berlin, 1971).

Barr, J., *The Semantics of Biblical Language* (Oxford, 1961).

—'The Symbolism of Names in the Old Testament', *BJRL* 52/1 (1969), 11-29.

Barth, C., 'Ezechiel 37 als Einheit', in *Beiträge zur alttestamentlichen Theologie. Festschrift für W. Zimmerli* (Göttingen, 1977), 39-52.

Barton, J., *Amos's Oracles against the Nations* (Cambridge, 1980).

Baumgärtel, F., *Die Eigenart der alttestamentlichen Frömmigkeit* (Schwerin, 1932).

Becker, J., *Der priesterliche Prophet. Das Buch Ezechiel*, Stuttgarter Kleiner Kommentar, Altes Testament, 12/1&2, 2 vols. (Stuttgart, 1971).

—'Erwägungen zur ezechielischen Frage', in Ruppert, L., Weimar, P. and Zenger, E. (eds.), *Künder des Wortes* (Würzburg, 1982), 137-49.

Begrich, J., 'Die priesterliche Tora', in *Werden und Wesen des Alten Testaments*, BZAW 66 (Berlin, 1936), 63-88.

Bertholet, A., *Das Buch Hesekiel erklärt*, KHC 12 (Freiburg, 1897).

—(with Galling, K.) *Hesekiel*, HAT 13 (Tübingen, 1936).

Bettenzoli, G., *Geist der Heiligkeit. Traditionsgeschichtliche Untersuchung des QDS-Begriffes im Buch Ezechiel*, Semitistica 8 (Florence, 1979).

Bietenhard, H., *Theologisches Wörterbuch zum Neuen Testament* (ed. G. Friedrich); ET: *Theological Dictionary of the New Testament* (ed. G.W. Bromiley), vol. V.

Blank, S.H., 'Studies in Deutero-Isaiah', *HUCA* 15 (1940).

Boadt, L., 'Textual Problems in Ezekiel and Poetic Analysis of Paired Words', *JBL* 97/4 (1978), 489-99.

—*Ezekiel's Oracles against Egypt—a Literary and Philological Study of Ezekiel 29-32*, Biblica et Orientalia 37 (Rome, 1980).

Brownlee, W.H., 'Ezekiel's Parable of the Watchman and the Editing of Ezekiel', *VT* 28 (1978), 392-408.

—*Ezekiel 1-19*, Word Biblical Commentary 28 (Waco, Texas, 1986).

Brueggemann, W., 'Trajectories in Old Testament Literature and the Sociology of Ancient Israel', *JBL* 98/2 (1979), 161-85.

—*Hopeful Imagination: Prophetic Voices in Exile* (Philadelphia, 1986).

Brunner, R., *Ezechiel*, Zürcher Bibelkommentare, 2 vols. (2nd edn, Zurich, 1969).

Bruno, D.A., *Ezechiel: eine rhythmische und textkritische Untersuchung* (Stockholm, 1959).

Burrows, M., *The Literary Relations of Ezekiel* (Philadelphia, 1925).

Carley, K.W., *The Book of the Prophet Ezekiel* (London, 1974).

—*Ezekiel among the Prophets*, SBTh II/31 (London, 1975).

Carroll, R.P., *From Chaos to Covenant: Uses of Prophecy in the Book of Jeremiah* (London, 1981).

—*Jeremiah* (London, 1986).

Childs, B.S., *Introduction to the Old Testament as Scripture* (London, 1979).

Clements, R.E., 'Patterns in the Prophetic Canon', in G.W. Coats and B.O. Long (eds), *Canon and Authority* (Philadelphia, 1977), 42-55.

—'The Ezekiel Tradition: Prophecy in a Time of Crisis', in Coggins, R., Phillips, A. and Knibb, M. (eds.), *Israel's Prophetic Tradition: Essays in Honour of Peter R. Ackroyd* (Cambridge, 1982), 119-36.

—'The Chronology of Redaction in Ezekiel 1-24', in Lust, J. (ed.), *Ezekiel and his Book: Textual and Literary Criticism and their Interrelation* (Leuven, 1986), 283-94.

Coats, G.W. and Long, B.O. (eds.), *Canon and Authority* (Philadelphia, 1977).

Cooke, G.A., *A Critical and Exegetical Commentary on the Book of Ezekiel* ICC (Edinburgh, 1936).

Cornill, C.H., *Das Buch des Propheten Ezechiel* (Leipzig, 1886).

Daube, D., *Studies in Biblical Law* (Cambridge, 1947, reprinted New York, 1969).

Day, J., 'The Daniel of Ugarit and Ezekiel and the Hero of the Book of Daniel', *VT* 30 (1980), 174-84.

Dhorme, P., *L'emploi metaphysique des noms de parties du corps en hébreu et en accadien* (Paris, 1923).

Driver, S.R., *An Introduction to the Literature of the Old Testament* (9th edn, Edinburgh, 1913).

Duhm, B., *Das Buch Jesaja*, HKAT (Göttingen, 1892).

—*Das Buch Jeremia*, KHC (Tübingen & Leipzig, 1901).

Eichrodt, W., *Theologie des Alten Testaments*, 3 vols. (Stuttgart, 1933, 1935, 1939) ET: *Theology of the Old Testament*, 2 vols. (London, 1961, 1967).

—*Der Prophet Hesekiel*, ATD 22 (Göttingen, 1959; 3rd edn, 1968); ET: *Ezekiel* (London, 1970).

—'Das prophetische Wachteramt. Zur Exegese von Ez. 33', in *Tradition und Situation. A. Weiser zum 70. Geburtstag* (Göttingen, 1963), 31-41.

Eissfeldt, O., *Der Maschal im Alten Testament*, BZAW 24 (Giessen, 1913).

—*Einleitung in das Alte Testament* (Tübingen, 1934); ET (of 3rd edn, 1964), *The Old Testament: An Introduction* (Oxford, 1965).

Fishbane, M., 'Sin and Judgment in the Prophecies of Ezekiel', *Interpretation*, 38/2 (1984), 131-50.

—(with Talmon, S.) 'The Structuring of Biblical Books. Studies in the Book of Ezekiel', *ASTI* 10 (1976), 129-53.

Fohrer, G., 'Die Glossen im Buche Ezechiel', *ZAW* 63 (1951), 33-53.

—*Die Hauptprobleme des Buches Ezechiel*, BZAW 72 (Berlin, 1952).

—'Das Symptomatische der Ezechielforschung', *ThLZ* 83 (1958), 241-50.

—'Remarks on Modern Interpretation of the Prophets', *JBL* 80 (1961), 309-19.

—*Einleitung in das Alte Testament* (Heidelberg, 1965) (10th completely revised edn of the work by E. Sellin, first published 1910); ET: *Introduction to the Old Testament* (London, 1970).

—'Neue Literatur zur alttestamentlichen Prophetie (1961-1970)', *ThR* NF 45 (1980), 121-29.

—(with Galling, K.) *Ezechiel*, HAT 13, (Tübingen, 1955).

Fontaine, C.R., *Traditional Sayings in the Old Testament: A Contextual Study* (Sheffield, 1982).

Freedy, K.S., *The Literary Relations of Ezekiel. A Historical Study of Chapters 1-24* (Dissertation; Toronto, 1969).

Fuhs, H.F., *Ezechiel 1-24*, Die Neue Echte Bibel (Würzburg, 1984).

Galling, K. (with Bertholet, A.) *Hesekiel*, HAT 13, (Tübingen, 1936).

—(with Fohrer, G.) *Ezechiel*, HAT 13, (Tübingen, 1955).

Garscha, J., *Studien zum Ezechielbuch: Eine redaktionskritische Untersuchung von Ez 1-39*, Europäische Hochschulschriften XXIII/23 (Bern & Frankfurt, 1974).

Gese, H., *Der Verfassungsentwurf des Ezechiel (Kap. 40-48) traditionsgeschichtlich untersucht*, Beiträge zur Historischen Theologie 25 (Tübingen, 1957).

Geyer, J.B., 'Ezekiel 18 and a Hittite Treaty of Mursilis II', *JSOT* 12 (1979), 31-46.

Gibson, A., *Biblical Semantic Logic* (Oxford, 1981).

Good, E.M., *Irony in the Old Testament*, (2nd edn, Sheffield, 1981).

Gottwald, N.K., *The Tribes of Yahweh: A Sociology of the Religion of Liberated Israel, 1250-1050 B.C.E.* (New York, 1979).

Graffy, A., *A Prophet Confronts his People: The Disputation Speech in the Prophets* Analecta Biblica 104 (Rome, 1984).

Gray, G.B., *A Critical Introduction to the Old Testament* (London, 1913).

Greenberg, M., 'On Ezekiel's Dumbness', *JBL* 77 (1958), 101-105.

—'Ezekiel', in *Encyclopaedia Judaica*, VI (Jerusalem, 1971), 1078-95.

—'The Vision of Jerusalem in Ezekiel 8-11: A Holistic Interpretation', in Crenshaw, J.L. and Sandmel, S. (edsd.), *The Divine Helmsman. Studies on God's Control of Human Events, Presented to L.H. Silberman*, (New York, 1980), 143-64.

—'The Meaning and Location of the "Lookout" Passage in Ezek. 3: 16-21', in *Proceedings of the American Academy for Jewish Research*, XLVI/XLVII (Jerusalem, 1980), 265-80.

—*Ezekiel 1-20*, AB 22 (Garden City, New York, 1983).

Gunkel, H., 'Die Israelitische Literatur', in P. Hinneberg (ed.), *Die Kultur der Gegenwart* (Berlin & Leipzig, 1906).

Harford, J. Battersby, *Studies in the Book of Ezekiel* (Cambridge, 1935).

Harvey, J., 'Collectivisme et Individualisme, Ezk. 18:1-32 et Jer. 31:29', *Sciences Ecclésiastiques* 10 (Montreal, 1958), 167-202.

Heaton, E.W., *The Old Testament Prophets* (rev. edn, London, 1977).

Hempel, J., *Das Ethos des Alten Testaments*, BZAW 67 (Berlin, 1938; 2nd edn, 1964).

Herntrich, V., *Ezechielprobleme*, BZAW 61 (Giessen, 1932).

Herrmann, J., *Ezechielstudien*, BWANT 2 (Leipzig, 1908).

—*Ezechiel, übersetzt und erklärt*, KAT (Leipzig, 1924).

Herrmann, S., *Die prophetischen Heilserwartungen im Alten Testament*, BWANT 85, NF 5 (Stuttgart, 1965).

—'Die konstruktive Restauration. Das Deuteronomium als Mitte biblischer Theologie', in *Probleme biblischer Theologie. Festschrift G. von Rad* (Munich, 1971), 155-70.

—*Geschichte Israels in alttestamentlicher Zeit* (Munich, 1973); ET: *A History of Israel in Old Testament Times* (London, 1975).

Hitzig, F., *Der Prophet Ezechiel erklärt*, KeH (Leipzig, 1847).

Hölscher, G., *Die Profeten* (Leipzig, 1914).

—*Hesekiel, der Dichter und das Buch*, BZAW 39 (Giessen, 1924).

Hossfeld, F.L., *Untersuchungen zu Komposition und Theologie des Ezechielbuches*, FZB 20 (Würzburg, 1977; 2nd edn, 1983).

Hurvitz, A., *A Linguistic Study of the Relationship between the Priestly Source and the Book of Ezekiel*, Cahiers de la Revue Biblique 20 (Paris, 1982).

Irwin, W.A., *The Problem of Ezekiel* (Chicago, 1943).

Jahn, G., *Das Buch Ezechiel auf Grund der Septuaginta hergestellt, übersetzt und kritisch erklärt* (Leipzig, 1905).

Jahn, P.L.D., *Der griechische Text des Buches Ezechiel* (Bonn, 1972).

Janssen, E., *Juda in der Exilszeit: Ein Beitrag zur Frage der Entstehung des Judentums*, FRLANT 69 (Göttirgen, 1956).

Johnson, A.R., *The One and the Many in the Israelite Conception of God* (Cardiff, 1942; 2nd edn, 1961).

—*The Vitality of the Individual in the Thought of Ancient Israel* (Cardiff, 1949).

Joyce, P.M., 'Individual Responsibility in Ezekiel 18?', *Studia Biblica 1978*, ed. E.A. Livingstone, JSOTS 11 (Sheffield, 1979), 185-96.

—'Ezekiel and Individual Responsibility', *Ezekiel and his Book: Textual and Literary Criticism and their Interrelation*, ed. J. Lust, Bibliotheca Ephemeridum Theologicarum Lovaniensium LXXIV (Leuven, 1986), 317-21.

Junker, H., 'Ein Kernstück der Predigt Ezechiels: Studie über Ez. 18', *BZ* NF 7 (1963), 173-85.

Kaiser, O., *Einleitung in das Alte Testament* (Gütersloh, 1969); ET: *Introduction to the Old Testament* (Oxford, 1975).

—*Der Prophet Jesaja. Kap 13–39*, ATD 18 (Göttingen, 1973); ET: *Isaiah 13–39* (London, 1974).

Kaufmann, Y., *The Religion of Israel*, ET by M. Greenberg (London, 1961).

Kessler, W., *Die innere Einheitlichkeit des Buches Ezechiel*, Berichte des theologischen Seminars der Brüdergemeinde 9 (Herrnhut, 1926).

Klein, R.W., *Israel in Exile: a Theological Interpretation* (Philadelphia, 1979).

Kittel, G. & Friedrich, G. (eds.), *Theologisches Wörterbuch zum Neuen Testament* (Stuttgart, 1932ff.), ET: *Theological Dictionary of the New Testament*, ed. Bromiley, G.W. (Grand Rapids, Michigan, 1964ff.).

Koch, K., 'Gibt es ein Vergeltungsdogma im Alten Testament?', *ZThK* 52 (1955), 1-42; ET: 'Is there a doctrine of retribution in the Old Testament?', in J.L. Crenshaw (ed.), *Theodicy in the Old Testament* (London & Philadelphia, 1983), 57-87.

—'Der Spruch "Sein Blut bleibe auf seinem Haupt" und die israelitische Auffassung vom vergossenen Blut', *VT* 12 (1962), 396-416.

—Both the above also collected in Koch, K. (ed.), *Um das Prinzip der Vergeltung in Religion und Recht des Alten Testaments*, Wege der Forschung 125 (Darmstadt, 1972).

Kraetzschmar, R., *Das Buch Ezechiel*, HKAT III 3/1 (Göttingen, 1900).

Kuhl, C., 'Zur Geschichte der Hesekiel-Forschung',*ThR* NF 5 (1933), 92-118.

—'Neuere Hesekielliteratur', *ThR* NF 20 (1952), 1-26.

—'Zum Stand der Hesekiel-Forschung', *ThR* NF 24 (1957-58), 1-53.

Kutsch, E., 'Gesetz und Gnade. Probleme des alttestamentlichen Bundesbegriffs', *ZAW* 79 (1967), 18-35.

—*Die chronologischen Daten des Ezechielbuches*, Orbis Biblicus et Orientalis 62 (Freiburg & Göttingen, 1985).

Lamparter, H., *Zum Wächter Bestellt: Der Prophet Hesekiel* (Stuttgart, 1968).

Lang, B., *Kein Aufstand in Jerusalem: die Politik des Propheten Ezechiel* (Stuttgart, 1978; 2nd edn, 1981).

—'A Neglected Method in Ezekiel Research: Editorial Criticism', *VT* 29 (1979), 39-44.

—'Die Geburt der jüdischen Hoffnungstheologie', in *Wie wird man Prophet in Israel?* (Düsseldorf, 1980), 59-68.

—*Ezechiel: Der Prophet und das Buch*, Erträge der Forschung, 153 (Darmstadt, 1981).

Lauha, R., *Psychophysischer Sprachgebrauch im Alten Testament: Eine strukturalse-mantische Analyse von leb, nepes und ruah: I. Emotionen* (Helsinki, 1983).

Lindars, B., 'Ezekiel and Individual Responsibility', *VT* 15 (1965), 452-67.

Liwak, R., Uberlieferungsgeschichtliche Probleme des Ezechielbuches. Eine Studie zu postezechielischen Interpretationen und Kompositionen (Dissertation; Bochum, 1976).

Lust, J., 'De samenhang van Ez. 36-40. Theologische relevantie van het ontbreken van Ez. 36,23c-38 in enkele handschriften', *Tijdschrift voor Theologie* 20 (1980), 26-39.

Lust, J. (ed.), *Ezekiel and his Book: Textual and Literary Criticism and their Interrelation*, Bibliotheca Ephemeridum Theologicarum Lovaniensium LXXIV (Leuven, 1986).

Lys, D., *Ruach. Le souffle dans l'Ancien Testament*, EHPhR 56 (1962).

May, H.G., 'The Book of Ezekiel', *IB* VI, (New York & Nashville, 1956), 39-338.

—'Individual Responsibility and Retribution', *HUCA* 32 (1961), 107-20.

Mayes, A.D.H., *Deuteronomy*, NCB (London, 1979).

Mendenhall, G.E., 'The Relation of the Individual to Political Society in Ancient Israel', in Myers, J.M. (ed.), *Biblical Studies in Memory of H.C. Alleman* (Locust Valley, 1960), 89-108.

Miller, J.W., *Das Verhältnis Jeremias und Hesekiels sprachlich und theologisch untersucht* (Assen, 1955).

Miller, P.D., Jr., *Sin and Judgment in the Prophets: a Stylistic and Theological Analysis*, Society of Biblical Literature Monograph Series 27 (Chico, California, 1982).

Morgan, D.F., *Wisdom in the Old Testament Traditions* (Atlanta & Oxford, 1981).

Mosis, R., 'Ez 14,1-11 - ein Ruf zur Umkehr', *BZ* 19 (1975), 161-94.

Muilenburg, J., 'Ezekiel', in *Peake's Commentary on the Bible* ed. M. Black and H.H. Rowley (London & Edinburgh, 1962), 568-90.

Mulder, M.J. (ed.), *The Old Testament in Syriac, according to the Peshitta Version: Ezekiel* (Leiden, 1985).

Nicholson, E.W., *Deuteronomy and Tradition* (Oxford, 1967).

—*Preaching to the Exiles* (Oxford, 1970).

—*God and his People: Covenant and Theology in the Old Testament* (Oxford, 1986).

Nielsen, K., *Yahweh as Prosecutor and Judge : An Investigation of the Prophetic Lawsuit (Rîb Pattern)*, JSOTS 9 (Sheffield, 1978).

Nobile, M., *Una lettura simbolico-strutturalistica di Ezechiele* (Rome, 1982).

Noth, M., *Überlieferungsgeschichte des Pentateuch* (Stuttgart, 1948); ET: *A History of Pentateuchal Traditions* (Englewood Cliffs, New Jersey, 1972).

—*Geschichte Israels*, (2nd edn, Göttingen, 1958); ET: *The History of Israel*, (2nd edn, London, 1960).

—'Noah, Daniel und Hiob in Ezechiel 14', *VT* 1 (1951), 251-60.

—'La catastrophe de Jérusalem en l'an 587 avant Jésus-Christ et sa signification pour Israel', *RHPhR* 33 (1953), 82-102 = 'Die Katastrophe von Jerusalem im Jahre 587 v. Chr. und ihre Bedeutung für Israel', *Gesammelte Studien zum Alten Testament*, (2nd edn, Munich, 1960), 346-71; ET: 'The Jerusalem Catastrophe of

587 BC and its Significance for Israel', *The Laws in the Pentateuch and Other Studies* (Edinburgh, 1966), 260-180.

Oesterley, W.O.E. and Robinson, T.H., *An Introduction to the Books of the Old Testament* (London, 1934).

Orelli, C. von, *Das Buch Ezechiel*, Kurzgefasster Kommentar zu den heiligen Schriften Alten und Neuen Testaments 5,1 (2nd edn, Munich, 1896).

Peake, A.S., *The Problem of Suffering in the Old Testament* (London, 1904).

Pedersen, J., *Israel: its Life and Culture, I–II* (London & Copenhagen, 1926).

Perlitt, L., *Bundestheologie im Alten Testament*, WMANT 36 (Neukirchen, 1969).

Pfeiffer, R.H., *Introduction to the Old Testament* (New York, 1941).

Phillips, A., *Ancient Israel's Criminal Law* (Oxford, 1970).

—'Double for all her Sins', *ZAW* 94/1 (1982), 130-32.

Porter, J.R., 'The Legal Aspects of the Concept of "Corporate Personality" in the Old Testament', *VT* 15 (1965), 361-80.

—*The Extended Family in the Old Testament*, Occasional Papers in Social and Economic Administration, 6 (London, 1967).

Procksch, O., *Theologisches Wörterbuch zum Neuen Testament* (ed. G. Kittel); ET: *Theological Dictionary of the New Testament* (ed. G.W. Bromiley), vol. I.

Rabenau, K. von, 'Die Entstehung des Buches Ezechiel in formgeschichtlicher Sicht', *Wissenschaftliche Zeitschrift*, Reihe 5 (1955/56), 659-94.

—'Das prophetische Zukunftswort im Buch Hesekiel', in *Studien zur Theologie der alttestamentlichen Überlieferungen*, ed. Rendtorff, R. and Koch, K. (Neukirchen, 1961).

Rad, G. von, *Das erste Buch Mose, Genesis*, ATD 2-4 (Göttingen, 1949ff.). ET: *Genesis* (London, 1961; rev. edn, 1972).

—'"Gerechtigkeit" und "Leben" in der Kultsprache der Psalmen', *Festschrift für Alfred Bertholet* (Tübingen, 1950), 418-37. ET: '"Righteousness" and "Life" in the Cultic Language of the Psalms' in *The Problem of the Hexateuch and other Essays* (Edinburgh & London, 1966), 243-66.

—*Der heilige Krieg im alten Israel*, ATANT 20 (1951).

—*Theologie des Alten Testaments*, 2 vols. (Munich; 1957, 1960); ET: *Old Testament Theology*, 2 vols. (London; 1962, 1965).

Raitt, T.M., *A Theology of Exile: Judgment/Deliverance in Jeremiah and Ezekiel* (Philadelphia, 1977).

Rendtorff, R., *Das überlieferungsgeschichtliche Problem des Pentateuch*, BZAW 147 (Berlin & New York, 1977).

—*Das Alte Testament: Eine Einführung* (Neukirchen, 1983) ET: *The Old Testament: An Introduction* (London, 1985).

Reventlow, H. Graf, 'Die Völker als Jahwes Zeugen bei Ezechiel', *ZAW* 71 (1959), 33-43.

—'Sein Blut komme über sein Haupt', *VT* 10 (1960), 311-27.

—*Das Heiligkeitsgesetz formgeschichtlich untersucht*, WMANT 6 (Neukirchen, 1961).

—*Wächter über Israel: Ezechiel und seine Tradition*, BZAW 82 (Berlin, 1962).

Rhymer, J. and Bullen, A., *Companion to the Good News Old Testament* (London, 1976).

Robinson, H. Wheeler, 'The Hebrew Conception of Corporate Personality', in *Werden und Wesen des Alten Testaments*, BZAW 66 (Berlin, 1936), 49-62.

—'The Group and the Individual in Israel', in Hughes, E.R. (ed.), *The Individual in East and West* (Oxford, 1937).

—Both essays reprinted in Robinson, H. Wheeler, *Corporate Personality in Ancient Israel*, (Philadelphia, 1980; with an introduction by G.M. Tucker & Edinburgh, 1981; with an introduction by C.S. Rodd).

—*The Cross of the Servant* (London, 1926).

—*Two Hebrew Prophets: Studies in Hosea and Ezekiel* (London, 1948).

Robinson, J.M. and Koester, H., *Trajectories through Early Christianity* (Philadelphia, 1971).

Rodd, C.S., 'Shall not the Judge of all the earth do what is just? (Gen. 18:25)', *ET* 83 (1972), 137-39.

Rogerson, J.W., 'The Hebrew Conception of Corporate Personality: a Re-examination', *JTS* 21/1 (1970), 1-16. (Reprinted in Lang, B. (ed.), *Anthropological Approaches to the Old Testament*, (Philadelphia & London, 1985), 43-59.

Rowley, H.H., 'The Book of Ezekiel in Modern Study', *BJRL* 36 (1953), 146-90.

Sakenfeld, K.D., 'Ezekiel 18:25-32', *Interpretation* 32/3 (1978), 295-300.

Schenker, A., 'Saure Trauben ohne stumpfe Zähne. Bedeutung und Tragweite von Ez 18 und 33:10-20 oder ein Kapitel alttestamentlicher Moraltheologie', in Casetti, P., Keel, O. and Schenker, A. (eds.), *Mélanges Dominique Barthélemy*, Orbis Biblicus et Orientalis 38, (Göttingen, 1981).

Schmid, H.H., *Der sogenannte Jahwist: Beobachtungen und Fragen zur Pentateuchforschung* (Zürich, 1976).

Schulz, H., *Das Todesrecht im Alten Testament*, BZAW 114 (Berlin, 1969).

Segert, S., 'Bis in das dritte und vierte Glied', *Communio Viatorum* 1, (1958), 37-39.

Seters, J. Van, *Abraham in History and Tradition* (New Haven & London, 1975).

Simian, H., *Die theologische Nachgeschichte der Prophetie Ezechiels. Form- und traditions-kritische Untersuchung zu Ez. 6; 35; 36*, FZB 14 (Würzburg, 1974).

Smend, R., *Der Prophet Ezechiel* KeH (2nd edn, Leipzig, 1880).

Smith, J., *The Book of the Prophet Ezekiel—a New Interpretation* (London, 1931).

Spiegel, S., 'Noah, Daniel and Job, Touching on Canaanite Relics in the Legends of the Jews', in *Louis Ginzberg Jubilee Volume* (New York, 1945), 305-55.

Stalker, D.M.G., *Ezekiel* (London, 1968).

Steinmann, J., *Le prophète Ezéchiel et les débuts de l'exil* (Paris, 1953).

Talmon, S. (with Fishbane M.), 'The Structuring of Biblical Books. Studies in the Book of Ezekiel', *ASTI* 10 (1976), 129-53.

Taylor, J.B., *Ezekiel* (London, 1969).

Thomas, D. Winton, 'The Sixth Century BC: a Creative Epoch in the History of Israel', *JSS* 6 (1961), 33-46.

Torrey, C.C., *Pseudo-Ezekiel and the Original Prophecy* (New Haven, 1930; reissued, New York, 1970).

Tucker, G.M., 'Witnesses and Dates in Israelite Contracts', *CBQ* 28 (1966), 42ff.

Verdam, P.J., '"On ne fera point mourir les enfants pour les pères" en droit biblique', *Revue Internationale des Droits de l'Antiquité* 3 (1949), 393-416.

Vogt, E., 'Textumdeutungen im Buch Ezechiel', *Sacra Pagina* I (Paris, 1959), 471-94.

—'Die Lähmung und Stummheit des Propheten Ezechiel', in *Wort-Gebot-Glaube. W. Eichrodt zum 80. Geburtstag*, ATANT 59 (Zürich, 1970), 87-100.

—*Untersuchungen zum Buch Ezechiel*, Analecta Biblica 95 (Rome, 1981).

Weiser, A., *Die Psalmen*, ATD 14/15, (5th edn, Gottingen, 1959); ET: *The Psalms* (London, 1962).

Wevers, J.W., *Ezekiel* NCB (London, 1969).

Whitley, C.F., *The Exilic Age* (London, 1957).

Whybray, R.N. *Isaiah 40-66* NCB (London, 1975).

—*The Making of the Pentateuch: A Methodological Study*, JSOTS 53 (Sheffield, 1987).

Wilson, R.R., 'An Interpretation of Ezekiel's Dumbness', *VT* 22 (1972), 91-104.

—'Prophecy in Crisis: the Call of Ezekiel', *Interpretation* 38 (1984), 117-30.

Wolff, H.W., 'Die Begründungen der prophetischen Heils- und Unheilssprüche', *ZAW* 52 (1934), 1-22.

—'Das Zitat im Prophetenspruch', *BhEvTh* 4 (Munich, 1937).

—'Das Thema "Umkehr" in der alttestamentlichen Prophetie', *ZThK* 48 (1951), 129-48.

—*Dodekapropheton 2, Joel und Amos* (Neukirchen-Vluyn, 1969; 2nd edn, 1975); ET: *Joel and Amos* (Philadelphia, 1977).

—*Anthropologie des Alten Testaments* (Munich, 1973); ET: *Anthropology of the Old Testament* (London, 1974).

—'Prophecy from the Eighth through the Fifth Century', *Interpretation* 32 (1978), 17-30.

Ziegler, J., *Ezechiel*, Septuaginta 16/1 (Göttingen, 1952; 2nd edn, 1977).

Zimmerli, W., (1) *Ezechiel*, BK 13, 2 vols. (Neukirchen, 1969; fascicles appeared from 1955; 2nd edn, 1979); ET: *Ezekiel 1* (Philadelphia, 1979); *Ezekiel 2* (Philadelphia, 1983).

—(2) 'Ich bin Jahwe', in *Geschichte und Altes Testament. Beiträge zur historischen Theologie, 16. A. Alt zum 70. Geburtstag dargebracht* (Tübingen, 1953), 179-209.

—(3) 'Die Eigenart der prophetischen Rede des Ezechiel. Ein Beitrag zum Problem an Hand von Ez. 14:1-11', *ZAW* 66 (1954), 1-26.

—(4) *Erkenntnis Gottes nach dem Buche Ezechiel. Eine theologische Studie*, ATANT 27 (Zürich, 1954).

—(5) 'Das Wort des göttlichen Selbsterweises (Erweiswort), eine prophetische Gattung', in *Mélanges A. Robert* (Paris, 1957), 154-64.

—(6) '"Leben" und "Tod" im Buche des Propheten Ezechiel', *ThZ* 13 (1957), 494-508.

—(7) 'Israel im Buche Ezechiel', *VT* 8 (1958), 75-90.

—(8) 'Der Wahrheitserweis Jahwes nach der Botschaft der beiden Exilspropheten', in *Tradition und Situation. Studien zur alttestamentlichen Prophetie A. Weiser zum 70. Geburtstag dargebracht* (Göttingen, 1963), 133-51.

—(9) 'The Special Form- and Traditio-Historical Character of Ezekiel's Prophecy', *VT* 15 (1965), 515-27.

—(10) 'Planungen für den Wiederaufbau nach der Katastrophe von 587', *VT* 18 (1968), 229-55.

—(11) *Der Mensch und seine Hoffnung im Alten Testament* (Göttingen, 1968); ET: *Man and his Hope in the Old Testament*, SBTh II:20 (London, 1971).

—(12) 'The Message of the Prophet Ezekiel', *Interpretation* 23 (1969), 131-57 [='Die Botschaft des Propheten Ezechiel', *ThB* 51 (1974), 104-134] .

—(13) *Ezechiel, Gestalt und Botschaft*, Biblische Studien 62 (Neukirchen, 1972).

—(14) 'Deutero-Ezechiel?', *ZAW* 84 (1972), 501-16.

—(15) *Grundriss der alttestamentlichen Theologie* (Stuttgart, 1972; 2nd edn, 1975); ET: *Old Testament Theology in Outline* (Edinburgh, 1978).

—(16) 'Vom Prophetenwort zum Prophetenbuch', *ThLZ* 104 (1979), cols. 481–496.

—(17) 'Das Phänomen der "Fortschreibung" im Buche Ezechiel', in *Prophecy: Essays Presented to G. Fohrer*, BZAW 150, (Berlin & New York, 1980), 174–91.

Note: Items 2, 3, 4, 5, and 6 above appear together in:
Zimmerli, W., *Gottes Offenbarung: Gesammelte Aufsätze I*, ThB 19 (Munich, 1963).

Items 8, 10, and 12 above appear together in:
Zimmerli, W., *Studien zur alttestamentlichen Theologie und Prophetie: Gesammelte Aufsätze II*, ThB 51 (Munich, 1974).

Items 2, 4, 5, and 10 above appear together in English in:
Zimmerli, W., *I am Yahweh*, ed. Brueggemann, W. (Atlanta, 1982).

Zyl, A.H. van, 'Solidarity and Individualism in Ezekiel', *Ou-Testamentiese Werkgemeenskap van Suid-Afrika* 4 (1961), 38–52.

INDEXES

INDEX OF BIBLICAL REFERENCES

INDEX OF AUTHORS

JOURNAL FOR THE STUDY OF THE OLD TESTAMENT
Supplement Series

* Out of print